Praise for

E. E. Cummings

"Effectively situates Cummings within a larger literary and cultural movement. . . . Cummings's life is inherently interesting, dramatic, and sad, and Cheever highlights its colorful and tragic aspects."
—*The Boston Globe*

"Deeply personal. . . . A textured inspection of some of the more intriguing faces of the multifaceted Cummings." —*The Plain Dealer*

"Cheever's biography stands as a welcomed introductory attempt to understand Cummings's impact. . . . One of the best efforts to situate a Modernist inside the larger historical context. . . . Filled in with entertaining research and deep thinking about the lives of artists."
—*The Daily Beast*

"[Cummings's] individualism makes him just about as American as apple pie; and as vital to the tradition of American poetry as Whitman, Dickinson, and Frost. I can only express gratitude to biographers like Cheever for keeping him alive today."
—J. P. Poole, *Bookslut*

"Affecting. . . . Deeply satisfying. . . . Ms. Cheever is the kind of biographer who can maintain both an intimacy and dispassionate relationship with her subject." —*New York Journal of Books*

"Cheever's reconsideration of Cummings and his work charms, rattles, and enlightens in emulation of Cummings's radically disarming, tender, sexy, plangent, and furious poems." —*Booklist* (starred review)

"This sympathetic life may win Cummings a new generation of readers." —*Kirkus Reviews*

Susan Cheever

E. E. Cummings

Susan Cheever was born in New York City and graduated from Brown University. Her work has been nominated for a National Book Critics Circle Award; she has
also received an Associated Press Award and the *Boston
Globe* Winship Medal. A Guggenheim fellow and a board
member of the Yaddo Corporation, she has taught at Yale,
Brown, Columbia, and Hunter College, and is currently
on the faculty in the MFA programs at Bennington College and The New School. She lives in New York City.

www.susancheever.com

E. E. Cummings

E. E. Cummings

A Life

Susan Cheever

Vintage Books
A Division of Penguin Random House LLC
New York

For my son, Warren,
and for our friend Liam Rector

What I propose, then, is this: that you give Mr. Cummings *enough rope*. He may hang himself; or he may lasso a unicorn.

—Edna St. Vincent Millay's
recommendation to the Guggenheim Foundation
for her Greenwich Village neighbor E. E. Cummings

Contents

A Visit to the Masters School

During the last years of his life E. E. Cummings made a modest living on the high-school lecture circuit. In the spring of 1958 his schedule brought him to read his adventurous poems at an uptight girls' school in Westchester where I was a miserable fourteen-year-old sophomore with failing grades.

I vaguely knew that Cummings had been a friend of my father's; my father loved to tell stories about Cummings's gallantry, and Cummings's ability to live elegantly on almost no money—an ability my father himself struggled to cultivate. When my father was a young writer in New York City, in the golden days before marriage and children pressured him to move to the suburbs, the older Cummings had been his beloved friend and adviser.

On that cold night in 1958, Cummings was near the end of his brilliant and controversial forty-year career as this country's only true modernist poet. Primarily remembered these days for its funky punctuation, Cummings's work was in fact a wildly ambitious attempt at creating a new way of seeing the world through language. Part of a powerful group of writers and artists, many of whom were Cummings's friends—James Joyce, Gertrude Stein, Hart Crane, Marianne Moore, Ezra Pound, Marcel Duchamp, Pablo Picasso, Henri Matisse—he struggled to reshape the triangle between the reader, the writer, and the subject of the poem, novel, or painting. As early as his 1915 Harvard College graduation valedictorian speech, Cummings told his audience that "the New Art, maligned though it may be by fakirs and fanatics, will appear in its essential spirit . . . as a courageous and genuine exploration of untrodden ways."

Modernism as Cummings and his mid-twentieth-century colleagues embraced it had three parts. The first was the exploration of using sounds instead of meanings to connect words to the reader's feelings. The second was the idea of stripping away all unnecessary things to bring attention to form and structure: the formerly hidden skeleton of a work would now be exuberantly visible. The third facet of modernism was an embrace of adversity. In a world seduced by easy understanding, the modernists believed that difficulty enhanced the pleasures of reading. In a Cummings poem the reader must often pick his way toward comprehension, which comes, when it does, in a burst of delight and recognition. Like many of his fellow modernists (there were those who walked out of Stravinsky's *Rite of Spring,* and viewers were scandalized by Marcel Duchamp's *Nude Descending a Staircase*), Cummings was sometimes reviled by the fakirs and fanatics of the critical establishment. Princeton poet Richard P. Blackmur said Cummings's poems were "baby talk," and poetry arbiter Helen Vendler called them repellent and foolish: "What is wrong with a man who writes this?" she asked.

Nothing was wrong with Cummings—or Duchamp or Stravinsky or Joyce, for that matter. All were trying to slow down the seemingly inexorable rush of the world, to force people to notice their own lives. In the twenty-first century, that rush has now reached Force Five; we are all inundated with information and given no time to wonder what it means or where it came from. Access without understanding and facts without context have become our daily diet.

Although in the 1950s and '60s Cummings was one of the most popular poets in America, he sometimes didn't make enough money to pay the rent on the ramshackle apartment in Greenwich Village on Patchin Place where he lived with the incandescently beautiful model Marion Morehouse. This bothered Cummings not at all. He was delighted by almost everything in life except for the institutions and formal rules that he believed sought to deaden feelings. "Guilt is the cause of more disauders / than history's most obscene marorders," Cummings wrote.

Cummings was an American aristocrat with two degrees from Harvard; my father had been headed for Harvard when he was expelled from high school, and he adored Cummings's combination of academic success and lighthearted lack of reverence for academic success. In spite of his establishment background, Cummings treated the establishment with an amused contempt.

At a time when *The New Yorker* annoyingly bowdlerized my father's mentions of kissing, Cummings got away with writing graphic erotic poetry, neatly stepping around the Mrs. Grundys of the magazine world. "may i feel said he / (i'll squeal said she / just once said he)," he wrote, in a famous poem that doesn't upset the apple cart as much as give it a new team of wild horses. He also wrote some of the sweetest love poems of the century:

> i carry your heart with me(i carry it in
> my heart)i am never without it(anywhere
> i go you go,my dear; and whatever is done
> by only me is your doing,my darling)

My father drove me to school that night—the Masters School, in Dobbs Ferry, was thirty minutes from where we lived in Scarborough. As we stepped into the entrance hall, Cummings bellowed "JOEY!"— my father's boyhood nickname. The two men heartily embraced as the school's sour founders and headmistresses glared down from their gold-framed portraits on the paneled walls.

Cummings was taller than my father and eighteen years older, but they both wore tattered Harris Tweed jackets. Cummings had developed an electrifying and acrobatic way to give poetry readings, sitting on a chair and moving around the stage instead of hiding behind a lectern, and timing his readings to the second. For this audience, he knew enough to skip his erotic masterpieces. His elegance and courtesy got him a standing ovation, especially for a powerful, moving evocation of his father: "my father moved through dooms of love / through sames of am through haves of give, / singing each morning out of each night . . ." After an encore, he appeared in his coat and scarf to let the audience know he had to go home.

My father and I drove him home to Patchin Place. "He was the most brilliant monologist I have ever known," wrote Malcolm Cowley; and that night, leaning forward from the backseat of our secondhand Dodge, I was treated to what Archibald MacLeish called one of Cummings's "virtuoso performances." Cummings was an unabashed and very funny rebel; he also had an astonishingly mobile face and a flexible dancer's body. He wasn't just an inspired mimic; he seemed to become the people he was imitating. To this day my ninety-four-year-old mother fondly remembers his imitations, his collapsible top hat, and his willingness to stand on his head for a laugh.

As we turned out of the school's genteel, tree-lined driveway and down the hill to Route 9, headed for the vibrant city, Cummings let out a deep, comic sigh of relief. My father drove, and Cummings talked, mocking the teachers who were making my life miserable—he said the place was more like a prison than a school. It was a hatchery whose goal was to produce uniformity. I was unhappy there? No wonder! I was a spirited and wise young woman. Only a mindless moron (Cummings loved alliteration) could excel in a place like that. What living soul could even survive a week in that assembly line for obedient girls, that pedagogical factory whose only purpose was to turn out so-called educated wives for upper-class blowhards with red faces and swollen bank balances? I had been told not to be so negative all the time. Cummings reminded me of his friend Marianne Moore's admonition: you mustn't be so open-minded that your brains fall out.

When we stopped for burgers at a White Castle in the Bronx, heads turned at Cummings's uncanny, hilarious imitation of the head of the Masters School English Department. In that well-lighted place, late at night, my father produced a flask and spiked the coffee. I was already drunk on a different kind of substance—inspiration. It wasn't those in authority who were always right; it was the opposite. I saw that being right was a petty goal—being free was the thing to aim for. My father, who had always sided with the school, listened. Within a year he had consented to send me to a different kind of school, an alternative school in South Woodstock, Vermont, where I was very happy.

History has given us very few heretics who have not been burned at the stake. Cummings was our generation's beloved heretic, a Henry David Thoreau for the twentieth century. He lived most of his life in Greenwich Village, at Patchin Place, during a time when experiments of all kinds, social, artistic, and literary, were being carried out. He knew everyone in the city's downtown hobohemia, from the iconic homeless Harvard alumnus Joe Gould, whose oral history was more myth than reality, to the sculptor Gaston Lachaise. In his almost three thousand poems he sometimes furiously, sometimes lovingly debunked anything or anyone in power—even death, in his famous poem about Buffalo Bill, with its spangled alliterations and intimate last lines: "and what i want to know is / how do you like your blueeyed boy / Mister Death."

Cummings despised fear, and his life was lived in defiance of all who ruled by it. This led him into some political carelessness. After a miserable stint trying to write screenplays in Hollywood, he wrote some stupidly anti-Semitic poems and sentences. His feelings about communism led him to become a fan of Senator Joseph McCarthy. On the other hand, when it came to writing about love and sex, Cummings did for poetry what Henry Miller was doing for prose.

Even more shocking, he was no respecter of social mores. "but it's life said he / but your wife said she / now said he) / ow said she / (tiptop said he / don't stop said she / oh no said he) / go slow said she . . ." Instead of using dialect as novelists do today, he explored phonetics in a way that urges the reader to speak the dialect in question: "oil tel duh woil doi sez, dooyuh unners tanmih." In a world where his antithesis Robert Frost was famously opining that free verse was like playing tennis without a net, Cummings—who, unlike Frost, had a rigorous classical education—showed that traditions like the sonnet form could be reinvented.

Cummings and my father met in New York City in the 1930s, introduced by the biographer Morris Werner; his wife, Hazel Hawthorne Werner; and Malcolm Cowley. (Malcolm was later my father-in-law, but that's another story.) "His hair was nearly gone," my father recalled of their first meetings, with the kind of exaggerated black humor both men loved; "his last book of poetry had been rejected by every estimable publisher, his wife was six months pregnant by her dentist and his Aunt Jane had purloined his income and had sent him, by way of compensation, a carton of Melba toast." Cummings's second wife was leaving him, and he was having trouble finding a publisher. Yet he urged my father to be proud. "A writer is a Prince!" he insisted. He also, with more success, urged him to abandon Boston, "a city without springboards for people who can't dive."

By the time I heard him read at the Masters School that night in 1958, I was steeped in Cummings stories that few people had heard. My father's credo was taken from a letter Cummings had written to cheer him when my father was an infantry sergeant in the Philippines in 1942. "I too have slept with someone's boot in the corner of my smile," my father often quoted, although he cleaned up Cummings's experimental language. "listen, moi aussi have slept in mmuudd with a kumrad's feet in the corners of my smile," Cummings actually wrote. The letter included an autumn leaf and a ten-dollar bill. I have it on my wall today.

In another favorite story of my father's, Cummings and Marion, literally penniless, used their last two tokens to take the subway uptown from Patchin Place to a fabulous New Year's Eve party. They were dressed to the nines: she, long-legged in a spectacular evening gown, and he in a glamorous gentleman's top hat and tails. The night was freezing cold; how would they get home? Neither of them worried at all as they dazzled the partygoers and had the time of their lives.

In the elevator on their way home in the early morning, the airy, beautiful couple noticed a leaden banker and his stodgy wife. They were all a little drunk on champagne. The banker admired Cummings's beautiful hat. "Sir," asked Cummings in his educated accent, "what would you give for the privilege of stepping on it?" The banker paid ten dollars, the hat collapsed on cue, and Cummings and Marion took a cab back to Patchin Place.

The way he died, in 1962, at Joy Farm, the Cummings family place in Silver Lake, New Hampshire, was another one of my father's often-told stories. Marion had called him in to dinner as day faded and the glorious sky lit up with the fires of sunset. "I'll be there in a moment," Cummings said. "I'm just going to sharpen the axe." A few minutes later he crumpled to the ground, felled by a cerebral hemorrhage. He was sixty-seven. That, my father let us all know, was the way to die—still manly and useful, still beloved, still strong. " 'how do you like your blueeyed boy / Mister Death,' " my father growled, his eyes wet with tears.

Fortunately, almost miraculously, Patchin Place is a corner of New York City that has been virtually untouched by the last fifty years. Still a small mews of shabby houses tucked off a tree-lined street in the West Village, it is home to a bohemian group of writers, eccentrics, and people who have lived there for decades. In the summer, through the open windows, you can see a woman reading in a room piled high with books. A gray tabby snoozes in the sun on the pavement. In the spring there are homemade window boxes and piles of literary junk from spring cleanings, and in the winter the snow falls softly on the peeling paint of white fences and sagging iron gates between the mews and Tenth Street. Two plaques are bolted to number 4, where Cummings rented a studio in the back on the third floor, and later a ground-floor apartment with Marion.

You step away from the traffic and trendiness of lattes and expensive baby clothes on Sixth Avenue and into a place where time stands still. When I wander there under the streetlights on warm evenings, it could be the night fifty years ago that my father and I drove Cummings home. When we got to Patchin Place that night, Cummings warmly invited us to come in for more conversation. We could talk awhile, have a coffee, and listen to some of his new poems; but it was late, and we had a long drive home. Now, in this book, I would like to take him up on that invitation.

New York City
June 2012

E. E. Cummings

I

Odysseus Returns to Cambridge

There was no aged dog to welcome him, and no murderous suitors for him to deceive, but E. E. Cummings was a nervous wreck. Professor John H. Finley Jr., introducing Cummings at Memorial Hall, kept saying that Cummings's return to Harvard after more than thirty years was like Odysseus' return to Ithaca, but the fifty-eight-year-old Cummings, held together by a neck-to-hip corset that he called "the Iron Maiden," and attended by his beautiful, homesick common-law wife, did not feel at all victorious or Homeric.

Many of the women in his audience, however, were as ecstatic as Penelope was when she finally recognized her long-absent husband. "There was a hush when he walked out onto the stage," says Joanne Potee, who was a Radcliffe student studying Greek with Professor Finley and who had been dragged to the lecture by her mother. "He was enchanting, captivating, and magnetic. He was very virile and sexual on the stage. I think he made some of the men uncomfortable."

Decades had passed since Cummings had jubilantly stood on the same vast stage and, with the cheekiness of youth, given a controversial class lecture as a magna cum laude for his own Harvard class. Back then, in 1915, he had a true son of Harvard College. He had grown up in a large frame house a few blocks away from Memorial Hall at the crossroads of Irving Street and Farrar Street, and he stayed on at Harvard for an extra year after graduation to get a master's degree in classics.

Now, on a late October night in 1952, with the crescent moon high over Harvard Yard, he was returning in glory as the distinguished Charles Eliot Norton Lecturer, to give a prestigious series of six lectures (for a total fee of $15,000) in Harvard's Sanders Theatre within the ornate Memorial Hall, a furbelowed Victorian Gothic giant that had been built after the Civil War to honor the Union dead.

His self-imposed exile from Cambridge—a town he had come to hate for its intellectualism, Puritan uptightness, racism, and self-righteous xenophobia—had seemed necessary for him as a man and as a poet. Soon after his 1915 class lecture and after serving in World War I, Cummings had permanently fled to sexy, law-breaking Greenwich Village, where he could hang out with other modernist poets like Marianne Moore, talk with writers like Hart Crane, be admired by Dylan Thomas and Edna St. Vincent Millay, have an affair with another man's wife, go to burlesque performances at the National Winter Garden, and ask William Carlos Williams for medical advice. He had no regrets about leaving his home-town of Cambridge, which liked to compare itself to Athens; one of his earliest poems, a sonnet, brilliantly, angrily takes its measure and finds it wanting:

> the Cambridge ladies who live in furnished souls
> are unbeautiful and have comfortable minds
> (also, with the church's protestant blessings
> daughters, unscented shapeless spirited)
> they believe in Christ and Longfellow, both dead,
> are invariably interested in so many things—
> at the present writing one still finds
> delighted fingers knitting for the is it Poles?
> perhaps.   While permanent faces coyly bandy
> scandal of Mrs. N and Professor D
> . . . . the Cambridge ladies do not care, above
> Cambridge if sometimes in its box of
> sky lavender and cornerless, the
> moon rattles like a fragment of angry candy

Still, he had come back, and standing at the polished maple lectern beneath a frieze of carved laurels, he was in the presence of some major ghosts, including the specter of his own notorious youth. Before Cummings was even born, his redoubtable father, the Reverend Edward Cummings, a Harvard professor and a member of the Harvard class of '83, had played Shakespeare's Julius Caesar in a college production on the boards of the Sanders Theatre.

Cummings had spent most of the summer before his first Charles Eliot Norton Lecture trying to calm his anxieties by writing and rewriting and rehearsing both the lectures—in a typical reversal, he titled them "nonlectures"—and the poems he planned to read. He decided that in the first lecture he would speak on the subject of his distinguished parents: his New Hampshire–born father and his mother, Rebecca, whose family came over on the *Mayflower*. His parents were Harvard royalty. They had been introduced by their friend and future Cambridge neighbor the philosopher William James. How would Cummings be able to take this haunted stage and make it his own?

"Please keep many fingers crossed (on my nonworthy bewhole) from 8 to 9 this coming Tuesday," Cummings had written his good friend Ezra Pound, who couldn't be there because he was incarcerated in St. Elizabeths, a Washington, DC, hospital. Both men loved to poke fun at their colleague T. S. Eliot, who had previously given the Norton Lectures, calling him "Old Possum."

Cummings had celebrated his birthday two weeks earlier in Greenwich Village before moving at the last minute to the borrowed house at 6 Wyman Road in the Cambridge woods, where he and Marion Morehouse lived while he was giving the lectures. He was encased in the corset that had been prescribed for his aching back by Dr. Frank Ober. (One drunken tryst he had while living with Marion in Greenwich Village was complicated by his carelessness in leaving the Iron Maiden behind. Cummings was too embarrassed to call Dot Case, the friend in whose bedroom he had left it; Marion called her and fetched it.)

"He strolled in with that elegant, erect bearing of his that expressed so well his apparent remoteness especially noticeable when he was on the lecture platform," wrote his friend Hildegarde Watson, who was in the Sanders Theater audience. "He didn't look nervous," remembers Hugh Van Dusen, a Harvard freshman who had been a Cummings fan since a Maine summer neighbor had introduced him to the poems. "He was erect, tall and slender and bald, cool and collected, reading at a small table and seated with a lamp." Van Dusen was thrilled by Cummings's manner on the stage, by his crusty New England manners, his haughty accent with its Massachusetts twang, and his animated reading. "I had a very strong impression of personality," he says. "Even in a good-humored way he was cranky. It made a deep impression to see one of my heroes in the flesh."

Sanders Theater was triumphantly crowded that October night, with dozens of students turned away at the door and others climbing the fire escapes or rapping at the windows hoping to be allowed to sit in the aisles. Harvard sophomore Ben La Farge, who sat in the packed audience, was one of the men whom Cummings apparently made very uncomfortable. The speaker was less than Homeric, La Farge thought, and in fact he gave an impression of disappointing frailty. "Cummings was not at all the man I expected from his photograph—at least, from the one picture I had of him, in Oscar Williams's *A Little Treasury of Modern Poetry*." La Farge was in the minority, but his disappointment persisted. Later, at a reception for Cummings, he remembers, "I found it somehow aesthetically annoying that his wife seemed to tower above him. I was especially disappointed that his head, which had looked so manly in the photo, seemed to wobble above his frail body."

Indeed, Marion's height—she was three or four inches taller than Cummings's 5'8"—had been a big part of his own first impression of her when he and his friends the Lights took her out for dinner at Felix's in Greenwich Village in June of 1932 after picking her up backstage after a play in which she had a small part. It was a blind date. At the time Cummings was a poetic prodigy with two awful marriages behind him. Marion was an actress who in spite of herself already had huge success as a model. Her long-necked, long-legged, wide-eyed beauty was praised by photographers like Cecil Beaton and Edward Steichen. Steichen said that she was the greatest model he ever shot because she could transform herself into the woman wearing the clothes. This girl's too tall for me, Cummings thought at first, but his doubts quickly vanished as she listened to him raptly and, later, spent the night in his studio at Patchin Place.

Before Marion, Cummings was a lonely and sometimes suicidal mess with a tendency to pick and marry women who seemed intent on little less than destroying him. His first wife, Elaine Thayer, who was married to Cummings's friend and patron Scofield Thayer when their affair started, was the mother of Cummings's only child, Nancy. Elaine divorced Cummings and abducted his child; Cummings didn't see his daughter for more than twenty years. His second wife tried to steal the family place in New Hampshire as part of their ugly divorce. Ultimately Marion's loving kindness and her appreciation of Cummings's talents made them an unusually close couple.

Harvard students are a notoriously tough audience, and this was so even in the buttoned-up 1950s under the calming influence of President James Bryant Conant, who would soon leave to join the Eisenhower administration, and would be succeeded by the conservative Nathan Pusey from Council Bluffs, Iowa. "We were all very polite and repressed," Van Dusen remembers. "This was the only time in Harvard's history when there were no panty raids. There was no friskiness even among college freshmen. The administration kept everything undramatic and laid back. Because of this we appreciated Cummings more."

The poet and editor Harvey Shapiro remembers that the audience was annoyingly packed with dewy Radcliffe girls—girls like Joanne Potee, who seemed to worship E. E. Cummings for no good reason, or no good reason that Shapiro could discern. These were the same girls who, when Shapiro was living across the mews from Cummings on Patchin Place in the Village, would show up at all hours to recite Cummings poems under his windows and leave scrawny bunches of wildflowers. Serious poets, Shapiro believed, felt otherwise; Cummings was for kids. "The fifties view of him handed down by Randall Jarrell was that he was a perpetual adolescent and you didn't have to bother with him," Shapiro says of Cummings. Except for the one Norton Lecture, Shapiro didn't. In almost ten years of living as Cummings's neighbor, in hundreds of evenings when Shapiro would come home to Patchin Place from his job at *The Village Voice* and find Cummings heading out with a sketchbook in his pocket, the two poets never exchanged one word.

Ever since the letter from the Harvard University provost, Paul Buck, had come in February, Cummings had agonized over whether to give the lectures at all, asking Harvard to limit the time he had to spend in Cambridge and badgering them over what was expected of him. Professor Finley, as the chairman of the faculty committee on the Charles Eliot Norton Professorship, was put in charge of keeping Cummings happy. In his letters, cleverly laced with admiration and flattery, Finley conceded that although the lectureship was a year-long appointment, Cummings could come in October, leave in May, and go home over the Christmas-and-January break.

Then Finley comfortingly wrote to him that a previous lecturer, Aaron Copland, had spoken for half an hour and then played some of his music, and Cummings hit on the idea of a short speech followed by a reading. For his first lecture he would talk about his parents and read the whole of William Wordsworth's "Intimations of Immortality," one of his favorite poems.

Although by the 1950s Cummings had tentatively begun lecturing at colleges and high schools—which would become a kind of new career for him, and the one that would support him in the final decade of his life—he timed and rehearsed obsessively literally to the second every time he spoke. Tortured by his own expectations and fears about returning to Cambridge, he still often thought of changing his mind and declining to give the lectures as he worked on them the summer before at his beloved New Hampshire house, Joy Farm. Marion wrote a friend that he had never worked as hard over anything as he did over the Norton Lectures.

Yet, for all these difficulties, Cummings was a sharp judge of his audience. Everything he stood for—a puncturing of pretension, an openness to adventure, a deliciously uncensored attitude when it came to sex, a sly sense of humor fueled by a powerful defiance—is in his opening phrases. He stood at the lectern under the fifty-foot carved ceilings and won the hearts of the audience in a few words. "Let me cordially warn you, at the opening of these so called lectures, that I haven't the remotest intention of posing as a lecturer," he told the students.

As he watched the audience settle down and heard the rustling of clothing and papers as the rows of listeners adjusted themselves and as he smelled the familiar, slightly lemony, well-waxed wood of Sanders Theatre, his doubts seemed to fall away. As rehearsed, he smoothly continued, calling himself "an authentic ignoramus." Then, having debunked the powers that be, he proceeded to talk about sex.

"For while a genuine lecturer must obey the rules of mental decency, and clothe his personal idiosyncrasies in collectively acceptable generalities, an authentic ignoramus remains quite indecently free to speak as he feels. This prospect cheers me, because I value freedom; and have never expected freedom to be anything less than indecent." Furthermore, Cummings explained to his thrilled audience, he was a man who loved naked women, a man addicted to striptease and burlesque theater, where he had "many times worshipped at the shrine of progressive corporeal revelation." He had their attention. He took control of the vast room in a way that was almost palpable. "Lucky the students who had you to distemper their easy comfort of thought," his friend Janet Flanner wrote him after reading *nonlectures,* which was published by Harvard University Press. "It's a wonder I thought . . . that you weren't jailed." Since, as Cummings explained to his audience, he knew nothing at all, he would not lecture on what he knew. He *would* lecture on who he was, and he would start with his astonishing parents, Rebecca and Edward Cummings.

How did Cummings get away with it? His academic bona fides—Harvard, Harvard again—helped, but he was also a true intellectual. After debunking his own credentials, praising naked women, and preaching freedom, Cummings attacked the literary critical establishment directly by reading a few revolutionary lines from Rainer Maria Rilke. "Works of art are of an infinite loneliness and with nothing to be so little reached as with criticism. Only love can grasp and hold and fairly judge them."

In a more satiric mood he might have recited an edgy autobiographical poem he had written years earlier but never put in a collection—"Ballad of an Intellectuall." Here his distaste for Harvard's intellectualism, its high-minded conversations and linguistic convolutions, is clear:

> Listen,you morons great and small
> to the tale of an intellectuall
> . . . .
> You know the rest:a critic of note,
> a serious thinker,a lyrical pote,
> lectured on Art from west to east
> —did sass-seyeity fall for it? Cheast!
> if a dowager balked at our hero's verse
> he'd knock her cold with a page from Jerse;
> why,he used to say to his friends,he used
> "for getting a debutante give me Prused"
> and many's the heiress who's up and swooned
> after one canto from Ezra Pooned . . .

By the fall of 1952, Cummings's speaking style had evolved over the dozen or so lectures he had given into something both powerful and eccentric. His voice, a whispery yet carrying sound, was magnetic as well as pleasing. Using it as an instrument, he read the poems as if they were arias without music. You leaned forward to hear him, and you were often rewarded with a joke or an inspired, wicked impression of someone like T. S. Eliot or a redoubtable English professor.

At fifty-eight, Cummings had had his share of illnesses—most of which were a series of aches and pains that defied diagnosis—but his body was also lithe and small, more feminine than masculine, more flexible than imposing. He had a kind of buoyancy and quickness that he used to great effect in acting out scenes and mimicking those he wanted to mock. He was a conversational genius, creating dazzling monologues in which words seemed to cascade over themselves in shining profusion. His close friend Gaston Lachaise, the sculptor, made huge, rounded women in bronze to float above the MoMA garden. Cummings was able to achieve this physical floating quality in the service of wit. When he was a schoolboy, his classmates joked that God would forgive them their short Cummings. "As a child he was puny; shrank from noise," he wrote, and his physical slightness as he grew was in sharp contrast to his father's righteous masculine bulk.

To describe his father to his Sanders Theatre audience, Cummings quoted a letter he had written about the redoubtable Professor Edward Cummings. "He was a New Hampshire man, 6 foot 2, a crack shot & a famous fly-fisherman & a firstrate sailor (his sloop was named The Actress) & a woodsman who could find his way through forests primeval without a compass & a canoeist who'd stillpaddle you up to a deer without ruffling the surface of a pond . . ."

The elder Cummings, his son explained to his young audience, was a great humanist who urged his own congregation on one sunny Sunday to get out into the beautiful world instead of listening to his sermon. He was the man who had the first telephone in Cambridge and one of the first automobiles. An Orient Buckboard with a friction drive, made by the Waltham Watch Company, the car was driven by chains not unlike bicycle chains. It had two kerosene lamps, open seating for two, and went as fast as fifteen miles an hour—dangerously fast on roads that were dominated by horse-drawn carriages. The car was started by pulling an ignition strap out of the rear end, a method that worked erratically. The ride was bumpy on primitive tires and dirt roads, and the car would often stall, leaving its driver to walk home. Edward Cummings loved machines and always had the latest technological invention, but it was Rebecca

Cummings who named the Buckboard *Bluebird* and offered rides to everyone she knew.

It was on the family's summer migration to New Hampshire that the car really came into its own. Before the purchase of the Orient Buckboard the trip was made by an equally temperamental and slow-moving train. Passenger trains at the beginning of the twentieth century were an uncomfortable series of cars with balky windows that failed to keep out the oily smoke from an engine that burned coal and gave off soot and cinders. The train was pulled by an impressive round-fronted steam locomotive with smoke pouring out of its smokestack and steam coming from the top of the gleaming engine, which often had a mind of its own. To stop a train, an engineer had to tell the fireman to stop shoveling, and apply the brakes judiciously, hoping that they would work against the remaining forward power of the engine. "It was both scary and exciting to see one of those locomotives come into a station," wrote Cummings's sister, Elizabeth. "The engineer would be leaning out of the cab, looking proud to be able to control such a great monstrous engine."

Now with the Orient Buckboard, and later with the Model T Fords they bought as soon as the new ones came off the line, the Cummings family could drive all the way up into New Hampshire, going north on the partially paved road that the state had named Route 3, and then veering off to the east, going through the picturesque small towns—Wolfeboro, Ossipee—until they reached the dirt road to their own houses at Joy Farm.

As the century progressed and the Model T became a more common sight on the roads around Boston, Edward Cummings decided that a Franklin car would better suit his station in life. The Franklin, manufactured by a die-cast maker named H. H. Franklin, was referred to as "the Car Beautiful." A luxury automobile, it was the first car to have a case-hardened crankshaft in regular production, to use Duralumin connecting rods in regular production, and to have a steel front body pillar construction. The Franklin boasted an air-cooled engine that was supposed to make it possible to drive for long distances without stopping.

In the Cummings family there were many annual adventures traveling to and from their house at the crossroads in Cambridge and Joy Farm and later the house that Cummings's father had built right on the shore of Silver Lake, New Hampshire, and most of these adventures included automotive disasters of one kind or another, in which overnight stays by the side of the road were narrowly averted by the resourcefulness and intelligence of Edward Cummings. His insistence on having the latest, most newfangled machines was an amusing part of his character that delighted his friends and family.

His mother, Cummings told the attentive audience in Sanders Theater, was "the most amazing person I have ever met." By 1952 she had been dead five years, outliving her husband by two decades. "Never have I encountered anyone more joyous, anyone healthier in body and mind, anyone so quite incapable of remembering a wrong, or anyone so completely and humanly and unaffectedly generous. I have the honor to be a true heroine's son," Cummings told the audience, his voice slowing with feeling.

In the final fifteen minutes of his lecture, Cummings—who refused to take questions or sign books after a lecture—read all of Wordsworth's "Intimations of Immortality," a seven-page poem, which suggested that he too had been born somewhere in heaven and had the benefit of having angels as his true parents. Even in 1952, after the war but before helicopter parents, when the invention of childhood was still young, Cummings suggested to a receptive audience of young people that the young were closer to heaven than their elders—than the parents and professors who thought they knew better because of their age and experience and who therefore tried to tell them what to do. Cummings used Wordsworth to point out that the opposite was true:

> Our birth is but a sleep and a forgetting:
> The Soul that rises with us, our life's Star,
>   Hath had elsewhere its setting,
>   And cometh from afar:
>   Not in entire forgetfulness,
>   And not in utter nakedness,
> But trailing clouds of glory do we come
>   From God, who is our home:
> Heaven lies about us in our infancy!
> Shades of the prison-house begin to close
>   Upon the growing Boy,
> But he beholds the light, and whence it flows,
>   He sees it in his joy . . .

As the first lecture ended and students streamed chattering out into the Cambridge night, Cummings and Marion headed down the street toward the house where he had grown up, on Irving Street, for a small reception given by William James and his wife, Alice. Gratified by the success of his lecture, Cummings was able to put aside some of his deep-seated anger against Harvard and all that it stood for. Marion, however, did not like Cambridge at all. As Cummings's biographer Richard Kennedy has pointed out in his book *Dreams in the Mirror* (1980), the conservative, anticommunist Cummings may also have felt politically uncomfortable in this bastion of fifties liberalism. "Have yet to encounter anybody in any manner connected with Harvard who isn't primevally pink," he complained to Hildegarde Watson.

Cummings devoted the second lecture to his own childhood, much of which had taken place a few hundred yards from where he stood on the Sanders stage. "My own home faced the Cambridge world as a finely and solidly constructed mansion, preceded by a large oval lawn and ringed with an imposing white pine hedge. Just in front of the house itself stood two huge appletrees; and faithfully every spring these giants lifted their worlds of fragrance toward the room where I breathed and dreamed," Cummings told his equally eager audience at the second nonlecture a month later. The woods he played in as a child had been donated to the town by the great Harvard professor Charles Eliot Norton, who had owned them; now he was giving lectures endowed by the same professor of poetry.

The first three lectures, as Cummings planned them, would be about himself and the world in which he grew up—which also happened to be the world of his audience. The second three lectures, delivered in February, March, and April, would be about poetry and the state of the world outside of Cambridge and the Harvard Yard. Each lecture concluded with Cummings reading for fifteen minutes to half an hour from his favorite works—which ranged from his own poems and plays to Wordsworth and Keats and Robert Burns to the Gospel of John from the New Testament to the final scenes of Shakespeare's *Antony and Cleopatra,* in which Cleopatra kills herself by putting a poisonous asp on her skin. "Dost thou not see my baby at my breast / That sucks the nurse asleep?" Cummings read to the enchanted audience at the Sanders.

Although after the first nonlecture, it was clear that Cummings was a huge success, he continued to write, rewrite, agonize and fret over the speeches, often staying up late the night before to try and bring them into alignment with the perfection he held in his mind. His back was killing him, and he took two or three Nembutal in order to get to sleep—a sleep that was rarely satisfying. Marion's unhappiness in Cambridge, where she felt isolated in the wilderness and consigned to being an old man's nurse, made Cummings's anxiety worse. Even after all his years of exile, Cambridge was still his place—his homeland—and Marion continued to feel left out. The Jameses snubbed her, she said, and other old friends and neighbors of Cummings paid no attention to her.

The third lecture, delivered on November 25, was so popular that it turned into a mob scene, with students trying to force their way into the door. Cummings was a star. Cummings and Marion had only been in Cambridge a little more than a month, but they could hardly wait to get back to Patchin Place. The second lecture series, after Christmas, was easier although the couple spent two months in the dreary house on Wyman Road. In the final lecture, before reading Keats's moving "Ode on a Grecian Urn" and the stirring lines from Percy Bysshe Shelley's *Prometheus Unbound* that he had chosen as his finale, Cummings delivered an excelsior that many in his audience would never forget. "I am someone who proudly and humbly affirms that love is the mystery-of-mysteries, and that nothing measurable matters 'a very good God damn': that 'an artist, a man, a failure' is no mere whenfully accreting mechanism, but a givingly eternal complexity . . . whose only happiness is to transcend himself, whose every agony is to grow."

These days you can walk from the Harvard Yard to Sanders Theatre in Memorial Hall in a few minutes. A new Harvard building is going up at the corner of Kirkland Street, but if you go left on Irving Street you enter into the leafiness of a Cambridge that, except for the paved streets and parking regulations, has not changed much in the past century. The Cummings house at the crossroads is walled off from the street by a flat wooden fence with a small plaque noting that Cummings was born and grew up there and that he was the poet who wrote that "the Cambridge ladies . . . live in furnished souls." It is far more elegantly maintained than it was in Cummings's day, but as you stand on the narrow street among the grand houses you can almost hear a past commotion coming from over the wall. Children are shouting and playing, an adult voice calls them inside, and a dog barks at the gate.

2

104 Irving Street

Edward Estlin Cummings was named after his father, Edward, and J. Estlin Carpenter, a British friend of Edward Cummings who also became the boy's godfather. To avoid confusion with his father, everyone always called the boy Estlin. He was the first child of his family and the only son. He was born on the evening of October 14, 1894, after a six-hour labor and a forceps delivery in the family's white clapboard mansion, with its three stories and thirteen fireplaces, at 104 Irving Street. He weighed eight and three quarters pounds and his astrological sign, Libra, the scales, predicted that he would be charming, romantic, and a bit gullible. Edward Cummings, who at thirty-three had just been appointed an assistant professor at Harvard, later told his son that the house on Irving Street was built "to have you in." Although the house may have been built in expectation of a first son, baby Estlin was the smallest of its many inhabitants, human and animal, who only increased in number as he grew up.

For starters, the bustling house was home to the baby's grandmother—his father's mother, who was called Nana. A New Hampshire grande dame, in long skirts and high-button shoes, Nana Cummings kept a sharp eye on everyone and sometimes said that she never relaxed until the entire family was safely in bed—often very late at night. Estlin's father's sister, the unmarried Aunt Jane, lived on the third floor. His mother's mother, Nana Clarke, and his aunt Emma Clarke lived in large bedrooms with their own fireplaces off the hall on the second floor. All of these female relatives were charged with being sure that young Estlin learned proper etiquette.

It was a big house, but it often seemed to be bursting with family.

The triangular yard attracted neighbors' children, and it was big enough for a touch football game. Cummings and his younger sister, Elizabeth, usually joined by a crowd of cousins and friends, were allowed a lot of freedom to play games like marbles and hopscotch, to get cold and dirty and to wander around the neighborhood. But they were also expected to be respectful, punctual, and bathed and ready for bed at eight o'clock at night. Rounding out the household were a cook, Julia, and a handyman named Sandy. Unlike many early-twentieth-century homes, the Cummings house was also filled with pets—cats, rabbits in a pen in the backyard, and the beloved family dog.

The children's favorite family member who lived in the house was their mother's charming, rule-breaking, beloved unmarried brother, Uncle George Lemist Clarke. "He was by profession a lawyer, by inclination a bon vivant, and by nature a joyous human being," Cummings recalled in his second nonlecture. George was a playful man who also wrote poems. Cummings's mother adored poetry, and she hoped her son would become a poet. As a result, Estlin started writing poetry before he went to school, and he was also a talented sketch artist. A drawing he made at the age of six features two buoyant elephants—an animal that would be Estlin Cummings's totem and favorite creature for the rest of his life. His pachydermophilia was also fed by family trips to the circuses that came through Cambridge.

When it came to writing, Rebecca Cummings encouraged George to encourage her son, and so Uncle George was Estlin's first poet and a man who provided a perfect model of the mischievous, aristocratic Boston gentleman. He was a man who knew the rules but found them a bit too boring to follow. It was a household filled with books, reading, and poetry. Even the children's games were punctuated by counting rhymes passed down through generations. When the children disagreed about who should be It in their games of tag, or who should turn the rope and who should jump, they ceded authority to the traditional choosing rhymes, like this one in which sound trumps sense: "Eenie, meemie, moanie, my / Huskaloanie, bonie, stry / Hultie, gultie, boo. / Out goes you."

Uncle George took on part of Estlin's education, and gave him a precious gift when he was in those impressionable years before puberty— a book titled *The Rhymester,* subtitled *The Rules of Rhyme: A Guide to English Versification, with a Dictionary of Rhymes, an Examination of Classical Measures, and Comments upon Burlesque, Comic Verse, and Song-Writing.*

This wonderful book is much more than a primer in poetry writing. Quoting Cicero's injunction that poets are born poets, its author, Tom Hood, includes a comprehensive discussion of everything about poetry from word sound to metrics, from subjects to syntax. Most important, it taught Cummings his first lesson in the basics of formalism and diverted him from the "what" of poetry and from thinking that poetry was only good if it had a political importance like Julia Ward Howe's "Battle Hymn of the Republic." *The Rhymester* focused on the "how" of poetry. Because of Uncle George and his gift, young Estlin's focus in poetry went from substance to structure, a shift that would characterize all his work.

Cummings's first word, according to the extensive journals of his behavior that his mother kept along with scrapbooks throughout her life, was "hurrah."

> if there are any heavens my mother will(all by herself)have
> one.   It will not be a pansy heaven nor
> a fragile heaven of lilies-of-the-valley but
> it will be a heaven of blackred roses
>
> my father will be(deep like a rose
> tall like a rose)
>
> standing near my
>
> swaying over her
> (silent)
> with eyes which are really petals and see
>
> nothing with the face of a poet really which
> is a flower and not a face with
> hands
> which whisper
> This is my beloved my
>
>   (suddenly in sunlight
> he will bow,
>
> & the whole garden will bow)

As a toddler Cummings wore a white sweater that his mother had embroidered with a crimson H for Harvard. The Cummings house was unusually relaxed. Children came over to play on the swings and in a sandbox and in a tree house built for their delight in spaces that, in neighboring houses, might have been groomed and manicured. They lived in and were part of a mythic neighborhood, and the Cummings house was within calling distance of a half-dozen other Harvard professors, including William James and Josiah Royce; it stood in the woodsy backside of Cambridge far from Brattle Street, behind the Divinity School on the Boston side of Massachusetts Avenue and close to the Somerville town line.

"Only a butterfly's glide from my home began a mythical domain of semiwilderness," Cummings told the audience in nonlecture two, "separating cerebral Cambridge and orchidaceous Somerville . . . Here, as a very little child, I first encountered that mystery who is Nature; here my enormous smallness entered Her illimitable being . . ." This love of nature as well as a passion for both the high and the low, the restrained and the showy, the cerebral and the vulgar, is another one of Cummings's characteristics as a writer and as a man. The Irving Street neighborhood was more populated by intellectuals than other, more Brahmin neighborhoods nearer the college itself. Their dogs had names like Hamlet. The Cummings house was filled with books, music, and adoration.

One day Professor Josiah Royce, chair of Harvard's Department of Philosophy, ran into young Estlin on the street and asked if he knew the sonnets of Dante Gabriel Rossetti. He invited Cummings in, led him to the study, and read him a few: "the ignoramus listening, enthralled; the sage intoning, lovingly and beautifully, his favorite poems." Cummings was delighted as Royce's rich voice read Rossetti's "The sonnet," an ode in sonnet form.

> A Sonnet is a moment's monument,—
> Memorial from the Soul's eternity
> To one dead deathless hour. Look that it be,
> Whether for lustral rite or dire portent,
> Of its own intricate fulness reverent:
> Carve it in ivory or in ebony,
> As Day or Night prevail; and let Time see
> Its flowering crest impearled and orient.

A Sonnet is a coin: its face reveals
The soul,—its converse, to what Power 'tis due:—
Whether for tribute to the august appeals
Of Life, or dower in Love's high retinue,
It serve, or, 'mid the dark wharf's cavernous breath,
In Charon's palm it pay the toll to Death.

The sonnet became Estlin Cummings's favorite form.

Long summers were spent at Joy Farm in Silver Lake, New Hampshire, near the White Mountains, where his education was still overseen by Uncle George and by his parents. By the time Estlin was enrolled at Miss Webster's School, he could already read and write fluently and he knew the Greek alphabet.

In many ways it was a golden childhood at a great moment of American history in one of the country's most interesting and beautiful places— a place where the seasons blazed out red and gold, faded to roof-high drifts of soft snow, and then burst into the bright, hot greens of summer in New England. Loving, attentive parents and servants kept a close eye on this beloved boy. His first poem, faithfully transcribed by his mother after he had announced that he wanted to be a poet, was thought to be precocious for a toddler: "O, the pretty birdie, O / with his little toe,toe,toe!" A few years later, in his first collection of poems, *Tulips & Chimneys,* he immortalized the mood of his childhood, a childhood of circuses and games and other kids in one of his best loved poems.

in Just-
spring   when the world is mud-
luscious the little
lame balloonman

whistles   far   and wee

and eddieandbill come
running from marbles and
piracies and it's
spring

when the world is puddle-wonderful

the queer
old balloonman whistles
far   and   wee
and bettyandisbel come dancing

from hop-scotch and jump-rope and

it's
spring
and
    the
            goat-footed

balloonMan   whistles
far
and
wee

"I am of the aristocracy of this earth," Cummings wrote during his fresh-man year at Harvard, when he still lived at home on Irving Street and slept in his boyhood room. "All the advantages that any boy should have are in my hands. I am a king over my opportunities."

Yet beneath this happy childhood melody were some chords of sadness and rage. Even the neighborhood had its dark side, as Estlin learned when he watched two smooth cows being driven to the slaughterhouse on one of Cambridge's larger streets near his home. The sight of the lovely crea-tures being whipped forward to their grisly death made the young Cum-mings stop: "I stand hushed, almost unbreathing, feeling the helplessness of a pity which is for some whole world," he wrote.

Cummings's father, Edward, a man so much larger than life that he looms over his son's entire story, had not had such an easy childhood. He was born in Colebrook, New Hampshire, in 1861 above his dour Calvin-ist father's general store, Cummings and Co. After a rough-and-tumble country childhood, during which he became a creditable carpenter, Edward Cummings managed to graduate from high school and get him-self to Harvard College, where he stayed on, intending first to get a law degree and then to get one in divinity. After two years he changed again, studying sociology as a graduate student and becoming Harvard's first instructor in sociology. "No father on this earth ever loved or ever will love his son more profoundly," Cummings told the Harvard audience in his first nonlecture.

Yet the older Cummings, an old-fashioned paterfamilias in a male-dominated world, could sometimes seem more frightening than loving, especially for a boy who grew up less interested in sports than in books and less interested in being a woodsman or a crack shot than in poetry and reading. Later, the older Cummings was appointed minister at the Cambridge Congregational Church, and the moment he appeared at home after work looking like an ordained messenger directly from God was a solemn one. He was a solid man morally and physically. His son, Estlin, was small, agile, and playful—all feminine attributes in the gender-challenged early twentieth century. Estlin, flexible and slight, loved to laugh and mimic and make fun of things and stand conventional wisdom on its head. In fact, he loved to flip upside down and stand on his own head. He loved to cheer people up with his antics. When the whole neighborhood came down with whooping cough and the children were going stir-crazy, it was Estlin who founded the "Whooper Club" to make a game out of a problem. His father was a sterner sort, a man who wore his Puritan morality on the black sleeve of his ministerial robes.

Cambridge and Joy Farm were the two poles of Cummings's youth. One he eventually came to despise; the other he adored increasingly throughout his entire life. Joy Farm, named after its owner Ephraim Joy, who sold it to Edward Cummings at the turn of the century, also earned its name in the joy of the Cummings children, Estlin's younger sister, Elizabeth Qualey, told Charles Norman.

The Cummingses had bought Joy Farm in 1899 after a few experimental summers at the shore, where Edward loved to sail his catboat, the *Actress*. Rebecca Cummings, however, didn't like the beach, so the family repaired to the mountains. Cummings's mother was the aristocrat of the family; her forebears on her mother's side had been distinguished Unitarian writers, judges, and adventurers. A family scandal—her father had gone to jail for a forged check, and her mother had their marriage annulled and took her three children home to live with her parents—just made the excellence of her bloodline more intriguing. Rebecca Clarke was an old maid of twenty-nine when William James introduced her to Edward Cummings in 1888. She had earned her happiness as a wife and mother, and she was appreciative and loving to the fullest measure.

On this farm, with its view of Silver Lake and its more distant view of the picturesque Mount Chocorua—a dramatic peak in the Ossipee range with a marked tree line and a craggy summit—the Cummings children were free to tumble in the hay and go on long expeditions in the woods. The entire Cummings family, with aunts, uncles, and cousins, left Cambridge in the spring to go north.

The state of New Hampshire is a landscape of lakes and rocks, granite outcroppings and thin growing soil, the land scraped clean by the ancient glaciers inching east to west, which went on to dump topsoil and rich loam in Vermont on the other side of the Connecticut River. Settled in the early nineteenth century by sturdy pioneers who desperately tried to grow things in the inhospitable soil and during the minute growing season, it became grazing land for sheep and cows. By the aftermath of the Civil War many New Hampshire towns and farms had been deserted, left behind by families who gave their sons to fight, or who had gone to Boston to work in the growing factories, or who just gave up.

The New Hampshire landscape is haunted by the ambitions of its first settlers. Walking deep in the woods, hikers like the Cummingses could come upon a long stone wall, perfectly stacked without mortar, built to keep the animals in a pasture that had long since grown up into oaks and maple trees; or upon the remains of a house foundation with the hearth made from granite boulders that some long-ago farmer pushed into place with draft horses in the hope of making a permanent home for his family. This lean landscape, with its dazzling moments of beauty—lakes all the bluer and trees all the greener for their endurance, and skies that blaze out with stars against a velvety night—suited the elder Cummingses perfectly. There this impressive father relaxed and became more of a carpenter than a preacher, rebuilding the original Joy Farm house with extensions and a second story, windows looking out to the view of Silver Lake and Chocorua, and a flat roof for watching the stars and the sunset.

Once the main house was insulated and expanded enough for his family, Edward Cummings built a study for himself at the edge of the woods, a many-sided structure with a wide walk around it. Then he built a gazebo for young Estlin under a nearby tree. As the children grew up and yearned to play in the water, he installed a cold freshwater pond where they learned to swim. During the summer months the family gravitated toward the lake, and Edward decided to build another house by the lakeshore. This boathouse, or summerhouse, which he built for his family with his own hands, also had a flat roof for sky watching.

Cummings was Rebecca's first child. As Cummings grew up and became a young man, as he moved out of the house at 104 Irving Street and into a Harvard dormitory and then into an apartment in New York City, there were painful frictions between him and his father. But his connection to his mother never wavered. She was always there for him with emotional and financial support. She sent him monthly checks her entire life and always responded to his needs. Even when she disapproved of his actions, she supported him.

A story told by Cummings's sister, Elizabeth, in her memoir, *When I Was a Little Girl,* and by Charles Norman in his authorized biography of Cummings, gives a whiff of the strength and self-reliance that were expected of many New England boys at the beginning of the twentieth century. Cummings may have been slight and unimposing—he played no sports at Harvard or at any of the three previous schools he attended— yet his spirit was as flinty and determined as anyone's.

The patriarchal Edward Cummings had grown up in New Hampshire with many pets and with a series of beloved dogs whose exploits became stories he told his children. There was Old Jack, a Newfoundland, who walked their aunt Jane to school, keeping the edge of her coat in his mouth so that she was in his care at all times. There was the amusing pug, James Blaine, who liked to nest and sleep in the silky hair of another dog's tail, making a bed out of a Newfoundland named Doctor. Edward Cummings's love of animals expressed itself in the dozens of pets his children adored and cared for: rabbits, including one particularly naughty lop-eared named Hong Kong; Elizabeth's Fluffy and other cats; and dogs—Don, a stray terrier they had found, and Mack, the family collie. When Estlin was about fourteen, his father decided that he should have his own dog, a puppy from a litter born in the village of Silver Lake, a brindle-and-white bull terrier with long, silky ears and a placid disposition.

"Rex was a wonderful dog, he was always cheerful and ready for a romp," Elizabeth recalled. "He would let my brother and me do anything with him, even swing him in the hammock and carry him upside down." Rex had a deep, authoritative bark; but when Estlin came into the house in Cambridge or at Silver Lake, Rex would let out a howl of joy, a kind of yodel that led to the family calling him Prince Ahoohaw. Boy and dog were inseparable. Rex slept on Estlin's bed at night, growling softly if any-one approached the room, and he waited patiently for him to come home from the Cambridge Latin School in the afternoons. After a bout with distemper, which made Estlin's feelings about him even more intense, Rex became a kind of family hero.

When neighborhood dogs attacked Fluffy the cat, Rex—seeing that he was outnumbered—picked her up by the scruff of the neck and carried her to safety around the corner of the house before returning to dispatch the other dogs. When Hong Kong got out of his pen and appeared to be lost forever, it was Rex who led the family to a pile of leaves by the fence where the bad rabbit had been hiding. Rex was also an astute guard dog, able to distinguish between sounds that were actually threatening and sounds that were just the creaks of an old house or the sighing of the wind in the maples. Other dogs had their foibles—Don chased cars, Martin disappeared for days at a time—but Rex was the perfect companion and family dog, and his bond with Estlin was as powerful as anything the young boy had known.

It was in the country at Joy Farm that Rex really thrived. He guarded the children when they camped out, sleeping in tents or the teepee Estlin had built. He went along on hayrides and caterpillar-collecting expedi-tions. As the children walked, Rex would run ahead and behind, checking out the country smells, the traces of night animals passing, the fascinat-ing scent of other dogs that might have quartered the same territory. On one of the family's many climbs up Mount Chocorua, Rex tangled with a porcupine and got a faceful of quills. Estlin held and calmed his dog while Edward Cummings pulled the barbed spears out one by one.

One summer evening after supper when the family had just moved to the new summer house on Silver Lake, Estlin and Elizabeth, along with the faithful Rex, decided to try out one of their father's latest acquisitions—a supposedly unsinkable folding canoe with two wooden box seats. As the sixteen-year-old boy and his sister crossed the lake in the late-afternoon light, with sunlight beginning to funnel into a shining path across the water, Rex snapped at a hornet that was flying around the children's heads. His lunge capsized the canoe, leaving both children far out in the lake fully dressed and holding on to the two skimpy boxes that had been used for seats. Estlin told Elizabeth to hold on to the canoe, which had turned turtle, but when she grabbed the side of the boat, there was a gurgling sound of air escaping and it sank to the bottom of the lake. According to Elizabeth, her brother's confidence and good humor kept her from being afraid.

At first Rex swam away from the children, furiously heading for the shore. At some point he realized he had left the children behind, and he started swimming back toward them. "He must have felt himself at the end of his strength and, hearing our familiar voices, turned back to us for help," Elizabeth wrote. Estlin raised himself as high as he could from the surface and shouted at Rex to go to shore, but the dog apparently did not understand. When he got to them there was no way for him to stop swimming. In a panic and splashing so much he apparently could hardly see, Rex tried to save himself by climbing up on Elizabeth.

"I felt his weight on my shoulders; then lost hold of my box and went underwater, I came up, sputtering, and got hold of the box again," Elizabeth remembered. "Again Rex tried to climb on, and again I lost hold and went underwater." Estlin yelled at Rex and called to him, but as he saw his sister about to go down for a third time he grabbed the frightened, panicking dog and held him underwater until he stopped struggling. Elizabeth was saved from being pushed underwater for the moment, but the children were by no means out of danger. They spent another exhausting hour in the water before Edward Cummings, luckily out for a ride in the motorboat, investigated two heads bobbing in the middle of the lake and rescued them. Estlin asked his father and other rescuers from nearby Camp Shawmut to search for Rex, hoping that he could be saved, but nothing was found that night.

The next day Estlin walked the edge of the lake until he found Rex's bloated body and carried it home for a burial. The family put up a marker, and Estlin did what he so often did when his feelings threatened to overwhelm him—he wrote a poem.

> Rex, you and I have loved each other
> > As dog and man
> > Only can,
> And you have given your silent best,

With silent cheerfulness to me,
And now that our great mother
Holds your poor body to her breast
I come to give you my best, you see
Dear dog, to that pure Rex whom we,
We two, know lies here not at rest.

Estlin Cummings never had another dog.

This was the end of his idyllic childhood. Edward Cummings kept the wooden boxes that had kept his children from drowning in the house by the lake for the rest of his life. "I keep them to remind me whenever things seem to me to be too bad," he said.

Indeed, father and son enjoyed an increased closeness as the boy approached puberty. The next March they took the train together up to Joy Farm to build a new room onto the farmhouse. On June 14, 1911, at the graduation ceremonies for his Cambridge Latin School class, Estlin Cummings attended the first of many momentous occasions of his life at Sanders Theatre in Memorial Hall.

There is a mystery at the heart of the story of the youthful Cummings. The young man who walked the few blocks to his first Harvard classes in September 1911 was above all things a loving and respectful son and a credit to his estimable parents and to their friends the professors and philosophers with whom he had grown up—the movers and shakers of Cambridge and its incomparable university. His parents abhorred drinking and all kinds of intemperance, and their only son agreed heartily. They were old-fashioned New Englanders who drew a veil—a thick muslin curtain—over all things sexual. They came from an era when piano legs were covered with fabric and women's clothes were dried inside special shams lest thinking about any kind of body part be too much temptation for the soul. Until he got to Harvard, Estlin went along without a qualm.

Something, during the years he was there, shifted tremendously. E. E. Cummings went from being the good boy of 104 Irving Street to being the bad boy of his Harvard class and later the bad boy of the national consciousness. He found that he loved to drink. He discovered the Old Howard and the burlesque delights of Kenmore Square, and one famous night he even left his father's car—the Ford of a distinguished minister—parked in front of a bordello, where the Boston police were very surprised to find it and towed it away. Cummings found that he loved going out with friends to pick up girls, get drunk on whiskey sours and gin rickeys, and end up hungover and loose in the early morning hours.

He even officially fell in love—with Amy de Gozzaldi, a woman whom he kissed onstage when they both joined the Cambridge Social Dramatic Club and had parts in *The New Lady Bantock*. Cummings played the role of the second footman, but the poet who played Lord Bantock—T. S. Eliot, another Harvard student—also had designs on Amy. Neither of these literary suitors won her over.

Soon enough, Cummings was in full rebellion against his father. He hated Cambridge; he scorned the prevailing American attitudes and tastes, and he associated with, as Richard Kennedy calls them, "a lively, spree-drinking, girl-chasing group of young men who were apprentices in the new artistic movements of the twentieth century."

At the same time that Cummings began to rebel against his parents and their culture, he began to aggressively experiment with language in a different kind of rebellion—a rebellion that would become his trademark. His friend S. Foster Damon at Harvard had introduced him to the poems of Ezra Pound, especially the powerful plaint "The Return," in which capital letters are used for emphasis within a line and the form of the poem on the page stutters along like the defeated men and dogs who are its subject. In contributing poems for his first book, *Eight Harvard Poets,* published by Laurence Gomme, Cummings included poems that played with punctuation, capitalization, and the form of the poem on the blank page. Cummings forged ahead, eager to be the first to do anything and also happy to follow paths that no one else had noticed. Pound's influence was added to that of his beloved Greek poets, who capitalized only the first letter in a poem, and his favorite comic strip, *Krazy Kat,* which also used capital letters for emphasis rather than according to the style manual.

Once he started experimenting, Cummings never stopped. In one poem he tried reverse lettering: "I will wade out / srewolf gninrub ni depeets era shgiht ym llit [Till my thighs are steeped in burning flowers]." What began with Pound deepened and doubled. At the same time, Cummings fell in love with the idea that became his trademark—the lowercase *i*. Perhaps he first saw it in the notes written by Sam Ward, the Yankee caretaker at Joy Farm. At any rate, the idea of an unassuming but very special lowercase *i* appealed to him for many reasons. As Kennedy notes, Cummings was smaller than his father, who was definitely an Important, Imposing capital letter. By using the lowercase *i* he was able to rebel, break the rules, adopt the Yankee humility of someone his family depended on, and present himself as playful rather than pompous. During the first ten years of his career, Cummings experimented with both upper- and lowercase in his own name and with all kinds of forms and punctuation. Not until the production of his play *Him* at the Provincetown Playhouse did he use the form of his name that has come to characterize everything he stood for—e. e. cummings.

At the same time, for all his playfulness and rule breaking, Cummings wanted his word taken seriously. In a letter to the poet and literary critic John Malcolm Brinnin, he explained that the lowercasing of his name was part of his work, not something he wanted every time his name was used. He didn't, he explained to Brinnin, want to be in any way "tricksy." When the question of his lowercase name came up, Cummings always answered that it was a poetic device, not some kind of gimmick he had embraced. In the 1950s, when Hugh Van Dusen wrote him to ask about the upper- and lowercasing of his name, Cummings replied charmingly on a postcard:

> perhaps(who knows?)the journalistic "image"
> behind that lower case signature myth was
> of some publicitymad smartalec who used "a
> small I" to call attention to himself
> Then signed his name with upper case capitals.

The most dramatic blowup during his more corporeal rebellion—his struggle with his father—happened after the discovery of Edward Cummings's car. When he finally returned home to Cambridge, Estlin found his father in full ministerial fig, greeting him at the door in pajamas with a sermon. Estlin taunted his father, suggesting that he could kick his only son out of the house. Edward burst into tears.

Cummings the well-behaved boy, the shy, slight mama's boy, the do-gooder and good-grade getter, became an angry young man. This anger, this shimmering energy of rage, characterized much of his greatness as he left his golden youth behind and struck out to places where there were fewer rules and more rebellion. Cummings's satirical poems, many of which are his greatest, seem to be thrown off by a great fire of fury at all authority and all established rules and customs. Yes, what happened with his father that night was partly teenaged rebellion, the pushing away of a distinguished parent so that Cummings could find his own identity. Still, he was an angry man and an angry poet; where did all that anger come from? Perhaps some of it came from having a slight, feminine body and a receptive character in a world of burly, overbearing men. Perhaps some of it floated up from the depths of Silver Lake, where a young man wrestled his beloved dog underwater on a summer afternoon a long time before.

3

Harvard

The Harvard University that Estlin Cummings entered in September 1911 was a place in the grip of enormous, conservative, regressive change. Harvard was the oldest and most prestigious college in the United States, and students traveled from all over the country and all over the world to use the observatory and science labs and to take courses with famous professors like George Kittredge on Shakespeare and LeBaron Briggs on poetry. Cummings was not like most of his classmates, who came by train or by one of the newfangled cars.

To get to college on his first day of classes, Cummings took a short stroll the few blocks down Irving Street past Memorial Hall to Harvard Yard. After school he would return to his childhood home on Irving Street for the formal family dinner with his father, the Reverend Edward Cummings, at the head of the table. He slept at home under the eagle eyes of his family, had breakfast as always in the dining room, and then left for school. Even as he sat in his freshman classes, his mother's apron strings were firmly tied to him.

Until 1909, the old Harvard had been run with the aristocratic liberal rigor of Charles William Eliot, who had been its president for forty years. Eliot was a populist democrat in an elitist world who believed that any man could be educated by reading a five-foot shelf of classics—books that became the Harvard Classics. Eliot was so liberal that he had overseen the creation of Radcliffe College from what previously had been the Harvard Annex for women. Radcliffe women had their own classrooms, of course; women weren't permitted in Harvard classes until 1943. Eliot had brought Harvard from being a provincial school to being a beacon of educational excellence for the entire country.

When Cummings got to Harvard two years after Eliot stepped down, the institution was slowly and painfully giving way to what would become the new Harvard under the conservative, anti-Semitic, racist aegis of A. Lawrence Lowell, a Brahmin's Brahmin who ran Harvard College for the next twenty-four years. Lowell "represented the conservative and exclusionary wing of the Protestant upper class as surely as Eliot represented its liberal democratic wing," writes Jerome Karabel. He was also a brilliant fund-raiser.

Under President Lowell, the university would thrive and prosper when it came to money, enrollment, and buildings. Its endowment would go from $23 million to $123 million, its student body would double from four thousand to eight thousand, and many of the buildings that identify the Harvard campus today—the Widener Library, the Memorial Chapel—were built. Even as the early years of Lowell's tenure were the years when the physical foundation was laid for Harvard to become Harvard, they were also the years when the foundation was laid for E. E. Cummings, Harvard B.A., M.A., to become the modernist poet e. e. cummings.

Under Lowell, the university would join the national mood of intolerance: for Jews, for homosexuals, and for women. President Lowell was distressed when the percentage of Jews in the 1922 graduating class rose to 22 from a genteel 7 in 1907. Lowell believed that democracy and universities should be homogeneous—"homogeneous" meaning that they should be peopled by white Protestant men. Lowell knew that his old-fashioned convictions would not be enough to change university policy or sway the disturbingly liberal Board of Overseers. Instead he argued, first, that having a class that was 22 percent Jewish hurt Harvard's applicant pool, because the right kind of parents didn't want to send their children to a college with so many Jews.

President Lowell also argued that admitting so many Jews might add to anti-Semitism; his stated theory was that the more Jewish students there were at Harvard, the greater the prejudice against them might be. No Jews, no anti-Semitism! "The anti-Semitic feeling among the students is increasing, and it grows in proportion to the increase in the number of Jews. If their number should become forty per cent of the student body, the race feeling would become intense," he wrote. President Lowell decided that Harvard should institute a 15 percent quota system for admitting Jewish students. He was also against letting African-American students live in the freshman dorms, where, beginning in 1915, all freshmen were required to live. This confused policy was quickly abolished. His policy regarding Jewish students was not so easy to resolve.

Lowell received a great deal of public criticism for his suggestion of a quota, particularly in the Boston press. Later, his rectitude was tested when he served on a three-member commission appointed by Massachusetts Governor Alvan Fuller to review the conviction of Nicola Sacco and Bartolomeo Vanzetti, two Italian anarchists and shoemakers who had been tried for murder and, through a series of legal injustices, sentenced to death. Lowell's commission found that Sacco and Vanzetti had been justly tried and sentenced. His role in sending Sacco and Vanzetti to their execution on August 23, 1927, is one of the ways he lives in history.

In response to Lowell's quota suggestion, Harvard's overseers appointed a thirteen-member committee, which included three Jews, to study the university's "Jewish problem." The committee rejected a Jewish quota but agreed that "geographic diversity" in the student body was desirable. At the same time the theoretically defeated President Lowell changed the application requirements to include a photograph and, if possible, an interview. As students began being admitted from the western and midwestern states, the student body became once again predominantly Anglo-Saxon. By the time Lowell retired in 1933, Jewish students constituted less than 10 percent of the Harvard student body.

Of course, during these decades of discussion about application policies for Jewish students and African-American students there was no discussion of a group that was even more definitely barred from the precincts of the country's most prestigious university—women. During the years when Cummings was at Harvard, in fact, women did not even have the vote. Ever since Elizabeth Cady Stanton and Lucretia Mott convened the Seneca Falls Convention in 1848, they had been campaigning. In 1914, by which time women had become one fifth of the American work force, a suffragette named Alice Paul pushed the movement into more militant tactics, which were brutally repelled with the consent of President Woodrow Wilson. Women were stripped and jailed, locked in solitary, and starved—all for the sin of demonstrating on behalf of women having the vote.

Lowell was not alone in his general intolerance or his anti-Semitism in particular. The freshman E. E. Cummings's favorite professor, Theodore Miller—his first Greek instructor and later a close friend—took a job at Princeton in Cummings's third year at Harvard. Miller visited Joy Farm in the summer and introduced Cummings to a world of poetry—Shelley, Keats, Sappho—that the young New Englander had not read. It was through Miller that Cummings discovered Greek literature as well as the Greek restaurants of Boston; it was under Miller's tutelage that he first started working on the art of translation and discovered the fragments of Sappho that appear in different patterns on the page. Miller directed Cummings to a letter from Keats that became a credo for the young poet: "I am certain of nothing but of the holiness of the Heart's affections and the truth of Imagination."

Yet even Dory Miller was immersed in and influenced by the repulsive anti-Semitic environment of this country at the turn of the century. After he went south to teach at Princeton, Miller wrote Cummings that he was glad to have moved, because at Harvard he had to teach poetry with students like Cummings "sitting next to some little rough-neck Irish Catholic or Polish Jew." Miller, who had been his mentor in his early years at Harvard, came to represent parts of the university that Cummings despised. There was accepted anti-Semitism in education and accepted anti-Semitism in literature. *The House of Mirth,* Edith Wharton's best-selling 1905 novel, features a slimy Jewish character named Simon Rosedale who is described as having the unattractive characteristics of his race. In *The Age of Innocence,* which won the Pulitzer Prize in 1921, Wharton deploys the same character in the form of Julius Beaufort. Although Cummings was disturbed by anti-Semitism at Harvard and in Cambridge, and this was one of the reasons he left, later in his own career the charge of anti-Semitism would be leveled at him and his work.

Another group that drew Lowell's furious drive for homogeneity was homosexuals. A purge of homosexuals on the Harvard campus was carried out when Lowell convened a secret tribunal that interviewed thirty students and expelled the ones accused. At a time when homosexuality was illegal in many states, it was so condemned that few people were courageous enough to admit to it. In those days, men like Cummings's Uncle George, for instance, were "unmarried" or "perennial bachelors," as if even homosexuality had to be defined in relation to heterosexual marriage.

Cummings himself certainly had bisexual yearnings—yearnings that were so unthinkable as to be entirely suppressed. Although he dutifully wrote poems to women, the great devotions of his early life were to men—to his Harvard friends S. Foster Damon and Scofield Thayer and especially to the tall, handsome James Sibley Watson Jr., a senior from a wealthy Rochester, New York, family who with his wife, Hildegarde, would become Cummings's lifelong patron and friend. Watson was not a poet, and he reminded Cummings sometimes of Edward Cummings. As Hildegarde reported in her memoir, *The Edge of the Woods,* when she met him Watson was already thrillingly scandalous in his hometown: "He is interested in rather depraved, even degenerate literature—reads Baudelaire, you know, that sort of thing," she was told before they met. With his small mustache and dark eyes, his fiancée noted, he looked like someone from another era. During the course of dozens of wildly drunken evenings, these men seem to have become physically as well as emotionally close to each other. "Homosexual feelings toward Watson," Cummings wrote in his journals. "time we drove fr. Boston–NY all night . . ."

Harvard was at a crossroads during Cummings's five years there, and so was Cummings. When he entered the college, he was younger than most of the freshmen—sixteen—and a slight 5'8" and looked even slighter standing next to his bulky father, who was more than six feet tall. A blond with refined, narrow features, he was painfully self-conscious about his body and his persistent acne. In public he often hid behind a newspaper. Because he commuted from home, he joined none of the clubs or fraternities that characterize most Harvard students' time in the Yard.

At the same time his writing lost its conscientious, conventional pleasingness and began to lurch and jump with a manic, angry energy. By the end of his freshman year he had found his intellectual soul mates and was publishing poetry in both *The Harvard Monthly,* which would be his home as a poet, and *The Harvard Advocate.*

At the *Monthly,* Cummings met S. Foster Damon, from Newton, Massachusetts, who edited the magazine. Damon took it upon himself to introduce the provincial Cummings to the world of the new art, taking him to the International Exhibition of Modern Art when it arrived in Boston in 1913. Known as the Armory Show because it opened at the New York City 69th Regiment Armory, it already had scandalized art lovers everywhere it went. It included 1,250 works by many emphatically nonrepresentational painters, such as Paul Gauguin and Henri Matisse. Cubism, with its effort to represent different points of view, was at the heart of the show. Cummings was thrilled and changed. At the center of the controversy was Marcel Duchamp's *Nude Descending a Staircase No. 2*. The Duchamp painting tries to show actual movement: instead of taking a moment from life and making it static on the canvas, Duchamp—with many of the goals that were still embryonic in Cummings's young imagination—decided to represent a whole series of moments in a series of modernistic forms descending from the upper-left to the lower-right corner of the canvas. A poem could do the same thing. "Practically everything I know about painting and poetry came from Damon," Cummings said later.

Cummings became a senior in the fall of 1914. Two years after he had first attended a Harvard College class, he was allowed to move out of the house in which he had been born and into a dormitory at Harvard Yard with his friends from the *Monthly*. His letter of acceptance to *The Harvard Monthly* had come from Scofield Thayer, a dapper, flamboyant figure on the Harvard campus, who was to become Cummings's close friend and who would have an incalculable effect on his personal and professional lives. Thayer was the handsome, dashing scion of a wealthy, distinguished Worcester, Massachusetts, family who had made their fortune in wool. His uncle Ernest had written the famous poem "Casey at the Bat."

Another friend, John Dos Passos, a social radical with a stormy background—he was the illegitimate son of a Chicago lawyer by his mistress, whom he later married—was to become one of the leading novelists of the 1920s with his *U.S.A.* trilogy. Dark, with protuberant eyes behind thick glasses, "Dos" also published in the *Monthly*, and he and Cummings found themselves sitting together in class. Then there was Stewart Mitchell, who was nicknamed "the Great Auk" because of his hatchet face.

Delighted with his independence as a senior, Cummings decorated his room with china elephants and *Krazy Kat* comic strips. He took full advantage of having his time to himself, especially the time after dark. With his gang of friends, he spent most nights in the fleshpots of Boston, where they drank, cuddled with women of questionable reputation, listened to jazz and ragtime, and danced silly dances like the turkey trot, standing on their toes and flapping their arms to the rhythms of music as unlike the music played in the parlor at 104 Irving Street as anyone could possibly imagine.

Now, liberated for the first time in his life from the Cummings schedule and the Cummings autocrat at the dinner table and the Cummings mother and the Cummings way of life, Estlin Cummings began to be angry, rebellious, rule-breaking, and provocative. Formerly neatly dressed, he wore dirty clothes and forgot to shave. His behavior changed from that of a rule follower and believer in the Unitarian Church and all its puritanical precepts, as embodied in his powerful, hulking father, to being a trickster, a Loki, a character like the poetic coyote, the character who was always working below the surface to challenge authority and blow up the foundations of the comfortable world. His experiences as a boy, after the death of Rex and with his overwhelmingly excellent father, may have laid the groundwork for his anger. At Harvard he grew into it and became confident. He wasn't just another young man striking out against his powerful father. He was a new man, an archetypal questioner, and with this newness would come a different kind of poetry. He began to love anything he could do that was truly original in poetry, truly first.

Now on his trips to Boston, he focused on getting into trouble with women. He haunted the Old Howard, a burlesque theater and strip club whose name never would have been mentioned at 104 Irving Street, and he had fallen in love collectively with the young girls who danced across the stage in increasingly daring states of undress. Begun as a church and then, in the nineteenth century, transformed into a serious theater, the Howard Athenaeum, the Old Howard in Boston's Scollay Square was already famous for its latest incarnation as the favorite of randy Harvard undergraduates. Cummings adored its vaudevillian stew of dancing, music, comedy, feathered fans, and female nudity. The Old Howard hosted the greats—Fanny Brice, Gypsy Rose Lee, Sophie Tucker—interspersed with comedians and acts like the Kouta-Kouta dancers. There were plenty of broad jokes and plenty of broads. "Would you hit a woman with a child?" one of the Old Howard tramps asked another one onstage. "No, I would hit her with a brick!" answered the second tramp. This joke, created by grammatic modification, inspired Cummings, who began switching out parts of speech and purposefully misplacing modifiers in his poems. Later he said that this joke was the basis of his mature style as a poet.

Another favorite haunt was Healey's Palace, memorialized in one of the poems Cummings wrote in LeBaron Briggs's class in pell-mell tetrameter rhyme with conventional punctuation. It's a little-known poem, but it's a lovely picture of that time in his life and it perfectly fits content to form in a way that came to be a Cummings trademark.

In Healey's Palace I was sitting—
Joe at the ivories, Irene spitting
Rag into the stinking dizzy
Misbegotten hall, while Lizzie,
Like a she-demon in a rift
Of Hell-smoke, toured the booths, half-piffed.

I saw two rah-rahs—caps, soft shirts,
Match-legs, the kind of face that hurts,
The walk that makes death sweat—Ted Gore
And Alec Ross; they had that whore
Mary between them.   Don't know which,
One looked; and May said: "The old bitch
Lulu, as I'm a virgin, boys!"
And I yelled back over the noise:
"Did that three-legged baby croak
That you got off the salesman-bloke?"

The beer glass missed.   It broke instead
On old man Davenport's bald head.
I picked a platter up, one-handed.
Right on her new straw lid it landed.
Cheest, what a crash!
                    Before you knew,
Ted slipped the management a new
Crisp five, and everyone sat down
But May, that said I'd spoiled her gown,
And me, that blubbered on her shoulder,
And kissed her shiny nose, and told her
I didn't mean to smash her...Crowst,
But I was beautifully soused!
I think Al called me "good old sport,"
And three smokes lugged out Davenport.

His angry rebellion also had an adolescent side. Everything his parents disapproved of, everything that Cambridge society disapproved of, from drinking to sex to Jews to foreigners, was what the young Cummings set out to embrace. "I led a double life," he wrote about his last year at Harvard. "getting drunk and feeling up girls but lying about this to my father and taking his money all the time."

The world was changing almost as fast as he was. During the summer after his junior year, while he was still living at home on Irving Street, on June 28, 1914, Austrian Archduke Franz Ferdinand and his wife were assassinated in Sarajevo, setting off a series of confrontations that led to the German declaration of war on Russia on August 1 and on France on August 3 and finally the British declaration of war against Germany on August 4. In literature there were the old world—the poet Joyce Kilmer's sentimental poem "Trees"—and the new world: James Joyce's *Portrait of the Artist as a Young Man* (1916), with its scathing indictment of unjust authority.

Authority everywhere was crumbling, and nowhere more than at 104 Irving Street. As Cummings's world began to open out in 1915, he made new friends and saw the paintings and read the works that would push his own work forward. In this year of freedom, Cummings, Thayer, Dos, and a few other friends formed the Harvard Poetry Society; they held meetings every few weeks, read each other's poems out loud, and invited an occasional speaker to come to Harvard and talk about poetry. Even Amy Lowell, President Lowell's renegade sister, came, smoking cigars and getting very cranky onstage when she was asked what she did when she didn't have anything to write about.

In June of his senior year, Cummings created a manifesto for his new, experimental world in a term paper for his composition professor, Le-Baron Briggs, titled "The New Art." It was a spring on the brink of a world that would change forever, and Cummings both consciously and unconsciously was thrilled. As President Woodrow Wilson desperately tried to avoid entering the war between Germany and Britain and France, writing a series of notes demanding an apology for the sinking of the unarmed British passenger ship *Lusitania*, Cummings submitted his essay to be an oral presentation at the June commencement exercises in Sanders Theatre. On June 24, 1915, he delivered it, alongside the traditional commencement orations, to the somewhat bemused crowd of graduates, parents, and visitors.

The new art, Cummings explained to his august audience, was happening in painting (he used Cézanne and van Gogh as examples), in music (he pointed to Debussy and Satie), and of course in poetry. As examples of the new art in poetry, he used Amy Lowell, and with a lascivious flourish he read out Lowell's deeply sensual lines:

> Why do the lilies goggle their tongues at me
> When I pluck them;
> And writhe, and twist,
> And strangle themselves against my fingers,
> So that I can hardly weave the garland
> For your hair?

"Is that our president's sister's poetry he is quoting?" hissed one of the Cambridge ladies in the audience. "Well, I think it is an *insult* to our president!" According to the class notes, President Lowell kept his face immobile, but flushed a deep brick red. There were stirrings of protest in the audience, and the next day one of the Boston newspapers ran the delicious headline HARVARD ORATOR CALLS PRESIDENT'S SISTER ABNORMAL. Other examples of the new art were a second poem by Lowell, a sonnet by Donald Evans, and twenty lines from Gertrude Stein's *Tender Buttons,* beginning with the spaced-out "A Sound": "Elephant beaten with candy and little pops and chews all bolts and reckless reckless rats, this is this."

Cummings was deadly serious about the new art, but his audience was largely outraged or amused. They were used to seeing paintings that represented the objects being painted, hearing music based on time-honored melodies, and reading poetry written in formal lines and stanzas, with the antique language of their beloved Longfellow or Emerson. Cummings had been deeply influenced by the man who had pulled off the trick of being a friend and mentor to both the experimental Cummings and his less-than-beloved colleague and classmate the experimental Tom Eliot. Ezra Pound was already famous for his help in encouraging and publishing James Joyce and Robert Frost. According to Matthew J. Bruccoli's *Hemingway and the Mechanism of Fame,* a later beneficiary, Ernest Hemingway, would write about Pound's epic, notorious generosity to other writers: "He defends [his friends] when they are attacked, he gets them into magazines and out of jail. He loans them money . . . He writes articles about them. He introduces them to wealthy women. He gets publishers to take their books. He sits up all night with them when they claim to be dying . . . He advances them hospital expenses and dissuades them from suicide." Pound, who would later require many of these services himself from his own generous friends, was living in Europe; but Foster Damon had showed Cummings his masterful, groundbreaking poem "The Return," written in 1913. As well as its experiments in language, the poem also uses the metaphor of hunting and hunters, which Cummings would soon use himself. The use of sounds to convey meaning, of form on the page to telegraph an emotion, of capital letters to underline importance—these were things that Cummings had somehow been searching for. "The Return," he wrote, "gave me [the rudiments] of my writing style."

See, they return; ah, see the tentative
Movements, and the slow feet,
The trouble in the pace and the uncertain
Wavering!

See, they return, one, and by one,
With fear, as half-awakened;
As if the snow should hesitate
And murmur in the wind,
        and half turn back;
These were the "Wingéd-with-Awe,"
        inviolable.

Gods of the wingèd shoe!
With them the silver hounds,
        sniffing the trace of air!

Haie! Haie!
    These were the swift to harry;
These the keen-scented;
These were the souls of blood.

Slow on the leash,
        pallid the leash-men!

Before he absorbed Pound, Cummings was writing well-behaved nature poems that leaned on Shakespeare and Wordsworth. A typical sonnet is one of the conventional poems published in *Eight Harvard Poets*:

> this is the garden: colours come and go,
> frail azures fluttering from night's outer wing
> strong silent greens serenely lingering,
> absolute lights like baths of golden snow.

Robert Frost later wrote in "The Figure a Poem Makes" that "like a piece of ice on a hot stove, the poem must ride on its own melting." Before Pound, Cummings didn't seem to be able to make this miracle happen. After Pound, and especially after reading and rereading "The Return," Cummings took a leap forward into the kind of poetry that became his signature. One early masterpiece has fourteen stanzas varying from two to three lines in iambic tetrameter:

> All in green went my love riding
> on a great horse of gold
> into the silver dawn.
>
> four lean hounds crouched low and smiling
> the merry deer ran before.
>
> Fleeter be they than dappled dreams
> the swift sweet deer
> the red rare deer.
>
> Four red roebuck at a white water
> the cruel bugle song before.
>
> Horn at hip went my love riding
> riding the echo down
> into the silver dawn.
>
> four lean hounds crouched low and smiling
> the level meadows ran before.

Softer be they than slippered sleep
the lean lithe deer
the fleet flown deer.

Four fleet does at a gold valley
the famished arrows sang before.

Bow at belt went my love riding
riding the mountain down
into the silver dawn.

four lean hounds crouched low and smiling
the sheer peaks ran before.

Paler be they than daunting death
the sleek slim deer
the tall tense deer.

Four tall stags at a green mountain
the lucky hunter sang before.

All in green went my love riding
on a great horse of gold
into the silver dawn.

four lean hounds crouched low and smiling
my heart fell dead before.

Pound and his friend the poet H.D. (Hilda Doolittle) and her husband,
the poet Richard Aldington, had all lived in London when Cummings
was at Harvard. They had produced three rules that became the basis of
a poetics they called imagism. (Later, when Amy Lowell had become so
identified with them that it came to be called Amygism, they changed
its name to vorticism.) The rules were simple: (1) The thing must be
treated directly; (2) no word that does not contribute should be used; and
(3) rhythm should be musical rather than metronomic. Pound's famous
haiku was the manifestation of these rules: "The apparition of these faces
in the crowd; / Petals on a wet, black bough."

becca Cummings in 1892 by Charles Sydney Hopkinson

e Cummings house at 104 Irving Street, Cambridge

A portrait of Cummings at age eight, c. 1902, by Charles Sydney Hopkinson

Cummings, age ten, with his father, Edward, and his younger sister Elizabeth, in 1904

e family at Joy Farm with, from right to left, a maid holding Rex the dog, Elizabeth on donkey,
in on horseback, Rebecca in white, and handyman Sandy Hardy leading the cows, c. 1904

in with his beloved dog, Rex, and Elizabeth in the hammock

Dean LeBaron Briggs, the Harvard professor who taught Cummings form

James Sibley Watson, Cummings's clos friend and patron

Young women at a burlesque theater in 1916

Scofield Thayer, Cummings's
friend and patron and Elaine's
first husband

Memorial Hall and Sanders
Theatre at Harvard College

Elizabeth Cummings, Estlin's sister, in her teens, c. 1917

ABOVE Cummings's Harvard graduation photograph, 1915
RIGHT A Cummings self-portrait, from the 1920s

Cummings's notes on the stationery of Collier & Son, where he was working: "Buffalo Bill is Dead"

Pound would become a close friend and mentor to Cummings, and the young poet was one of the friends who did not desert him even during his period of repulsive support of fascism or his incarceration after World War II in St. Elizabeths Hospital in Washington, DC. Before the war, Pound, who came from Idaho, was at the center of the vibrant, changing world of twentieth-century poetry. He was friends with William Butler Yeats; the two spent summers together talking about a new kind of poetry. He married Yeats's lover's daughter, Dorothy Shakespear. He was friends with William Carlos Williams and Ford Madox Ford. A flamboyant character who sometimes wore a huge hat and colorful earrings, Pound was shaken by the British experience of World War I, and in 1921 he moved to Paris.

Cummings and Pound finally met after the war on a Paris street, introduced by none other than Cummings's friend and *Harvard Monthly* colleague Scofield Thayer. As Thayer and Cummings walked down the Boulevard Saint-Germain one July night, Pound appeared before them and bowed. "Mr. Ezra Pound is a man of my own height," Cummings wrote his parents, "reddish goatee and ear whiskers, heavier built, moves nicely, temperament very similar to J. Sibley Watson (as remarked by Thayer)—same timidity and subtlety, not nearly so inhibited. Altogether, for me, a gymnastic personality." Pound and Cummings spent the evening together, two comrades on the barricades of a new way of writing poetry.

Pound, who was in some ways the brightest star of his generation, the most talented and the most generous, seemed to come completely unraveled during World War II. His civic grandiosity began with furious letters criticizing the design of the New York Public Library and ended with him being thrown into prison for being a traitor to his country. History has pushed this man to the sidelines, unable to tolerate his treachery. Perhaps his attacks on his own country might have been forgiven. The form those attacks took—voluntary radio speeches denouncing the Jews and on behalf of Mussolini—was unforgivable.

In the study of art and literary history, one of the great problems is how to separate the art from the artist, how to separate the masterworks of a Wagner or a Richard Strauss, a Pound or even a Cummings, from the terrible things they said and wrote in their roles as puny, deluded human beings—men. On the one side of the spectrum of possible reactions we have the silliness of political correctness—students who are denied the joys of Dickens or even Salinger because of those writers' behavior as men and their identity as men. When literature is divided into categories based on the politics or even the worldly identity of the writer, everyone loses. On the other side of the spectrum, we have Pound.

In some ways Cummings's experience at Harvard was typical of a young man's first experience away from home. Of course, for Cummings Harvard was not far away from home, and perhaps this made his experience even more vivid. In an early poem about the college, Cummings imagined seeing through the shadow-walls and ghost-toned tower of the "ancient-moulded" Yard to a heart of fire where sweating men worked at a smithy on the massive-linked chain "which is to bind God's right hand to the world." In other ways his group of young friends were clearly extraordinary. From the ranks of the *Harvard Monthly* writers who met on the third floor of the Harvard Union, one of them, Stewart Mitchell—the Great Auk—decided to produce a book that would be entitled *Eight Harvard Poets*. The anointed were Mitchell himself, Cummings, Dos Passos, S. Foster Damon, Robert Hillyer, William A. Norris, Dudley Poore, and Cuthbert Wright. Many things conspired to make this book hard to finish, difficult to produce, and late in reaching the press, but it was finally published with a great deal of financial help from Dos's father, a Chicago lawyer, in July of 1917. The publisher was Laurence Gomme, who ran out of money more than once, closed his publishing house and opened a new one for the purpose of publishing the book. Gomme printed two thousand copies and sent one hundred out to each of the contributors. The collection established Cummings as a poetic prodigy.

Between 1914 and 1917, Cummings and his friends lived in a kind of paradise. That world would accommodate even Cummings's silliest rebellions and respond to him with love and acceptance. World War I, with its unbearable death toll and new visions of the horror humans inflict on each other, would change all that. It would change what seemed possible for a whole generation of writers; and specifically, in the most gruesome and physically painful way, it would change that for one wide-eyed volunteer, E. E. Cummings.

4

The Western Front

Cummings entered Harvard as a slight, frightened, well-behaved boy, and he left it a confident, angry, rebellious young man who knew the rules so well he could break them in fresh and imaginative ways. In his fifth year there, after his controversial Class Day speech, "The New Art," he moved back in to the family house, where he abandoned his childhood bedroom and holed up in the attic to paint and write poems.

Harvard gave Cummings a sense of self, but one of his final classes there in English versification with LeBaron Briggs may have been the one that made him a great poet. Briggs, the dean of the Faculty of Arts and Sciences, was an extraordinary teacher of the old school. Although he was a father figure to his students, he was stern when it came to principles. He came from a tradition of privilege and service, as Cummings did. A quotation from him, passed on by his student George St. John, who became the headmaster of the Choate School when John F. Kennedy was a student there, has been documented as being the basis for JFK's famous "Ask not what your country can do for you, but what you can do for your country." According to Chris Matthews's biography, *Jack Kennedy: Elusive Hero,* the famous inversion was first used by the Harvard dean when he said, "Ask not what your alma mater can do for you, but what you can do for your alma mater."

Briggs was conventional when it came to poetry and radical when it came to teaching. He required a huge amount of writing from his master's students outside class—writing that was heatedly discussed in the classroom. He led his students through poem after poem in almost every poetic form invented: haiku, four-line stanzas with various rhyme schemes, sestinas, and Italian and English sonnets. They wrote in iambs, dactyls, and trochees, in tetrameter and trimeter and pentameter. They wrote with alliteration and assonance and without it. They used similes and metaphors until they dreamed in similes and metaphors.

This rigorous education in form was exactly what seemed to free Cummings to invent a new kind of form. His experiments with language became more extreme. Almost all his poems relied on the beauty of nature: a sunset, flowers, the moon. Now he put words on the page to telegraph meaning through the literal form of the poem as Pound had done. He tried to write the way people spoke, using casual language and direct address. He began switching parts of speech. Somewhere in his final year at Harvard and the year or two after that, Cummings found a kind of poetic sweet spot—he was able to string words and forms together in an electrifying and entirely original way.

"It was something absolutely new when it appeared," Malcolm Cowley wrote to Cummings later on, "as your poems in the first issue of the *Dial* were absolutely new. There had been a big change since 1915 . . . you found something new and your own—the real question is what started you looking for it?" Certainly Cummings's year with Dean Briggs, in which a newly confident poet and scholar drilled and redrilled the poetics of the English language, had something to do with the freedom he found within the ancient forms.

Like many poets, Cummings wrote his most startling and most famous work when he was a young man in his twenties. "All in green went my love riding," "Buffalo Bill's," "In Just-spring," "the Cambridge ladies"—all are poems from after he gave his class speech at Sanders Theatre in 1915 and before he enlisted to fight in World War I in 1917. The energy in Cummings's poems comes from the strict forms that seem to be barely containing their passionate subjects and images. Perhaps the tension between form and formlessness, between poetics and content, is sharper in these poems because his immersion in form was more recent. Much of Cummings's poetry plays with form in the way that only a formalist can play—this was the whole idea behind modernism as he embraced it. In the early poems, this revolutionary inversion—the way form can create freedom—seems livelier than it became in some of the more accomplished later work.

There was plenty of sentimental backsliding. Scofield Thayer asked him to compose a wedding poem for his June 21, 1916, marriage to the beautiful nineteen-year-old heiress Elaine Orr. Cummings, who was half-smitten with Orr himself after one meeting, composed the endless, bloviating, alliterative, faintly Keatsian "Epithalamion":

Thou aged unreluctant earth who dost
with quivering continual thighs invite
the thrilling rain . . .

Thayer paid Cummings a thousand dollars for writing the poem, which Cummings used to move to New York City, free from Cambridge at last.

Cummings already sensed that he was destined to live in Greenwich Village, that seething mass of poets, writers, and rule breakers. He rented his first apartment, at 21 East Fifteenth Street, near Fifth Avenue, with a friend, Arthur "Tex" Wilson, another writer. "In New York I also breathed: and as if for the first time." From this apartment, Cummings suited up and went to his first job, which had been found for him by one of his Harvard professors, William Allan Neilson. Cummings had thought the job would be writing or editing for a weekly magazine, *Collier's,* but instead he found himself working for the Collier publishing house, where for the handsome sum of fifty dollars a week he answered letters and packed books for shipping. Cummings was so bored by his job that he read both the poetic and the prose Eddas—dense Icelandic sagas—while he worked there.

Although the job was tedious, Greenwich Village was everything he had hoped it would be. Cummings soon found new friends, like the sculptor Gaston Lachaise; he spent hours over inexpensive meals at places like Khoury's, where he ate the eggplant paste called baba ghanoush, which he and Dory Miller had discovered in Boston, and Romany Marie's, where everyone from Eugene O'Neill to Buckminster Fuller gathered for thick, cheap beef stew. He discovered the National Winter Garden, the New York City version of the Old Howard and Healey's Palace, and soon he felt perfectly at home—more at home than he had felt at home for years.

Young, poor, and furiously ambitious, Cummings could feel ideas igniting in his mind like a string of firecrackers. On January 10, 1917, reading the *New York Sun* during one of those boring days at Collier, he came upon a headline announcing the death of Buffalo Bill Cody. "Buffalo

Bill is Dead," noted Cummings on a piece of P. F. Collier & Son stationery already a scrawl of penciled notes incomprehensible to anyone but himself—"Tasmania," "netsuke of Japan," "imprimatur," "hernia," "like a best-seller." Buffalo Bill Cody had been a symbol of glamour and sadness for Cummings and all those who followed his career; once one of the most famous men in the world, with long, flowing white hair, a silver stallion, and the adulation of millions, Cody went bankrupt and spent his last years trying to resuscitate his famous show. Later, at home on East Fifteenth Street, Cummings started fooling with the idea of writing a poem about Buffalo Bill that would take a spoken pattern on the page—as Pound had in "The Return"—and use all the alliteration and metric mastery he had learned in Briggs's class to express his anger and sadness.

Cummings was an angry young man in a generation of angry young men—many of whom would be destroyed by the war. "We were young, we were poor, and we were ambitious," wrote Allen Tate, another poet friend of Cummings's. "We thought that the older generation was pretty bad, and we were later going to replace them." Perhaps because of his education, or perhaps because of his intensity, or perhaps because of a stroke of great good luck, Cummings was one of those rare geniuses who were able to use their anger to create sublime, incandescent art. The short poem he wrote that January would become one of his most famous, and its few, short lines are some of the most powerful ever written in English. He uses the word "defunct" to create a syllabic meter in the second line—shades of Dean Briggs—and runs words together to create speed and visual imagery. Then he uses spacing and language forms to create the impression of speech. The work shimmers with anger: at loss, at the end of beauty, and most of all at death.

> Buffalo Bill's
> defunct
>   who used to
>   ride a watersmooth-silver
>
>   stallion
> and break onetwothreefourfive pigeonsjustlikethat
>   Jesus
> he was a handsome man
>   and what i want to know is
> how do you like your blueeyed boy
> Mister Death

The regular job at Collier was to be Cummings's first and last; after three months he quit. Armed with letters of recommendation from Amy Lowell, he decided to take his chances on magazine work. As a twenty-two-year-old and always, Cummings's attitude toward money was gallant and carefree. He returned his father's checks, sent to help the two young men set up housekeeping, and chided his sister about an overcoat his parents had sent. "We are alright and not really in need of a single thing (in fact, the trouble is to find a reputable burglar to remove our superfluous stuff)," he wrote home.

Although the winter of 1916–17 was bitterly cold, and New York was all pavement and streetcars and yelling, unlike peaceful Cambridge, Cummings fell in love with Greenwich Village, the neighborhood he would come back to and live in for the rest of his life. This was a first casual sighting of the city that would become one of his true loves—a place where the photographer who lived upstairs invited young women to pose nude for his camera, hoping they would not discover that he had no lens; a place where races and religions mixed with "colossally floating spider-webs of traffic; a stark irresistibly stupendous newness, mercifully harboring among its pitilessly premeditated spontaneities immemorial races and nations." In nonlecture 3, Cummings told his audience he was led to self-knowledge by a "phenomenon and a miracle." The miracle would be Paris; the phenomenon was New York.

Cummings and Wilson reveled in the city. Cambridge was everything old and stodgy; New York was everything new and adventuresome. New York had no quota system, no puritanical ideas about sex, no uptight restrictions on drinking and partying. There was no bullying, racist President Lowell; no smothering, adoring mother or meddling Aunt Jane to tell him what to do or to make him feel guilty about what he wanted to do. When he got home drunk after a night of partying and drinking, staying up late with his new friends to argue the state of the world or the ethics of prosody, there was no terrifying ministerial presence waiting up for him.

In the middle of enjoying himself, as a poet who was part of a brilliant community of New York poets and as a young man sowing his very wild oats, Cummings was still vaguely aware of the shadow of war and the possibility of being drafted. As Germany declared that it would use all available weapons to stop ships going to and from Great Britain, Cummings spent evenings enjoying the dancing girls at the National Winter

Garden. In the first months of 1917, German submarines sank thousands of ships; in April alone, allied and neutral nations lost 122 ships to the German sea offensive. Cummings and his friends in the Village didn't really care. The war seemed very far away and not very serious. "I don't know why I talk of this 'pseudo' war as I have no interest in it—and am painting and scribbling as ever . . . I read but one paragraph of Wilson's speech, being taken with a dangerous fit of laughter," he wrote to his mother as late as April 1, the day after the United States had entered the war. Even then it all seemed unreal, if not amusing. Wilson's stirring declaration of war accused Germany of seeking to rule the world through any means. "The challenge is to all mankind," the president said. "Each nation must decide for itself how it will meet it. The choice we make for ourselves must be made with a moderation of counsel and a temperateness of judgment befitting our character and our motives as a nation."

As ever, there were special protocols for Harvard men. In order to avoid being forcibly enlisted, Cummings went to see Eliot Norton, the wealthy son of the late Harvard professor, in his office at 2 Rector Street in New York to sign up along with a group of Harvard friends, including Dos Passos and Robert Hillyer, for the private ambulance corps that Norton's brother, Richard, had organized to help the French. The young men would be driving old Fords, Packards, Renaults, and Fiats in support of French and American troops near Noyon on the Western Front, where there had already been furious fighting.

While Harvard boys had been distracted, the French and German armies had suffered a million casualties on the Western Front, including the horrors of the trench warfare during the Battle of the Somme in the summer and fall of 1916. Three of Cummings's fellow poets of the Western Front—Wilfred Owen, Siegfried Sassoon, and Robert Graves—had already been emotionally destroyed by what had happened to them in the trenches, and had been sent to Craiglockhart War Hospital to recover from shell shock. Owen would return to the battlefield and be killed the next year.

Not only was the war far away, but Cummings at Harvard was halfway to being a pacifist. Still, under the threat of conscription into the infantry, joining an ambulance corps seemed wise. This cautious choice didn't make him any more enthusiastic about the prospect of war in general or war against the Germans in particular.

Writing to his parents on April 18 about his plan to sail for France on the ship *La Touraine* ten days away, Cummings wrote, "Hope the war isn't over before I get there." He wasn't alone in not being able to take the war seriously. As Malcolm Cowley wrote in *Exile's Return*, "We were eager to get into action, as a character in one of Dos Passos's novels expressed it, 'before the whole thing goes belly up.' " The Norton-Harjes American Volunteer Motor Ambulance Corps, loosely associated with the American Field Service (where Malcolm Cowley drove an ambulance) and the American Red Cross, was the enlistment of choice for Harvard men. The *Harvard Crimson,* announcing that twenty undergraduates had already signed up, explained that "for those who wish to go over . . . , the requirements are briefly these: A man should pay his way over and back, and have at least $150 in spending money. His uniform will be furnished him in Paris. He should have considerable driving experience, but not necessarily mechanical experience. His physical and nervous condition must be good. Transportation will be paid for some but they must have had considerable experience with driving the larger types of cars."

Cummings was seasick on board the *Touraine,* and so prone to think of the war as a great lark that he wrote his parents that the French ship's discomfort had made him pro-German. His misery was so great that if a German U-boat were to "waste a torpedo" on the *Touraine,* he would be delighted, he wrote. After the first few days of the voyage things improved. Someone introduced him to another young man headed for the Norton-Harjes Ambulance Corps, William Slater Brown, a Massachusetts aristocrat (his family had founded the town of Webster) who had been studying journalism at Columbia. Brown was two years younger than Cummings, but almost immediately the two men became close friends. Cummings's natural skepticism of any authority, heightened by liberal amounts of alcohol, was probably aggravated by Brown's equally devil-may-care attitude. Later this would get both of them into more trouble than they ever could have dreamed of. The war had been raging in Europe for three years; but crossing the Atlantic on their way to a battlefield, Brown and Cummings, two indulged young men, seemed determined to behave as if they were back on an Ivy League campus. "The amazing vulgarity of the whole deal—I mean La Croix Rouge, Voluntier Cummings—keeps one from jubilations on one's successful escape from conscription," Cummings wrote from the *Touraine.* Soon vulgarity would be the least of his problems.

If he had trouble taking the war seriously, his problem was compounded by what happened when he and Brown debarked from the *Touraine* and headed for Paris. Somehow, perhaps because they were deep in a private conversation, or perhaps because they were drunk, or perhaps because of some misunderstanding that had nothing to do with them, the two got off the train from Bordeaux at a different stop from their future colleagues-at-arms—or at least their colleagues at the steering wheel. Conscientiously, they made their way to the Norton-Harjes offices at 7 Rue François Premier, only to find that they had fallen through a delightful bureaucratic rabbit hole. The office was closed, and they were directed to the Hôtel du Palais, a lovely spot on the right bank of the Seine. Although they reported again at the office the next day, their assignments had somehow been lost or sidetracked. While their classmates and peers hunkered down in trenches or risked their lives in the primitive airplanes of the RAF, Cummings and Brown were detained in Paris for five weeks because of a bureaucratic glitch. Detained in Paris in the spring! For Cummings it was enough to begin to take the war with a bit more gratitude, if not any more seriousness.

April in Paris: if Cambridge was the question, Paris seemed to be the answer. Brown and Cummings walked everywhere and did everything. In Paris, scented by horse-chestnut blooms, the war still seemed far away, signified only by an absence of young men in the streets, the obvious deformities of the men left behind, and the presence of airplanes and dirigibles flying overhead. "Last night I sat in the Champs (with my feet in a running gutter) for half an hour, watching an eclairee aeroplane come from perhaps fifty miles off, through a night bursting with stars," he wrote home. The two young men had coffee at the Deux Magots on Saint-Germain-des-Prés and haunted the Louvre on the Right Bank. They read *Le Matin* and *Le Figaro* at breakfast near the Champs-Élysées. They reveled in the casual beauty of the Tuileries and of the Pont Alexandre III. They found a favorite restaurant, Chartier, and discovered couscous. Cummings, a talented linguist, soon picked up enough French to understand and speak. They read French poetry. Cummings bought Cézanne and Matisse reproductions and dozens of books from the stalls along the Seine.

They plunged into Parisian culture with the momentum provided by limited time. They went to the Ballets Russes to see *Petrushka* and liked it so much they went again. They were moved by the premiere of Erik Satie's *Parade,* with its sets by Picasso, and horrified by the audience's negative reaction. Cummings sketched everything: soldiers, children, a woman carrying a baguette, horses. He grew a mustache and wore a beret.

The great liberation of Paris was sexual. Still a frightened and confused virgin at twenty-two, Cummings had grown up in a household where sex was never discussed and sex outside of marriage was a sin. In Cambridge, men's evil animal desires were tamped down with cold showers, a no-touch zone around one's own genitals, constant warnings of moral boundaries and the dreadful price one paid for breaking them. For all his mischievousness and desire to break the rules, this was one rule that Cummings hadn't broken. He had taunted his parents by letting them know he loved burlesque. He had left his father's car outside a bordello, but he had not apparently gone so far as actually having sex.

Added to the moral strictures imposed on him by Cambridge was the fear of disease. Harvard physiology classes stressed the ease of contracting syphilis and its terrible symptoms. Sex was wrong and it was dangerous. Harvard men could look, but they had better not touch. So although Cummings and Brown were thrilled by the Folies Bergère and the city where prostitution was legal, and although they found two young prostitutes to hang out with—Mimi and Marie Louise—the frightened Puritan in Cummings was very much on the alert. According to Richard Kennedy (the biographer with the fullest account of Cummings's time in Paris, because he interviewed Brown after Cummings's death), Marie Louise was genuinely fond of Cummings, who wrote poems for her and cherished her. She called him "Edouard," and the two girls even invited the young men to dinner at their own apartment.

For Cummings, Marie Louise was an awakening—a woman who actually enjoyed her body and its sexual aspects. The two spent the night together in bed, a willing courtesan and a still-frightened Yankee, and although there was no sexual intercourse there was everything else. It was a delirious, passionate night for Cummings, and one that was really his first sexual experience. "the finest girls god ever allowed to pasture in the air of this fresh earth," Cummings wrote to his mother. For the rest of his life Cummings spent as much time as he could in Paris, the city he called "the miracle." It was the epitome of liberation from the dusty parlors of Cambridge, the furnished souls of the Cambridge ladies, and the rocks and cold water and severe landscape of New Hampshire. Paris was beauty; Paris was freedom.

This revelry of artistic, architectural, and sexual delight ended with a summons from an irritated Monsieur Harjes at the Norton-Harjes office, who scolded Cummings and Brown for dereliction of duty. They felt entirely innocent. Perhaps this set the stage for the disaster that was to follow. On June 13, they were sent to the village of Ham on the Western Front for duty.

When Cummings and Brown got to Ham (in the district of Noyon near Saint-Quentin, a few miles from the Somme), the Western Front was already a synonym for horror and death. Noyon itself had been held by Germans and temporarily abandoned by them. Somehow, Cummings and Brown failed to understand this. They were two American princes in this officially named Section Sanitaire XXI, confident at the worst of times but now coming off five weeks of delight and revelry in Paris. Like many young men who fall in love with Paris, they adored all things French and detested all things American. They both spoke better French than their peers, who found them off-putting and effete. They despised their American commanding officers, and they quickly made friends with the French soldiers, laughing and chatting about the American officer who was the *chef de section.* In their first weeks at Ham their commanding officer was John T. Phillips, a Harvard man from New York. When Phillips was replaced by Harry Anderson, things took a turn for the worse. Anderson, a former garage mechanic from the Bronx, had absolutely no use for the aristocratic cutups. He told his men that it was their job to "show those dirty Frogs what Americans were like." This, of course, didn't sit well with the bereted Francophile from Cambridge, Massachusetts.

Cummings and Brown, with their gallantry, their aristocratic attitude, and their sympathy for the French, actually belonged to another tradition, which may have been despised by Anderson but which thrived on the Western Front. The Great War is now seen as the end of a kind of civilized, fearless spirit. Bravery and cluelessness sometimes take the same form. Cummings and Brown were like the British officers who went "over the top" out of the trenches in soccer formation dribbling a ball, like the heroic class of British young men who brought more courage than sense to the ugly business of trench warfare. Robert Graves had been fighting just to the west of Noyon. Siegfried Sassoon had been called "Mad Jack" for his coolness under fire.

In a situation that had no precedent in human history, it was hard to know whether the right thing to do was to allow oneself to be slaughtered or to refuse to go along with the orders when one knew that slaughter was imminent. "They were all so brave, to suffer," D. H. Lawrence wrote of the thousands who were killed at the Somme, "but none of them brave enough, to reject suffering." As Geoff Dyer points out in his book *The Missing of the Somme*: "Perhaps the real heroes of 1914–1918, then, are those who refused to obey and to fight, who actively rejected the passivity forced upon them by the war, who reasserted their right not to suffer, not to have things done to them."

Cummings came from a long tradition of gallantry. Having been the little guy himself, he always sided with the little guy. In the encampment at Ham the French were the little guys, forced to be grateful for American help. Even in wartime, it was hard for Cummings to feel sympathetic to the victors. The boredom of life behind the lines, where the food was terrible and his principal work was cleaning the old Fords that served as ambulances and waiting for something to happen, wore on Cummings. Both he and Brown wrote furious letters home freely criticizing everything.

One day in Noyon there was a rumor of a gas attack. The German army had begun using mustard gas as a weapon late in the war as it retreated to the Hindenburg Line. It was those gas attacks about which Wilfred Owen had written one of the most famous poems of World War I, which ends with the bitter statement:

> My friend, you would not tell with such high zest
> To children ardent for some desperate glory,
> The old Lie: Dulce et decorum est
> Pro patria mori.

Owen would passively return to the Western Front and be killed in the last weeks of the war in 1918. In *Good-Bye to All That,* his memoir of World War I, Graves describes the aftermath of life under the threat of a gas attack a few miles from where Brown and Cummings were polishing the fenders of Anderson's ambulance. "Since 1916, the fear of gas had obsessed me: any unusual smell, even a sudden strong scent of flowers in a garden, was enough to send me trembling. And I couldn't face the sound of heavy shelling now; the noise of a car back-firing would send me flat on my face, or running for cover."

Cummings and Brown, intensely literary and determinedly light-hearted and gentlemanly in the face of death, were just a few miles too far south to have fought—and probably died—with men who would have understood them.

The American soldiers and commanders were worlds away from any of this; they had *not* been taught that it was a sweet and decorous thing to die for their country, and it wasn't even their country. They were Americans; they were there to win. Alerted to the oddness of the two recruits, their possibly treasonous oddness, the French censors began giving special attention to the letters of Brown and Cummings. In the spirit of rebelliousness that also caused him to wear his uniform and bathe as little as possible, Cummings not very cleverly used French to telegraph his whereabouts and elude the censors, some of whom were French, in his letters home. "I hope M. le Censor won't mind my saying that nothing exciting is going on where I am," he wrote his mother in July. "Every day French aeroplanes are shot at by German anti-aircraft guns, without the slightest effect." Bored, badly fed and restless, Cummings and Brown got less and less easy to handle. They wrote to the Lafayette Escadrille offering to become pilots. Once, the sirens went off and a few German shells fell nearby, but that was as close as they got to the historic battles being fought all around them.

Although in July of 1917 the Western Front was still one of the most heartbreaking and dangerous places on earth, in the tiny district of Noyon very little was going on. Occasionally, while driving in what seemed aimless forays, Brown and Cummings found themselves under fire, but they quickly fled, and the enemy was never engaged. Brown and Cummings took a walk one afternoon and found a small chapel in the willows; they noticed the wounds sustained by the rolling pastoral landscape with its islands and alleys of poplar trees, the churned mud and blasted trees. But still nothing happened.

Their long conversations with the French soldiers at camp revealed a deep demoralization in the troops. Cummings and Brown heard all about the mutiny in the French army after General Robert Nivelle's campaign had failed earlier in the spring. Twenty thousand French soldiers had deserted. Brown's letters about the low morale among the French troops and the possibility of a German victory probably further alarmed the censors. Anderson, whom Brown and Cummings both had come to despise, organized a lottery for a trip to Paris for a few of the soldiers. Of course Cummings and Brown felt delighted by the idea. They lost, and it turned out that Anderson had not even entered their names. "This made me angry," Cummings wrote home to his mother. "I took a mouthful of cigarette smoke and blew it flat in his face."

By August, Cummings and Brown had made a lot of people angry. Some combination of Anderson's rage and the alarm of the French army finally tripped a switch. Their names were given to someone as possible traitors. Treason, especially during the dreadful battles of 1916 and 1917, was punishable by death. By the first of October, as in other parts of the front, Americans joined their new French comrades on the field of battle, Cummings and Brown were in custody, picked up by two policemen and transported to holding cells in Noyon.

5

The Enormous Room

Even now, almost a century later, the wheat fields of northwestern France are distorted and pocked by the scars of World War I battles. The great upheavals of hundreds of trenches, barbed wire, bombs, fires, and explosions that scorched the vegetation to the ground still mark the weirdly beautiful landscape. Trees grow in gnarled and stunted shapes in the districts around Noyon. A few poppies dot farmers' neat rows and bales of hay. The collision of thousands of tragic deaths with the stubborn fertility of the soil haunts the villages. Here and there a cemetery with rows of white stones or a monument to the dead rises out of the rolling farmland. They are remembered.

Yet the greatest and most immortal monuments are not the marble memorials but the dozens of books and poems that were left behind—a generation of literary geniuses fought and often died there: Yeats, Owen, Brooke, Sassoon, Graves, Hemingway, Cummings, and many others. More than any other before or since, World War I was our literary war.

"I know that I shall meet my fate / Somewhere among the clouds above; / Those that I fight I do not hate, / Those that I guard I do not love," William Butler Yeats wrote after the death of his friend Robert Gregory in his plane in 1918. This kind of acceptance and willing shouldering of an obligation that didn't really make sense—an obligation that was nevertheless sacred—is part of the character of the soldiers of the Western Front and part of the yearning for a better world that makes great literature. "Death is not an adventure to those who stand face to face with it," wrote Erich Maria Remarque in his novel about the German soldiers on the other side of the trenches in northern France, *All Quiet on the Western Front.* "It will try simply to tell of a generation of men who, even though they may have escaped its shells, were destroyed by the war."

Fate had different plans for E. E. Cummings and William Slater Brown. Soon their defiance and outrageous behavior would take them out of immediate physical danger, although that was the last thing they wanted. On September 23, an otherwise quiet day when Section Sanitaire XXI was camped near the Somme in a formerly picturesque town named Ollezy with a bombed-out church, Officer Anderson commanded the two men to polish and grease his personal car. As they were finishing this unwelcome job, a crowd of officials—soldiers and policemen, including the local minister of health—arrived in camp. They ordered Brown and Cummings to collect their belongings and then drove them into Noyon, where they were separately interrogated by a panel of petty bureaucrats. Cummings was delighted by the three functionaries assigned to him, whom he nicknamed "the moustache," "the rosette," and "Noyon." At last his war was happening. The French bureaucrats were less than delighted by their prisoners. They warned Cummings that Brown's letters home had shown that he was no friend of France.

After many unimportant questions, the panel had a final very important question for Cummings, as he recalled later. " *'Est-ce que vous detestez les boches?'* Did he hate the Germans? I had won my own case. The question was purely perfunctory. To walk out of the room a free man I had merely to say yes. My examiners were sure of my answer," he wrote. "The rosette was leaning forward and smiling encouragingly. The moustache was making little *ouis* in the air with his pen. And Noyon had given up all hope of making me out a criminal." Unfortunately, these small-town French officials had no idea whom they were dealing with—an irrational Yankee who prized perversity over safety, a Harvard boy who had been taught that gallantry was all, a poet whose defiance would carry him happily right up to the edge of death. No, Cummings responded; he did not hate the Germans. *"J'aime beaucoup les français."*

Not surprisingly, Cummings found himself separated from Brown and spending the night in a primitive jail cell. Back home in Cambridge, the Cummingses received a telegram from Ambulance Corps chief Richard Norton: EDWARD E CUMMINGS HAS BEEN PUT IN A CONCENTRATION

CAMP AS A RESULT OF LETTERS HE HAD WRITTEN STOP AM TAKING UP THE MATTER THROUGH THE EMBASSY TO SEE WHAT CAN BE DONE. The next day in Noyon, two policemen escorted Cummings to a railroad junction where he spent another night in jail. After a second day of traveling he was taken off the train at Briouze in southern Normandy, well south and west of the worst fighting. To Cummings, at least in retrospect, anything was better than the alternating boredom and mindless obedience of Noyon. In his first cell he wrote: "An uncontrollable joy gutted me after three months of humiliation, of being bossed and herded and bullied and insulted. I was myself and my own master." That night he was ordered into another building—the Dépôt de Triage at La Ferté-Macé, a holding camp for all kinds of undesirables.

In the dark Cummings stumbled through a huge door and lay down on the straw bed he had been given. He did not know where he was and could see very little in the darkness. "I fell on my *paillasse* with a weariness which I have never felt before or since," he wrote. "But I did not close my eyes: for all about me there rose a sea of most extraordinary sound . . . the hitherto empty and minute room became suddenly enormous: weird cries, oaths, laughter, pulling it sideways and backward, extending it to inconceivable depth and width, telescoping it to frightful nearness. From all directions, by at least thirty voices in eleven languages . . . at distances varying from seventy feet to a few inches . . . I was ferociously bombarded." This room would be Cummings's home for the next three months.

Cummings took a determinedly positive and amused view of being imprisoned, which, he claimed, was far better than being the flunky of the moronic Harry Anderson, among other things. "I couldn't possibly want anything better in the way of keep, tho you have to get used to the snores, and they don't allow you a knife, so you can't cut the air at night which is pretty thick, all windows being shut," he wrote on October 1 from the Dépôt de Triage at La Ferté-Macé. "You can't imagine, Mother mine, how interesting a time I am having. Not for anything in the world would I change it. It's like working—you must experience it to comprendre—but how infinitely superior to Colliers! If I thought you would excite yourself I wouldn't write from this place, but I know you will believe me when I reiterate that I am having the time of my life!"

For the American troops who poured into France during the same month and started joining the trench war, charging barbed-wire barriers and being picked off by German snipers while Cummings was still in jail, the battleground was presumably a lot less superior than a job at Collier. In fact, being in jail may well have saved Cummings's life. The story of his arrest makes sassing yourself into deep trouble look like an act of grace. The sector of Noyon where he and Brown had been suffering under Anderson was later the scene of the war's most dreadful battles as American troops under General John "Black Jack" Pershing turned the tide of the war and desperately and successfully fought off the German army's final offensive at the Marne.

Ypres, Passchendaele, Belleau Wood: the killing fields of the Allied final offensive were all within a tank-drive distance of the Noyon sector. At the end of November the famous American Rainbow Division, with men from every state of the Union under the command of Colonel Douglas MacArthur, would be among the two million Americans who landed in France and swept east across the torn-up wheat fields. While Cummings worried about fleas and thin soup and took notes and sketched the interesting characters with whom he shared the enormous room at La Ferté, 49,000 American soldiers were killed and 230,000 wounded. Another 57,000 died from disease.

In spite of Cummings's bravado, his parents were outraged and beside themselves with worry. For them, Norton's telegram set the tone. Edward Cummings, using his Harvard connections and writing as a Unitarian minister, first contacted the American embassy in Paris and the State Department, only to be jerked around. His fears for his son began turning into anger at those who refused to help. As the days and weeks passed and the Cummingses didn't hear from officials about the whereabouts of their son, who appeared to have dropped off the map somewhere in a war zone, Edward Cummings's fury and fear increased. This was a man who wasn't used to bureaucratic blow-offs. If his son was being treated badly—and certainly incarceration was a high price to pay for some relatively innocent high jinks—the senior Cummings would find a way to save him and then to tell the world about it. The Cummingses now found themselves in their own enormous room.

The U.S. State Department didn't seem to be inclined to help—and then they did something to make the situation much, much worse. On October 26, Edward Cummings received a message saying that his son, one H. H. Cummings, had gone down on the S.S. *Antilles,* torpedoed by a German submarine. Terrified, anguished, and grief-stricken, Edward kept this information from his wife. After what might have been the worst two days of the Reverend Edward Cummings's life, the State Department let him know that this information was erroneous and that H. H. Cummings was not the E. E. Cummings who was still incarcerated at La Ferté-Macé.

Finally, beside himself at the beginning of December, Edward Cummings wrote to President Woodrow Wilson himself—a long, pleading, passionate letter. "Pardon me, Mr. President, but if I were President and your son were suffering such prolonged injustice at the hands of France," he wrote to the White House on December 8, "and your son's mother had been needlessly kept in Hell as many weeks as my boy's mother has, —I would do something to make American citizenship as sacred in the eyes of Frenchmen as Roman citizenship was in the eyes of the ancient world."

Due partly to his father's constant work on his behalf, but also due to French scheduling—La Ferté-Macé was a depot designed for three-month stays—Cummings was finally released without fanfare on December 19. Brown was moved from La Ferté-Macé a few days earlier and then released a month later. Cummings took the train to Paris on his way home and wandered around the wintertime, wartime city, finding it much less charming than on his last visit. He could not find Marie Louise; although he left a note at her apartment, he never heard from her. He was debilitated and sick. He was determined to lose his virginity; and after dinner in a restaurant he went home with a waitress named Berthe and, apparently without much joy, accomplished the longed-for consummation.

Finally, on the first of January, 1918, he landed in New York Harbor after crossing on the *Espagne* and was welcomed home at an elegant luncheon given by his friends Hildegarde and Sibley Watson. Cummings was not in the mood for elegant celebratory lunches. He seemed depressed and silent compared with the energetic, playful Cummings who had left for France the previous spring. Hildegarde sadly noted that he had lost his smile.

That wasn't all he had lost. "He was in bad shape physically as a result of his imprisonment," Edward Cummings wrote to the Judge Advocate's Office in Paris with some of the sarcasm and bottled-up rage that seemed to live in the family genes. He was "very much under weight, suffering from a bad skin infection which he had acquired at the concentration camp. However, in view of the extraordinary facilities which the detention camp offered for acquiring dangerous diseases, he is certainly to be congratulated on having escaped with one of the least harmful."

Cummings would have been the first to admit that his incarceration had probably saved his life, and he certainly knew almost at once that his sketches and notes would be a large part of his young writer's capital. *Eight Harvard Poets* had been published while he was in prison. Freed for the moment from military service, Cummings focused on trying to get his strength back. It was relatively easy to recover from his malnutrition and open sores; his father was having a harder time recovering from his son's ordeal. He was in a towering, ministerial, Harvard rage. He was furious at the Red Cross and the U.S. embassy in France and the little help they had given him. He was on fire with outrage at the French government and planned to bring an international lawsuit to show the world the injustice that had been done to a U.S. citizen.

For once, the younger Cummings took on the job of calming his father down. He had changed. He offered to write a book that would be a scathing indictment of the powers that be. His father agreed that a book would be better than a lawsuit and even offered to pay his son for writing it. This would be his best revenge. But having made the deal to write a book about La Ferté-Macé and accepted a down payment from his father, Cummings did everything but write it.

First he moved back to Greenwich Village, this time renting a place with Brown. There he began to get into even more trouble than he had managed to attract on the Western Front. He and Brown, outraged first by the idea and then by the imminent passage of Prohibition, made plans to hop a merchant steamer and go to a country that suited their habits—perhaps somewhere in the Orient or South America. In the meantime, Cummings began to fall in love with Elaine Thayer, his friend and patron Scofield Thayer's wife, who was living alone on Washington Square.

While the elder Cummings waited for his son to settle down and write the book that would finally express his fury and exonerate him, Cummings wrote poems, hung out at Khoury's, and spent altogether too much time at Elaine's apartment. This idyll ended when he was officially drafted in July of 1918 and ordered to report to Camp Devens in Massachusetts. According to the letters he wrote his worried parents, making himself available for the draft had been the right thing to do and he was glad to go. Again, he didn't want to act like an elite Harvard man; his heart was with the ordinary men who had no recourse from being drafted. Furthermore, as an artist it was his job to go everywhere and see everything. "The artist keeps his eyes,ears,& above all his NOSE wide open, he watches while others merely execute orders he does things. By things I do not mean wearing gold bars or pulling wires or swallowing rot-in-general or nonsense-in-particular. I mean the sustaining of his invisible acquaintance with that life which, taken from his eyes, makes itself a house in his very-brain-itself," he wrote his mother.

He declined officer training; he wanted to stay an enlisted man. Assigned to Company Three, First Battalion, Depot Brigade, Cummings trained as an infantryman. His identification with the ordinary, with the little man, with the people normally shunned by society, was becoming more and more intense. Partly an elitist noblesse oblige and partly a heartfelt desire to avoid the success that also seemed to avoid him, it came to be a characteristic of his work and his life. He began using even more of the lowercase *i* in his poems.

The six months Cummings spent in the 73rd Infantry Division at Camp Devens were far less memorable than his time at La Ferté-Macé. Perhaps because there was little danger and scant adversity, the experience wasn't vivid or particularly interesting. One thing did interest Cummings: a big blond conscientious objector who was reading Sir Thomas Browne was brutally interrogated and transferred to an army prison. When the man refused to say he wanted to kill Germans, his interrogator furiously asked if he would kill a German who raped his sister. The CO replied that he didn't have a sister. Cummings from the sidelines vividly imagined his fate. Although he hardly had a chance to speak with this man, and didn't even catch his name, the CO showed up soon enough in Cummings's great, angry antiwar poem:

> i sing of Olaf glad and big
> whose warmest heart recoiled at war:
> a conscientious object-or

his wellbelovéd colonel(trig
westpointer most succinctly bred)
took erring Olaf soon in hand;
but—though an host of overjoyed
noncoms(first knocking on the head
him)do through icy waters roll
that helplessness which others stroke
with brushes recently employed
anent this muddy toiletbowl,
while kindred intellects evoke
allegiance per blunt instruments—
Olaf(being to all intents
a corpse and wanting any rag
upon what God unto him gave)
responds,without getting annoyed
"I will not kiss your fucking flag"

straightway the silver bird looked grave
(departing hurriedly to shave)

but—though all kinds of officers
(a yearning nation's blueeyed pride)
their passive prey did kick and curse
until for wear their clarion
voices and boots were much the worse,
and egged the firstclassprivates on
his rectum wickedly to tease
by means of skilfully applied
bayonets roasted hot with heat—
Olaf(upon what were once knees)
does almost ceaselessly repeat
"there is some shit I will not eat"

our president,being of which
assertions duly notified
threw the yellowsonofabitch
into a dungeon,where he died

Christ(of His mercy infinite)
i pray to see;and Olaf,too

preponderatingly because
unless statistics lie he was
more brave than me:more blond than you.

What he primarily observed at Camp Devens was the horror of the monotony of war, broken only by the bloodthirsty warmongering of his commanding officers, men who said there should be guts at *both* ends of their bayonets. He would have preferred the enormous room at La Ferté to having to hear drill instructors talk about the pleasures of disemboweling the enemy. Although the war officially ended on November 11, 1918, Cummings still managed to spend a few more weeks at Camp Devens, mostly on KP peeling potatoes. But by January of 1919 he was ecstatically back in New York.

Living with Brown in a fourth-floor walk-up with no running water, he saw Elaine and started painting her portrait, commissioned by her husband. He exhibited at the rooftop gallery of the Waldorf Astoria Hotel. He also worked on his poems, but he was not one word closer to writing the book he had promised his father.

Finally, ensconced or incarcerated at Silver Lake with his parents in the summer of 1920, Cummings began to write the book he had titled *The Great War Seen from the Windows of Nowhere,* but which came to have the title *The Enormous Room.* His restlessness seemed to fuel the book. He couldn't wait to get back to New York and his delicious real life. Each morning he would canoe out from the shore on the crystalline water to a remote campsite and tent at a place called Hurricane Point. After a day's work he would canoe home for dinner, which often included fending off inquiries from his anxious father; then he would return to his tent for the night.

The notebooks he had kept at La Ferté were little help—he had done more drawing than writing—so Cummings reconstructed scene by scene from memory. Brown came up and lived with him and the two men went over every detail. Cummings wrote in a furious outpouring of memory and longing. To give structure to chaos, he decided to pattern the book on

John Bunyan's classic seventeenth-century religious work, *The Pilgrim's Progress*. Like Bunyan's Christian Everyman, the Cummings character in *The Enormous Room* journeys valiantly through all kinds of hazards and Apollyons and even into the Valley of the Shadow of Death before reaching redemption and the Delectable Mountains.

Some of his best descriptions mix his memories of French inquisitors with the farm he saw every day as he was writing. One of his questioners reminded him of Ichabod Crane:

> His neck was exactly like a hen's: I felt sure that when he drank he must tilt his head back as hens do in order that the liquid may run down their throats. But his method of keeping himself upright, together with certain spasmodic contractions of his fingers and the nervous "uh-ah, uh-ah" which punctuated his insecure phrases like uncertain commas, combined to offer the suggestion of a rooster; a rather moth-eaten rooster, which took itself tremendously seriously and was showing-off to an imaginary group of admiring hens situated somewhere in the background of his consciousness.

By September, when the lake got too cold for swimming and the nights began to come on earlier, he had finished enough to give to his father when the elder Cummings decamped for Cambridge. His father's response was totally positive—no small feat, since he seemed to feel that his own reputation was in his son's hands. "I am sure now that you are a great writer," his father wrote. By October, as the leaves around Silver Lake began to turn red and gold, Cummings was finished with the manuscript of his first and most famous book. He had written a vivid war memoir without describing war. Publishing the book was another matter. *Harper's, The Atlantic Monthly,* and *Scribner's* all turned it down. Edward Cummings had some kind of leverage over Horace Liveright; eventually, after some discussion, Boni & Liveright decided to take it on. When Horace Liveright later met Cummings, he exclaimed, "Your father turned my hair white!"

The Enormous Room is an often-ignored piece of the astonishing literary output that characterized the survivors of the Western Front in England and America. Fittingly, Robert Graves wrote an introduction to the British publication, praising Cummings's language. "He uses some new alloys of words, and has rare passages as iridescent as decay in meat . . . It seems to me so much the best American war-period book," he wrote.

Although it was not published until 1922, five years after Cummings's actual experience on the Western Front, *The Enormous Room* is still the best account of his months there, and one of the best accounts of the hidden war in which thousands of citizens were haphazardly and quixotically held in makeshift prisons. Every war has its little guys—the people and families who, because of what is happening on the battlefields, have their rights and freedoms pushed aside in one way or another. On the Western Front Cummings was their spokesman. He couldn't write about the trenches or the horrors of the mud on the Somme, because he hadn't been there. His portrait of what we now call collateral damage is one of the most vivid ever written.

His first morning in *The Enormous Room,* when he is awakened at 5:30 for cold, sludgy coffee in a tin cup, Cummings is able to see his surroundings in the grim dawn light. The room was vaguely ecclesiastical and "my mattress resembled an island: all around it . . . reposed startling identities." To his great relief and delight, he was directed to his friend Brown— the book's B—wrapped up like a mummy in a blanket. "Am I dreaming," Cummings asked his friend, "or is this a bug-house?" Brown laughed and quickly persuaded his friend that incarceration in the enormous room was so far superior to the annoyances and limitations of service in the Ambulance Corps, with its killjoy leader constantly badgering them about their hygiene, and their doughy-faced fellow soldiers, that both men embraced prison as well as each other in a spirit of gratitude and relief.

Most of *The Enormous Room* takes place at the Dépôt de Triage, a setting that Cummings deftly transforms into the enormous room of his own mind and memory. He and Brown appear to have a wonderful time in spite of buckets for toilets, two meals a day of soup, infestations of various types of insects, and little more than a glimpse of the female prisoners. The other prisoners—some cultured, some not; one a man who knew Cézanne—are, he writes to his mother, "splendid comrades . . . You can't begin to imagine our unimaginable glee at living safe and sound out of the nagging reach of our former owners." The inhabitants of *The Enormous Room* are most of them imprisoned by mistake. They are sailors who have missed their ships, tradesmen whose stores have gone broke, men who happen to have been in the wrong place at the wrong time—

which in the France of 1917, as the German army poured into the cities and countrysides, was very easy to be.

The startling identities included a gnome, a Norwegian seaman, and a disenfranchised nobleman in a swallowtail coat with impeccable, courtly manners named Count Bragard, who formerly had been a successful equine portrait painter in England. "Indeed for the first time since my arrival at La Ferté I was confronted by a perfect type: the apotheosis of injured nobility, the humiliated victim of perfectly unfortunate circumstances, the utterly respectable gentleman who has seen better days," Cummings wrote. "You know Cornelius Vanderbilt perhaps?" Count Bragard asked Cummings as other inmates pissed in buckets or picked bedbugs off their straw mattresses. "I painted some of his horses. We were the best of friends, Vanderbilt and I." Bragard produced Vanderbilt's card with an affectionate note for Cummings's perusal.

Another prisoner, Monsieur Ree-shar (Richard), was the self-appointed doctor for the shifting population although, as Cummings pointed out, "he knew probably less about medicine than any man living."

Because the only requirement for membership in the community was a hatred of authority and a sometimes humorous recognition of the absurdity of the situation, Cummings and Brown were welcomed as charter members. They had money from home that could be spent on chocolate from the commissary, and this also made them popular.

Cummings, steeped in literature and remembering his experience, was not about to write a simple memoir. Although his language is relatively conventional, he doesn't hesitate to twist punctuation or change parts of speech in the service of description. A great deal has been written about *The Enormous Room*. Richard Kennedy hailed it as a unique achievement. Charles Norman devoted an entire chapter to the mixed but thoughtful reviews the book received on publication—publication at a time when memoirs were rare and experiments with words and syntax were even rarer.

Now, decades later, Cummings's energy and nerve are evident both in the experience he describes and in his prose. The book has two great strengths. One is Cummings's spiritual attitude. In his pages, gallantry meets acceptance. Nothing that happens—nothing: not privation, being threatened with a gun, miles of trudging along under heavy burdens, or lack of food—will alter his ebullient and defiant attitude toward authority and everything associated with authority. Like John Bunyan's Pilgrim, he takes the world as it is and spurns the role of victim. Even his own trag-edies delight him. Whether it's a protest over bad coffee or the sadness of seeing a fellow inmate headed for a real prison farther south, whether it's being conned or watching as someone else sickens, all of life is expe-rienced by the character Cummings would later call i—experienced as a lighthearted passage in which often the only leavening is humor.

Cummings's other great achievement is his genius at setting scenes and using sensual details. Every inch of his skin and all his senses are alight with experience. "He makes us see and smell and sometimes hear, taste, and touch," writes Kennedy. "We experience vividly the daily life in the Dépôt de Triage—its oozing walls, its overflowing pails of urine, its encrusted dirt, its greasy soup, the piercing cold, the noise and confusion."

Once he had finished writing, Cummings sprang back to Greenwich Village like a man at the end of an elastic band. This was his home now. He was hard at work on paintings and on a book of poetry, which he had titled *Tulips & Chimneys*. He was twenty-six years old all of a sudden, and he felt the pressure to translate his early promise into some kind of significant life. And Elaine—oh, Elaine! She belonged to someone else—a friend, a patron, and a colleague—but he could not seem to resist her. He had finally lost his virginity, but this was different: scary, delightful, exciting, vibrant. Elaine was a beautiful princess, and although he was terrified by her marital situation and abashed by her wealthy, profligate way of living, he slipped into a delicious fugue state that would provide the central trauma of his life—a trauma that made his months at La Ferté look like a carefree summer vacation.

6

Greenwich Village: Elaine and Nancy

On a winter evening in January of 1917, a ragtag bunch of revolutionaries—including the artists Marcel Duchamp and John Sloan and actors from the nearby, experimental Provincetown Playhouse—staged a takeover of Washington Square Arch, the Stanford White–designed marble wedding cake that had been built at the bottom of Fifth Avenue in 1892. After climbing the 110 iron stairs to the top, they posed next to the statue of George Washington that gives the arch its name and proclaimed the "free and independent republic of Greenwich Village." Duchamp released a cloud of red balloons into the snowy air. These hardy, inspired, and somewhat tipsy souls were members of the bohemian Liberal Club and the harbingers of what would be the most fruitful and fervent decades in this country's history of arts and ideas.

Greenwich Village has always been more a state of mind than another urban neighborhood. Its golden age began at the end of World War I, when artists, writers, actors, and creative camp followers flooded the twisty, Old World, tree-lined streets between Fifth Avenue and the Hudson River below Fourteenth Street, drawn by low rents, a hobohemian lifestyle (including lots of drinking and sex), and the thrilling prospect of a new way of seeing the world, a new way of painting, and, especially, a new way of writing. They came from Harvard (Cummings, Dos Passos, John Reed, Malcolm Cowley); they came from Princeton (Edmund Wilson, John Peale Bishop, Eugene O'Neill). William Carlos Williams drove his Ford flivver in from New Jersey after a long day's work as a doctor. They came, as one of them famously wrote, to burn their candles at both ends.

Although Edna St. Vincent Millay was from Maine, she was already an honorary Villager at birth—she had been named in gratitude after the local Greenwich Village hospital, St. Vincent's, where her uncle had been nursed back to health after an accident. And they wrote about it. O'Neill's *The Iceman Cometh* is set in the Village dives of this era, the Golden Swan and Romany Marie's. O'Neill, Millay, and the novelist Theodore Dreiser were all Greenwich Village veterans who would be on hand to help the blue-blooded young aristocrat from Harvard.

When O'Neill, the resident playwright at the Provincetown Playhouse on Macdougal Street, migrated north to Broadway in 1920 for the production of *Beyond the Horizon,* which won the Pulitzer Prize, he was replaced, among others, by the twenty-nine-year-old E. E. Cummings and later with his irreverent first play, *Him. Him* was experimental, revolutionary, and sassy, and included a send-up of O'Neill. In those early days, Malcolm Cowley published Cummings and nearly everyone else in *The New Republic,* which he helped edit; his wife, Peggy, later ran off to Mexico with Hart Crane. Edmund Wilson and John Peale Bishop were both hopelessly in love with Edna St. Vincent Millay. When she decided to sleep with them simultaneously, all of them remembered, there were heated discussions about who would get the top of her and who the bottom.

John Reed returned to Russia and became the only American to be buried inside the Kremlin. Millay would meet Dutch businessman Eugen Boissevain at a house party in Croton-on-Hudson, marry him, move to the country, and win a Pulitzer Prize. On the way home from Mexico on the ship *Orizaba* Hart Crane jumped over the side to his death. Cowley moved to Connecticut. Cummings stayed on in the Village.

When he got there, the Village was already a storied place, once home to Edgar Allan Poe, Walt Whitman, Mark Twain, and Henry James. Typically for the Village, Reed was Mabel Dodge's lover while she ran a salon that boasted Sigmund Freud and Margaret Sanger as visitors. Typically, too, Reed's wife, Louise, was also having an affair with Eugene O'Neill.

In the forty-four years that Cummings lived in the Village, his neighbors and friends included a dozen influential poets, writers, and photographers, including Crane, Cowley, the famous bum Joe Gould, Wilson, Marianne Moore, Thomas Wolfe; Walker Evans and James Agee started the collaboration that became *Let Us Now Praise Famous Men* while walking the streets of the Village.

Yet Cummings's first return to Greenwich Village from Camp Devens in 1919 was shadowed by the complicated and passionate feelings he was coming to have for his patron Scofield Thayer's beautiful and unhappy wife, Elaine, whom he had first met in the spring of 1916. Cummings was then already a young success; his work would soon appear in *Eight Harvard Poets*.

When he first met Elaine, Thayer's nineteen-year-old fiancée, Cummings was immediately stunned by her retiring, soft-spoken, slender beauty. Her ethereal delicacy was the opposite, he noted, of his mother's stout, good-humored kind of femininity. Elaine, Cummings thought, was like a princess, and indeed she was a kind of Jamesian American princess, educated in the finest finishing schools, but shadowed by the tragedy of her very wealthy father's early death.

Cummings's life, as he wrote in his journals, had already been upended by the influence of Scofield Thayer—dapper, sophisticated, feminine, very rich, and on his way to Vienna to be psychoanalyzed by none other than Sigmund Freud. Thayer was an admirable antithesis of the masculine archetype of Edward Cummings with which Cummings had been raised. "ST—the world, money, Freud—&took me away from EC (Whereby nyc supplanted Cambridge) much to his rage." If it was Scofield Thayer who had enabled Cummings to break with his parents, partly through his payment of $1,000, then it was the fragile Elaine who would wean Cummings away from her husband. Freud himself, Cummings wrote, had urged Thayer to make Cummings marry Elaine.

Cummings was fascinated by sex, but he was a Puritan through and through. Still almost a virgin himself, he had written "Epithalamion" out of what seem to be his own vivid fantasies of sex between Thayer and Elaine: "Love, lead forth thy love unto that bed . . . ," and then, changing the point of view, "felt on her flesh the amorous strain / of gradual hands and yielding to that fee / her eager body's unimmortal flower . . ."

Later, in an investigation of what Cummings believed was his perversion and enantiodromia, a term from Heraclitus coined by Jung to mean the compulsion toward opposites and which Cummings used to explore what would become his love-hate relationship with Elaine, he wrote: "the first time I saw Elaine—she belongs to my friend Thayer (money*I-XXinferior, playing up to him . . . he:rich aggressive, i: passive."

"I never saw anything prettier than Elaine," wrote Hildegarde Watson after a lunch at Chicago's Blackstone Hotel with the Thayers on their way home from their European honeymoon. Hildegarde, who had been courted by Thayer before he met Elaine while traveling in England, was happily married to Cummings's other best friend, James Sibley Watson, and living with him in the Midwest. But even the newlywed Hildegarde sensed that all was not marital bliss with the Thayers. "What an unsettled luncheon that appeared to me, full of unrest," she wrote of their meeting. "The Thayers were, before long, to separate, there was the prospect of war, and all were confused by patriotic and pacifist feelings."

So when the sexually confused Cummings and the sexually rejected Elaine both found themselves in Greenwich Village and within a few blocks from each other, the girl who Cummings had written "would make any man faint with happiness" and the witty young poet were suddenly free to be friends and even more than friends. Thayer lived in a luxurious apartment on Washington Square East in a building reserved for bachelors; Elaine rented a first-floor apartment on Washington Square North. Sex was meant to be free, everyone said. And as Cummings's friend Dos Passos wrote, "Those of us who weren't in love with Cummings were in love with Elaine."

For months, Cummings was just one of many who gathered at Elaine's cozy apartment of an evening to drink and dance and chat about this and that. Seeing that she was lonely, he often tried to get her to come with him to a party or a restaurant. Cummings began to sympathize with Elaine's plight. She was married to a man who wasn't interested in her and who sometimes publicly belittled her. Thayer had paid Cummings for the wedding poem, and now he sent Cummings another check to help with his expenses in entertaining Elaine.

Thayer himself seemed to be having some kind of sexual crisis over his preference for adolescent boys, and he didn't seem concerned at all with Elaine. It was springtime in the Village; the cherry blossoms bloomed on the narrow streets with their romantic wrought iron and billowy brick fronts and flowers and trailing vines blooming in the stairways. Birdsong caromed around the big trees in Washington Square, where fountains

William Slater Brown, 1917

Cummings's drawing of the
view from one of his Paris
windows in the 1920s

Cummings's drawing of Marie Louise
Lallemand, his Paris friend from 1917

Paris artists in the 1920s. Ezra Pound stands in the middle row to the right.

American ambulance drivers in France near the Western Front in 1927

Dépôt de Triage at La Ferté-Macé where Cummings and Brown were incarcerated

Scofield and Elaine Thayer in the summer of 1916

Edward and Rebecca Cummings in the mid-1920s. Edward was killed in 1926.

Elaine near her Washington Square apartment just after Nancy was born, 1920

Private Cummings after his return from France at Fort Devens, Massachusetts, 1918

Cummings in Paris, age twenty-seven, early 1920s

Nancy Thayer Cummings, age fiv
in 1925

splashed just beyond Elaine's windows. Springtime in New York City is irresistible after the long city winter, and Elaine was equally irresistible in a way that Cummings didn't seem at first to notice. In his conscious mind, Cummings had embraced this new world of honesty, openness, and freedom; but one night in the spring when Elaine made it clear that she would like to sleep with him, he was as horrified as he was delighted and left the apartment as fast as he could.

"I see E. not as she is—a dissatisfied girl who needs a fuck . . . nor do I want to fuck her, much—no, no I want to love, PROTECT deserve her," Cummings wrote in his journal. "I HAVE AN IDEE FIXE OF RIGHT & WRONG." Cummings was still a prude, but he couldn't stay away from Elaine. "there's no way out," he wrote in his journal. "she is the only beautiful person (UNCANNY), small deli-cate, exquisite . . . incredible refinement . . . mind: unfoolable . . . no pose . . . interested-in-everything, everyone, everywhere utterly alive." He cast her as the unhappy Guinevere with Thayer as King Arthur and himself as a gallant Lancelot. Soon the two were spending nights lying in bed together trading caresses and kisses. Cummings tried to persuade himself that the whole thing was Elaine's idea and that he had no real responsibility. Then he tried to persuade himself that screwing her would be an act of gallantry. He was more successful in persuading himself that Thayer wouldn't mind.

In his own musings, the falling in love with Elaine brought up all of Cummings's confusion about what it means to be a man. If Edward Cummings was a man—bluff, large, loud—then what kind of man was his fine-boned, agile, quiet-loving son? He could only woo Elaine in the conditional. "If I hadn't changed," he told her after one night when he had put on evening clothes at her apartment, "I'd have come in here . . . & fallen on you & I wouldn't have cared, I'd have been so happy." Elaine moaned. Cummings wanted her to take responsibility for what was hap-pening between them; he held back physically while courting her with words. Cummings, he noted, was as much as asking if Elaine would be won, "instead of being aggressive, a man, & and winning her." By early summer, with Elaine urging him to "go in, oh please go in,! . . . You took me & put me inside with your hand . . ." the two were lovers.

"I didn't want to possess her," he wrote, "I wanted: to do as she liked, to please her."

Then, disaster. In May of 1919 Elaine told Cummings that she was pregnant with his child. It was one thing to be free, gloriously free, about sex and love and art. It was quite another thing to contemplate taking on the financial and emotional burdens of a child. How could he continue to work as an artist and as a poet if he was saddled with a family? Cummings balked. He urged Elaine to have an abortion. Thayer also urged her to have an operation to terminate the pregnancy. A doctor was consulted who apparently prescribed a pill to induce a miscarriage, which didn't work. But Elaine, until now so delicate and pliable, decided that she wanted to have the child. For once in her life she would not be bullied by men.

Thayer agreed to adopt the child, and the Thayers became closer again, inviting Cummings to spend a summer month with them in Martha's Vineyard. There the three pretended that the events of the last three years had not happened. Cummings slept apart from the married couple. What kind of man was he then? Elaine confided in him that she still loved Thayer; Thayer confided in him that he no longer loved Elaine. All these people believed, or said they believed, in the twin principles of freedom and creativity. Under the civilized surface of their lives, a lot was going on.

Over the next four years all would be buffeted about by their own feelings: Cummings was still in love with Elaine and would soon love the child she was carrying. Thayer himself was still attached to Elaine and might also have been a little bit in love with Cummings. Cummings himself had once had *that* serious physical crush on Sibley Watson. Elaine was naturally terrified, as most mothers-to-be are, and couldn't see herself finding safety with any of the alternatives available to her. For the moment, though, the façade of principle was intact. Soon enough it would come dreadfully undone.

Later that summer, at Silver Lake, far from the pregnant Elaine, Cummings wrote the poem that enshrines her in memory from the golden time before she had the temerity to get pregnant. "Puella Mea" is a long love poem to the "fragile lady," the "dexterous and fugitive," "the immanent subliminal," and in many ways it reads like a farewell. Certainly the blithe sexuality, the world without responsibility, the freedoms that seemed so important but that were so dependent on other people's money and other people's tolerance, had all come to an end for Cummings and Elaine, even in the free air of Greenwich Village.

Back in New York on Washington Square with her pregnancy showing, Elaine felt deserted by both Thayer and Cummings, a bitter experience that may have shaped what happened later. She was only nineteen when she first met Thayer; and the dramatic and painful few years of her marriage, her time as Cummings's mistress, and now the birth of her child may well have wounded her in ways that are hard to measure. On December 20, 1919, she gave birth to a baby girl, who was named Nancy Thayer. It was Thayer who went to the hospital for the birth and posed as the child's father. Cummings learned of his only child's birth in a phone call—he was not asked to visit. Thus began the long and difficult musical-chairs fathering to which Nancy would be subjected for much of her life. Using the image of a wheelmine from her father's play *Santa Claus,* Nancy Thayer later described her own origins. "Out of a very ancient wheelmine comes my folktale, like a family pieced together from precious fragments recovered or missed," she wrote in an introduction to a book of poems, *Charon's Daughter,* after the death of both her parents.

Cummings and Thayer didn't have time for a baby anyway; they were preoccupied with Thayer's acquisition of the fortnightly literary magazine *The Dial.* As an editor, Thayer promised not to edit Cummings and was ready to publish seven poems from his new manuscript titled *Tulips & Chimneys* as well as four Cummings drawings of the ladies of the National Winter Garden burlesque show.

On the surface, Cummings, Thayer, and Elaine were a highly civilized threesome dedicated to personal freedom and the idea that creative work had to come before personal lives. Still, Cummings couldn't help crowing over the adorable, tiny daughter who was finally put in his arms when she was a bit more than a month old. He boasted to his sister that she had a lot of hair. Before Nancy turned a year old, her parents seemed to have come back together in a permanent reunion—although of course the idea of anything permanent was anathema to them and to their community. After spending the summer in New Hampshire writing *The Enormous Room* at his father's insistence—and because his father agreed to pay for his travel in Europe if he finished the book—Cummings moved back to the Village to an apartment he shared with Brown on Bedford Street.

It was sweet to be with Elaine and play with Nancy, whom Cummings always called Mopsy. He had the freedom of being an artist and the loving joy of being a father. To underscore his freedom, Cummings took off for Lisbon in March of 1921, with Dos Passos as his companion on the

Mormugão—this trip was courtesy of Edward Cummings as payment for the completion of the book that the senior Cummings seemed to care about more than his son did, perhaps because of what he and Rebecca had been through while their son was incarcerated. Cummings didn't like Lisbon much, and by May he and Dos were back in Paris, the city that Cummings liked to think of as his second home.

They wandered the streets and ate beautifully, and in June Elaine and Nancy arrived, almost as they would have if they had been part of a more conventional kind of family. With Paris in the background, Elaine and Cummings seemed to fall in love all over again. Paris allowed them to retain their fantasies of who they were: Elaine and Nancy were wealthy Americans who stayed at the Hôtel d'Iéna with a full staff; Cummings was a romantically impoverished itinerant poet who lived in a cheap hotel on the Left Bank.

They saw each other every day and night, and being in Paris enabled them to play family in a new and unencumbered way. When Thayer arrived in Paris on his way to Vienna and Sigmund Freud, he and Nancy were officially divorced on July 28. Thayer settled a fortune on Nancy ($100,000, or about a million in today's dollars), introduced Cummings to Ezra Pound when they ran into him on the street, and, like the gentleman he was, left them all alone together again as he headed west for Austria and what he hoped would be increased mental stability.

Throughout the summers and falls of the next two years, Cummings and Elaine played at being the family with no strings attached, the uncommitted parents of the increasingly adorable Nancy, who was now a toddler and had begun to speak enough to be great company for her father. It is from this time that Nancy's only recollection of her father survived. "One solitary recollection in Paris of my father (who was later to celebrate his own home as supremely natural) would be guillotined and muffled in confusion so total, that many years later in America between two families of my own, I met him as a stranger."

Elaine left Paris for New York in December 1921, but she was back with her full entourage of nanny and personal maid to check in to the Hôtel Wagram on the Right Bank's Rue de Rivoli in May. She brought two copies of the American edition of *The Enormous Room*. Cummings was delighted to see her but furious when he examined his book, which had been altered by editing and cutting in ways he found horrifying.

Still, for a while it seemed as if they had it all. Cummings was passionate about his work and free to be passionate. His first solo volume of poems, *Tulips & Chimneys,* was published by Thomas Seltzer while Cummings was still abroad, and well reviewed in New York. He painted when he felt the urge to paint; he wrote when he felt the urge to write. Most of the time he could also husband and father when he felt the urge to husband and father. In June of 1922, Cummings, Nancy, and Elaine traveled to the south of France so that Cummings could paint in Cézanne country. The next summer they all decamped to the Atlantic coast of France, with Elaine and Nancy checking in to the Hôtel Carlton in Biarritz and Cummings renting a maid's room in a nearby village. They loved each other, and they left each other free—that was the idea. It's an idea that has often cropped up in human history; an idea that rarely works out, especially when there are children involved.

Cummings was poor and Elaine was rich, but that didn't matter! They weren't married, but that didn't matter! Their daughter was still legally the daughter of another man, but that didn't matter! They (or at least Cummings) occasionally slept with other people, but that didn't matter! They had left all those rules and oppressive customs behind and broken through into a new way of living. In the ancient struggle between the rights of art and the rights of living artists and their families, Cummings and Elaine seemed to have reached a happy compromise. "I am essentially an artist, secondarily a man," Cummings wrote. "but SHE is primarily a woman."

By March of 1924, Elaine was restless and wanted to marry him. When it came to his work, Cummings was furiously defensive; in his life he seemed strangely passive. In his journals he is aggressively furious at himself for being so passive. Elaine wanted to get married, so they got married. The Reverend Edward Cummings married his son, E. E. Cummings, to Elaine Orr Thayer at noontime in the living room at 104 Irving Street in Cambridge. Marriage didn't change much, and both promised that they would immediately release the other if that was wanted. Cummings half-moved into Elaine's apartment on Washington Square and kept his old apartment as a studio. By April the three were so much a family that Cummings even legally adopted his own child. Was this altogether too much bourgeois claptrap?

Although his private journals have dozens of pages of exploration of his relationship to Elaine and Nancy, what it all adds up to is a lot of confused feeling. In his own way, Cummings seemed quite happy to be married and even happier to be a father to the increasingly companionable Mopsy. He loved telling her stories and playing with her. His parents now recognized Nancy as their grandchild and adored having her as a visitor in Cambridge and New Hampshire. It all seemed like paradise.

The utopian strain in American belief is one of the strongest in our history. Greenwich Village in the 1920s was, in its own way, just another utopian community within the confines of an urban neighborhood. Cummings and Elaine were not alone in believing that the human soul—if left unencumbered—could grow and create beyond all previous accomplishments. Like Amos Bronson Alcott at the beginning of his utopian experiment Fruitlands, or like George Ripley at Brook Farm or John Humphrey Noyes at Oneida, Cummings and his fellow writers and the community they drew around them seemed to believe that, free from the ancient social institutions that had bound them and their parents, human beings would thrive. The restrictions had caused the problem, they believed, not the other way around.

Soon after Elaine and Cummings were married, Elaine's sister Constance, who had seen her through her pregnancy and childbirth, caught a bad cold that became a fatal pneumonia. Elaine was devastated. The woman who had mothered her was gone. An old-fashioned husband would have been on hand to help with the legal and emotional complications of such an intimate loss. There was the funeral in Troy, Elaine's hometown, to manage; the estate to be settled; the grieving to be done. Cummings, however, was the new kind of husband, and he hardly paid attention. Cummings may have had an idée fixe of right and wrong, but when it came to managing the adult world with all its aggravations and necessities, he was useless. Because a third sister was abroad, and perhaps because she wanted to be away from her new husband, Elaine, taking Nancy along with the nurse, left for Paris. It was May, and Cummings had a lot to do as the author of *The Enormous Room* and *Tulips & Chimneys* and as a contributor to *The Dial*. Because of Elaine's absence, he moved his easel and paints into the nursery in Elaine's Washington Square apartment.

Something had pushed Elaine to a breaking point. The form her unhappiness took was a love affair with a handsome Irish banker, Frank

MacDermot, almost the minute she stepped onto the boat to France. Cummings was happily oblivious.

First, Elaine wrote Cummings a letter that he experienced as a lightning strike. She told him that she was in love with another man and she wanted a divorce. Then she appeared in New York, showing up in his studio just as he was painting a portrait of Nancy. Cummings could hardly believe his ears: Elaine was adamant. It's easy to guess why she was overwhelmingly attracted to a man like MacDermot, the son of a self-made man, who had been attorney general for a British-ruled Ireland. MacDermot didn't have time for poetry and jokes and the vicissitudes of the creative life. For him, life was serious, and he was seriously in love with Elaine. For Cummings, nothing was serious—or at least that was the myth he had lived by.

Cummings was devastated, and the loss of Elaine was to lead to the most serious breakdown of his life. He turned for help to his family and friends. His father came to New York to urge him to hire a good lawyer, to sue MacDermot, and if necessary, to attack the man physically. Cummings visited Cambridge and Maine, and he found some comfort in the Adirondacks with his dear friends the Watsons. From Watson he also obtained a .38 caliber pistol, and this gun was the prop for scene after scene that would have led to an arrest and institutionalization in a less free society. Cummings threatened MacDermot; that's what a real man would do. Then he showed up at Elaine's with the gun and threatened to kill himself. He also considered murdering Elaine and then killing himself, but the thought of Nancy stopped him. In the end he capitulated to Elaine and agreed to a divorce. Watson found his broken, deserted friend a place to live in a third-floor room at Patchin Place, a quiet mews of tenements off Tenth Street near the elevated train tracks that ran above Sixth Avenue. Women would come and go in Cummings's life; he worked in the third-floor studio at 4 Patchin Place for almost forty years.

Built as housing for the Basque workers of the long-gone Brevoort House hotel, Patchin Place is land given to Aaron Patchin by his father-in-law, Samuel Milligan, who built Milligan Place next door. Built in the 1840s before the Civil War when Tenth Street and even Sixth Avenue were sleepy thoroughfares, the three-story brick row houses, adorned with fire escapes, look like a stage set, complete with one of the oldest lampposts in the city, whose gas has been changed to electricity. In

1917 the houses were modernized, with indoor plumbing and steam heat, and in 1920 the last member of the Patchin family sold the cul-de-sac to a realty company, which split the houses up into small one-room apartments—usually two rooms to each floor, divided by narrow hallways and staircases. Across the street stood the campanile of the Jefferson Market Courthouse.

The poet's relationship to the enchantment of Patchin Place was one of the strongest and most benevolent in his life. Cummings hated noise—a radio two floors away could drive him nuts. He despised size for the sake of size, as in the vast drawing rooms of Cambridge and Boston, which seemed to be built for intimidation. The small, cozy, cramped landscape of Patchin Place, with its eerie quiet and old-time details, could not have been farther away from the majestic, self-conscious architecture of Harvard College. If Patchin Place had not existed, Cummings would have had to invent it. "For a couple of decades the topfloorback room at 4 Patchin Place,which Sibley originally gave me,meant Safety & Peace & the truth of Dreaming & the bliss of Work," Cummings wrote in a letter to Hildegarde Watson in 1949.

By November, at Elaine's request, Cummings was again in Paris, but this time it was to get their divorce. He saw more and more of the delightful Nancy, although later she would remember only a scrap of their time together. They rode the merry-go-round at the Champs-Élysées. He once again tried to argue Elaine out of the divorce. He had brought the pistol to Paris and again contemplated shooting MacDermot or himself or both.

He was so disturbed that he came close to shooting a friend who was visiting Elaine one afternoon—he had been listening to voices behind the door of her apartment and convinced himself that one of them was MacDermot's. Cummings's journals of this time are agonizing to read. He excoriates himself, and draws diagrams showing where he went wrong with Elaine and where he went wrong as a man. He anguishes over the loss of his daughter. "I love her more than anything alive," he wrote, "she does not love me . . . I will help her—although it's the last thing I desire to do, I will give her up. BUT!! If the motivation really is: I REALLY DON'T WANT Elaine and Mopsy ENOUGH TO FIGHT for them both: . . . I am giving them up because I am a coward then_____I had better DIE." The divorce decree was issued on December 4, and a devastated Cummings headed back to New York on the *Leviathan*.

During the two years after Cummings and Elaine were finally divorced, all kinds of things seemed to come between him and his daughter. Although Elaine married MacDermot and they moved back to New York—first to the suburbs and then to the city—Elaine was sick, Nancy was sick, lawyers got involved, Cummings was distracted by his work and by a new love affair and by a fresh family tragedy. Although he was able to visit with Nancy two or three times, always chaperoned—and once, as he heartbreakingly remembered years later, got to hear the seven-year-old sing—the visits were short and uncomfortable. Cummings and MacDermot hated each other, and in 1926 the MacDermots moved with "their" daughter permanently back to Ireland. Their plan was to obscure Nancy's history with both her adoptive father and her real father. Nancy was not told until many years later that E. E. Cummings was her father, and then it was a piece of information that would tilt her world on its axis. She didn't see him again for twenty-two years.

7

Anne Barton and Joseph Stalin

William James was an unofficial godfather to the young Estlin Cummings. He was Edward Cummings's close friend, and the Cummings house on Irving Street in Cambridge was built to be close to the James house on the other side of Irving Street. Joy Farm in New Hampshire had also been purchased close to the James family summer house on Silver Lake. After all, James had indirectly been responsible for Cummings's existence when he introduced his own research assistant, Rebecca Clarke, to his friend Edward. William James's son Billy would become a close friend of Estlin Cummings's.

William James helped Cummings believe that writing was a noble profession, and his work was as instructive to the young man as his life was. This was especially true with his greatest and most important book, *The Varieties of Religious Experience,* originally written as a series of lectures to be given at Edinburgh University in Scotland in 1901 and 1902. In *The Varieties of Religious Experience* James wrote about the different kinds of characters men might inhabit—especially men like Cummings who found themselves somehow on the outside of their own childhood world.

In Lecture 8, James writes about a question that fascinated him and has fascinated many creative people since: how can two or more seemingly opposite characters inhabit the same body and personality? In his lecture, James put the question through the renegade French novelist Alphonse Daudet and his confession of amoral doubleness.

"Homo duplex, homo duplex!" writes Daudet.

> The first time that I perceived that I was two was at the death
> of my brother Henri, when my father cried out so dramati-
> cally, "He is dead, he is dead!" While my first self wept, my
> second self thought, "How truly given was that cry, how fine it
> would be at the theatre." I was then fourteen years old.
> "This horrible duality has often given me matter for reflec-
> tion. Oh, this terrible second me, always seated whilst the
> other is on foot, acting, living, suffering, bestirring itself. This
> second me that I have never been able to intoxicate, to make
> shed tears, or put to sleep and how it sees into things, and how
> it mocks!"

As an adult, Cummings faced his own divided self and was sometimes
sabotaged by it. The most obvious way he did this was in the use of the
word "I." In his poems and some of his prose he had created a personality
for the lowercase *i*. There are many sources for the lowercase *i*, from the
notes left by the unpretentious handyman at Joy Farm to the Greek poets.

On one particular summer morning at Joy Farm, while writing in
his journal, Cummings looked back on his early life and contemplated
the problematic dual nature of the uppercase I—in other words, E. E.
Cummings. "It's significant for me to distinguish clearly two Is,& decide
which I'll be." In writing that reveals his self-hatred, his playfulness, and
his robust sense of self, he described Cummings Duplex.

One I was his "before breakfast self," Cummings wrote. "he's short,
hateful,& and dogmatic—especially re women. Women are either bitches
or morons. They have no soul. They are always taking from you—never
giving to you." This side of Cummings's character was bitter, snobbish,
and lonely, Cummings wrote in a playful moment of self-satire. "What a
pity he had to be born into this lousy world at all!"

The other I, his after-breakfast self, was "warm, cheerful, adventurous,
with a quick sense of humor—the world is a perpetual amazement to
him . . . If he makes a blunder he's the first to laugh over it. If someone
meets his affection with love,he's loyal to the death."

Furthermore, Cummings explained as the sun began to dry the dew
on the pasture and the birds swooped in and out of the maples outside

his window, he understood Montaigne's statement that "fortune does us neither good nor evil," for "he's aware of millions upon millions of individuals inside him—& according to who he becomes,so will fate prove hostile or benevolent. It's up to him. Wholeheartedly he accepts this responsibility;and recognizes it as the supreme one."

The year 1926 and the years just after it were a time when Cummings's divided self was under enough pressure to shatter a stronger soul. His custody battle with Elaine was reaching its final, sad chapter. He would be granted a visit with Nancy in March of 1927 after he furiously refused to cancel his adoption of her. Elaine had been sick. There were many excuses for Nancy's unavailability. His mother had even written to Elaine in her own version of a fury at losing Nancy. Finally he was allowed an hour with his own daughter. She looked small and pale but was as spirited and playful as ever. This was the last time they would see each other until Nancy was a married adult with two children of her own.

Another loss was in the wings. Early in 1926, Edward Cummings— a man who seemed to embody the power and the mercy of God when he stood in the pulpit—lost his job as a minister. Two Cambridge churches merged and he was asked to step aside. Estlin Cummings was delighted that for once he was able to cheer his father instead of the other way around. "You can only see that you've lost the church, but that isn't so," Cummings admonished his grieving father. "He looked at me. 'In losing the church,' I said, 'you've entered the world. You're a worldly person: why deny it?' We stood face to face. 'Only a small part of you could possibly fit in that church' I said almost angrily—'all the rest of you had to remain outside.' "

His father, Cummings told him, was like a child who had slammed his finger in a door; the incident was painful, but now he was free. "I congratulate you," he told the older man, and the conversation ended in a tender hug. In spite of Edward Cummings's dejection, the family had a wonderful summer at Joy Farm.

Later, when Cummings was back at the studio on the third floor of 4 Patchin Place, with the low roofs of the city outside his windows and the rumble of the elevated tracks on Sixth Avenue in the distance, and his parents were at home on Irving Street in Cambridge, Rebecca sent her son a long letter as well as some neckties—for which Cummings naturally had scant use, but a mother can hope—and handkerchiefs. Cummings's lighthearted thank-you letter to his mother was the last he would send to the house in Cambridge for a long, long time. He recommends to Rebecca the works of Sigmund Freud, which he had read on the train home to New York after the summer. He reports that he is churning out articles for *Vanity Fair* and that his play *Him* is almost finished.

With Cummings, clarity in writing seemed to come when he was happiest, almost as if obscurity were a refuge from unwanted feeling. This particular letter has all the syntactic originality of a Cummings letter but none of the veil. "Myself seems to be quite on the rampage as usual," he writes. "If keeping busy were synonymous with keeping happy, your humble servant would claim a palm or three."

And Cummings the poet was certainly keeping busy in the summer and fall of 1926. *Tulips & Chimneys* had been out for three years, and its astonishing poems were still reverberating in the public consciousness as he embarked on more poems, more paintings, and a play. He followed it up with two more collections of poems, *&(AND)* and *XLI Poems,* in 1925 and another, *Is 5,* in 1926. *Tulips & Chimneys,* published when Cummings was a very young man and inspired by the huge relief of being free from a variety of prisons, including puritanical Cambridge and La Ferté-Macé in France, collects most of the poems for which Cummings is justly famous. "All in green went my love riding," "In Just—," "Buffalo Bill's," "I was sitting in mcsorley's," "the Cambridge ladies": the book is a treasure trove of astonishing poems written by a young man who was still a gallant adventurer in a world of wonders. Great losses were about to change that world.

In the old days the drive from Cambridge to Silver Lake could be a long day's trip, first north to Concord, New Hampshire, and then west over small local roads, leaving Lake Winnipesaukee to the north and turning north again toward the Ossipee range and the sharper peaks of the White Mountains, dominated by the rocky summit of Mount Chocorua at Silver Lake and Mount Washington in the distance. On November 2, 1926, Cummings's parents were headed back to Joy Farm for a mid-autumn visit. The couple, both in their sixties and with undiminished physical energy, drove their elegant, air-cooled Franklin, which with its huge, shiny fenders, long engine block in front of the passenger seat, and small windshield was Edward Cummings's latest automotive pride and joy.

They were eager to get to the house at Silver Lake. Problems that darkened the world in Cambridge—Edward Cummings's rejection by his own church, the loss of Nancy—often seemed to dissipate as they headed north. It was a clear day as they left Irving Street and drove the 122 miles north. The air still smelled of autumn apples and crushed leaves. Soon the seasonal foliage, which had been reds and golds in Cambridge, turned darker. When they crossed into New Hampshire, they saw that winter had come to the north country—many of the trees were already bare. As they approached the Ossipee range on the eastern side of New Hampshire near the Maine border, it began to snow lightly, slow flakes twirling down from what had been a blue sky. Then it began to snow in earnest. It was very early in the year for snow even this far north, and the Cummingses weren't well prepared.

Although the Franklin was a huge improvement over the Cummingses' first car, which had run on a chain engine, driving in 1926 was still something of an adventure, especially in northern New Hampshire. The roads were dirt as often as they were paved, and the family had had many encounters with livestock and horse-pulled country traffic on their trips in a car from Cambridge to Silver Lake. Cars in the 1920s were still prone to unpredictable breakdowns and roads to unanticipated problems.

Rebecca was driving the Franklin, and as they climbed higher into the mountains, the snow increased. Snow began to build at the sides of the road as they passed Lake Wentworth and the small town of Wolfeboro. As the snow got heavier and visibility diminished, Edward Cummings insisted that Rebecca pull the car over to the side of the narrow road and stop so that he could clear the small, high windshield. The wipers were short and primitive, doing little more than pushing the snow back and forth. He cleared off the glass with his hands, but in a few minutes the view was again obscured as Rebecca drove on, partially blinded, to the metronomic rhythm of the wipers.

Ahead, there were railroad tracks embedded in the road, cutting across the pavement at a sharp angle and now hidden by the snow. Rebecca entered a straight part of the road where, in better weather, they always had their first glimpse of Mount Chocorua's dramatic rocky summit. The tracks are still there, with no signal and no change in the road's surface at a place where trees line the shoulder. It's easy to see how Rebecca, concentrating on driving forward, failed to see what was bearing down on her from her right side. The huge Boston & Maine steam locomotive emerged from the trees as it took its last run of the day north to Intervale, New Hampshire, from Rochester on the spur line. The locomotive's engineer saw the Franklin heading for the tracks through the snow, and desperately tried to brake the engine and the coal car with their ten sets of deadly iron wheels arrayed behind the cowcatcher. It was too late. The steam-belching engine loomed above the Franklin and then cut it in half. Edward Cummings was killed instantly. Rebecca Cummings was miraculously thrown clear.

By this time the train had screeched to a stop. "When two brakemen jumped from the halted train, they saw a woman standing—dazed but erect—beside a mangled machine," Cummings wrote. "These men took my sixty six year old mother by the arms and tried to lead her toward a nearby farmhouse; but she threw them off, strode straight to my father's body, and directed a group of scared spectators to cover him. When this had been done (and only then) she let them lead her away." Rebecca Cummings was taken to the hospital in Wolfeboro, the small town that the couple had driven by earlier. The unseasonable snow had knocked out the electricity all over New Hampshire, even at the hospital, and Rebecca's head wounds were stitched up by a country surgeon working by candlelight.

Cummings was having a festive dinner at his friend Morrie Werner's apartment with his new lady love—the sexy, forthright Anne Barton—when his sister, Elizabeth, arrived at the door with the awful news. Brother and sister took the train north the next day to Rebecca's bedside. "My sister and I entered a small darkened room in a country hospital," Cummings recalled. "She was still alive . . . why the head doctor could not imagine. She wanted only one thing: to join the person she loved most. He was very near her, but she could not quite reach him. We spoke, and she recognized our voices. Gradually her own voice began to understand what its death would mean to these living children of hers; and very gradually a miracle happened. She decided to live." Somehow the vision of her children seemed to give her a new strength, and over the next month she was moved to Boston's Peter Bent Brigham Hospital and continued to recover.

Within a year Cummings had lost a daughter and a father. When Scofield Thayer was institutionalized later in 1926, it was just more of the same. Cummings threw himself into his work and into his ill-fated love affair with Barton, a woman who, even at the beginning of their relationship, didn't know how to be faithful to one man.

Cummings and Anne Barton had been introduced by Werner, a new friend of his who had been at Columbia with Brown. A biographer who had worked for the *New York Herald Tribune,* Werner had written books on P. T. Barnum and Brigham Young. He was married to the classy writer Hazel Hawthorne.

A pretty girl from a poor family who had been molested by her father, Anne Barton had already been married to the glamorous, unstable New York artist Ralph Barton and had a daughter with him who was a year younger than Nancy. Cummings's typically sardonic eulogy of her, written years later, is a concise portrait:

> annie died the other day
>
> never was there such a lay—
> whom,among her dollies,dad
> first("don't tell your mother")had;
> making annie slightly mad
> but very wonderful in bed
> —saints and satyrs,go your way
>
> youths and maidens:let us pray.

In character and circumstances, Anne was the opposite of Elaine; she was wild and funny and always in need of money and so sexual that she could electrify all the men in any room she entered. Not at all like the precious, protected, princessy, wealthy woman who had turned on him so bitterly, Anne represented a kind of freedom Cummings admired and craved.

The problem with Anne Barton was that she also claimed that freedom for herself, in practice as well as in principle, and as she and Cummings became a couple she continued to see other men—especially a wealthy suitor who bought her pretty things and promised to settle money on her daughter, Diana. For all his talk of liberty, this bothered Cummings a lot.

About the same time he met Anne, Cummings got a letter from his friend Sibley Watson conferring on him the annual award for poetry given by the magazine that Watson now published—the Dial Award, which came with a check for two thousand dollars and an irresistible pedigree; Tom Eliot had gotten it in 1922 and Marianne Moore in 1924.

All in all, it had seemed like a great idea to Cummings to take Anne and Diana to Paris, with a side trip to Venice, using the Dial Award money to get her away from her other boyfriends, provide her with something that no amount of money could buy, and cement her loyalties to him. Of course, this grand and expensive experiment didn't work; but Cummings came home with more work done on his play about betrayal. He immediately went up to Silver Lake to work while Anne stayed behind and returned to her flirtations. From this New Hampshire intensity developed the revolutionary play *Him,* which he continued writing in the fall when he got back to New York. Just as he finished the play, he heard about the accident in West Ossipee.

It was Marianne Moore who started Cummings on drama when she asked him to do a theater issue for *The Dial.* Although not an intimate friend of Cummings, Moore was one of his solid patrons and admirers. As editor of *The Dial* she had a hand in getting him the Dial Award as well as many assignments and publications. Moore, who would later win the Pulitzer Prize and the National Book Award for her poems, was already a formidable figure in Cummings's community. With her capes and her tricorne hats she looked as eccentric as she was; she was also a good friend of Pound's and a subject for Lachaise. Hildegarde Watson remembers being spellbound when she finally met Moore at a concert. "As she quickly rose to meet me I noticed her eyes, shafts of meaning darting from under the broad brim of her black sailor hat, and the shining bands, just visible, of her red hair."

Writing about the theater, Cummings came to believe that there was no contemporary theater, no *new* theater as there was new poetry, written by him and Pound and Stein and Lowell, and new art, painted by Picasso and Braque and Léger. The revolution of modernism had somehow skipped the theater. The real contemporary theater was outside the theater: it was the burlesque at the National Winter Garden, vaudeville, and the circus.

Cummings hoped that *Him* would be the first modernist drama. Using an open stage in which the actor's fourth wall was the invisible space between the actors and the audience, he wrote a strange play about men and women—*Him and Me*—filled with surreal imagery and wild dramaturgical swings. In one scene, in which Him tries to seduce Me—a scene that follows a scene in which Me gets an abortion—Cummings seems to be influenced by Freud, or perhaps by some kind of wisdom heard or learned from his experiences with Elaine and Anne. "Think that I am not a bit the sort of person you think," Me warns Him. "Think that you fell in love with someone you invented—someone who wasn't me at all. Now you are trying to feel things; but that doesn't work, because the nicest things happen by themselves."

The play seems to be ahead of the playwright when it comes to understanding the complicated dance between men and women in love. Perpetually engaged to Anne Barton, a woman who seemed to love him passionately but to love many men passionately, Cummings once again found himself in a kind of emotional agony. This time, he went to see a friend and student of Sigmund Freud's, Fritz (Siegfried) Wittels, an Austrian who had recently set up a psychoanalytic practice in New York. Wittels was a graduate of the erotic emphases of Freud and of fin-de-siècle Vienna. He had left one sex scandal behind him when he came to New York to lecture at the New School for Social Research, and he was on the second of three wives.

Although Cummings did not submit to a full psychoanalytic treatment, he went to Wittels as a patient beginning in 1928, just after Wittels arrived in Greenwich Village, and for the rest of Wittels's life. Wittels immediately zeroed in on Cummings's fears about his manhood. Was he still just a boy in a man's body? Had he acted the part of the careless, powerless boy when it came to dealing with Elaine and the manly Frank MacDermot? Was Anne Barton unable to be faithful to him because of his own failings as a man? Was his slight stature part of the problem?

Cummings did not want to marry Anne for very good reasons; but Wittels seemed to persuade him that this was his boyish, irresponsible self and that a real man would want to bear the burdens of a wife and child—even a crazy wife and someone else's child. Wittels made the decision to marry seem like a gateway to adulthood: now, in marrying Anne, Cummings would become a man. Perhaps this was a way of mourning his father; perhaps it was just a bad idea. "We knew from Freud that repressed sex instincts made men neurotic to such an extent that an entire era was poisoned," Wittels wrote. "What we did not know then was that former puritans running wild would not help either."

Cummings was one of these puritans running wild. He didn't want to marry Anne, but Wittels and Anne together were hard to resist. Cummings and Anne were married on May 1, 1929, at the Unitarian Church of All Souls on Fourth Avenue and Twentieth Street, with Rebecca and Elizabeth Cummings in attendance. Both the bride and the groom were drunk. "They had been stewed for days," wrote Edmund Wilson, who was there. "Cummings had taken several baths, one after the other; he had felt his arms and legs getting numb . . . Anne went to sleep and slept for days and couldn't wake up . . . awful moment just before the ceremony . . . when, after everything had been most nonchalant and amiable, they all began snapping at one another."

As Cummings's personal life took another disastrous turn, seemingly disproving his belief that fortune does us neither good nor evil, his professional life continued to get respectful attention. As a man he was spiraling toward agonizing loneliness; as a writer he was never more popular or successful. Throughout his life the personal and the professional seemed strangely divided. When one went well, the other sank, and vice versa. Now, in the 1920s, it was his professional life that seemed on a trajectory to greatness. Partly because Cummings was produced by the Provincetown Playhouse *Him* had gotten a great deal of review attention. Cummings adored the jacket copy, which hailed the play's "lucid madness, adventurous gayety and graceful irreverence." Edmund Wilson gave it a good review in the *New Republic.*

Him inspired loyalty and despair. Its twenty-one scenes and seventy-two characters for a cast of 105 were thrown together with Cummings's playful energy. Some critics said they couldn't understand it. "Fatiguing, pretentious and empty," said Alexander Woollcott. Others embraced it. At a time when the hit plays were things like *The Trial of Mary Dugan* and *The Shannons of Broadway, Him* was more than unusual and eccentric—it was almost completely fresh and different. Walter Winchell wrote a long, mixed review, but he did say something so memorably negative that it is still often quoted by people who do not remember its subject or its author—he wrote that watching *Him* was "every now and then like stepping on something extremely nasty in the dark." Only through the support of James Light and Eleanor Fitzgerald, forward-thinking directors of the Provincetown Playhouse along with Eugene O'Neill, was the play produced at all. Thus Cummings's career in the theater was launched, controversial and over budget as it was always to be.

After the production of *Him,* and his honeymoon in Europe with

Anne—this time without his mother or Diana, who was parked in a Swiss boarding school, the babysitter of choice for upper-class children in the 1920s and '30s—he and Anne moved to Paris. From there Cummings decided to try to get a visa for a trip to Russia.

Russia in the 1920s was a kind of antiauthoritarian promised land, especially for men and women who were fed up with American capitalism, commercialism, and venality. For many artists, the idea of a society in which competition was replaced by a benevolent state seemed genius. They heard all about it. Russia was the scene of a successful revolution on the part of the proletariat, and most artists identified with the proletariat. The idea that goods and services should be distributed according to need rather than according to, well, greed, was immensely appealing. The John Reed Clubs, named after Cummings's former neighbor at Patchin Place, thrived among the New York City artists and writers who abhorred the money-worshipping culture in which they found themselves. Reed himself was a kind of hero—a Harvard hero to boot.

The Russian Revolution had overthrown the twin doxologies of religion and money—two things about which Cummings had complicated and passionate feelings. As the son of a minister he had rejected religion, and as a son of Harvard and the wealthy Cambridge neighborhood where he grew up he had rejected money. So in 1931, while he was living in Paris with Anne, Cummings decided that he would like to go and see for himself what the great and glorious revolution looked like on the ground. Friends had visited Russia and come home with glowing reports of this new world where creativity was rewarded and the humble were as looked after as the wealthy. Dos Passos had been there. Morrie Werner had as well. Cummings's Paris friend Louis Aragon couldn't say enough great things about this new model of government. For Cummings, who had based both his life and his work on the principle of revolution and the toppling of all authority, the Russian Revolution was fascinating and irresistible. One of his Russian friends urged him to go, saying, in a suspiciously Cummings-like way, "Spring is nowhere else." In April of 1931, Cummings cabled his mother for money. He applied for a visa to travel to Moscow and Kiev. In May, carrying gifts and his typewriter alone and in high spirits, he boarded the train for Moscow.

Trouble started on this dream excursion as soon as the train crossed the border into Russia from Poland. There it was stopped and repeatedly searched by unsmiling men in uniform. This train ride, in a second-class carriage crowded with suddenly fearful passengers, became a centerpiece for Cummings's very funny stories about his visit to Russia. Puffing and panting as if he were a steam engine, Cummings communicated to his listeners the sharp difference between the relatively benevolent Polish landscape and the terrified citizens and terrifying officials on the wrong side of the Russian border. "Inexorably has a magic wand been waved; miraculously did reality disintegrate; where am I? . . . in a world of Was—everything shoddy; everywhere dirt and cracked fingernails—guarded by 1 . . . soldier," so Cummings described the change from Poland into Russia in *Eimi,* the memoir he wrote about his journey.

When the train finally pulled in to Moscow, Cummings somehow missed a connection with the man who was supposed to meet him at the station. He ended up at the very expensive Hotel Metropol, being shown around by exactly the kind of person he had spent his life avoiding—the Harvard Brahmin Henry Wadsworth Longfellow Dana. Dana appointed himself Cummings's guide to this revolutionary new world—he became in *Eimi*'s satiric pages Cummings's personal Virgil. Part Ancient Mariner, part propaganda machine, Dana drove Cummings nuts.

As the Hotel Metropol drained Cummings's bank account, his guide exhausted his patience. Dana's conversion to everything around them, including the abolishment of religious freedom and every other kind of freedom, did not sit well with Cummings. "The whole trouble with you," Dana tells Cummings, who is trying to take a nap, at one point, "is that, like so many people who were brought up on religion, you can't bear the idea of anything doing away with it." Cummings can barely grunt a response, "What?" "Of Science doing away with religion," Dana explains. Cummings is unresponsive as Dana harangues him and calls him trivial, childish, and cheap. They went to the theater and to the Writers' Club, and Dana introduced him to other Americans. Dana was a seemingly mindless believer when it came to communism, and it took Cummings a while to notice that their conversations were often followed by the same unsmiling men in uniform, who turned out to be members of Stalin's feared GPU, the forerunner of the KGB.

Cummings spent a little more than a month in Russia, visiting Kiev and leaving the country through Constantinople and Turkey. In the end he met wonderful people there: Joan London, the daughter of Jack London, and her husband; Lili Brik; the great director and actor Vsevolod Meyerhold, whose ideas about the theater were parallel to his own. Yet he found Russia more than disappointing. It wasn't just that the people were terrified of the government—perhaps totalitarianism was worse than capitalism—or that Stalin's purges were somehow in the air. Although he and Meyerhold seemed to speak freely, for instance, Meyerhold was arrested and tortured by Stalin's police in 1939, and in 1940 he was executed for the crimes he had confessed to under torture.

Worse, for Cummings, the Communist propaganda machine seemed to have otherwise intelligent people in its thrall. They did not seem to see what he saw. Their hypocrisy was astounding and terrifying. In spite of the fear and the searches and the disappearances that were already going on before their eyes, men and women like Henry Dana continued to spout platitudes about the noble experiment of the Russian Revolution. The combination of the general fear and the specific mindlessness of those who chose to ignore it was anathema to Cummings. The insanity and the power sucking of the men who were leading Russia under Stalin in the late 1920s were later to be perfectly lampooned in George Orwell's *Animal Farm*. Cummings saw through the sham of propaganda right away.

At the time of Cummings's visit, Stalin was just beginning the first of his great purges, sweeps in which anyone who spoke against the government or who just happened to get in the way was sent off to the gulags of Siberia or executed in the Moscow jails. Cummings was in the shadow of one of the great waves of cruelty in history, and he felt it.

Cummings had been carried along by the leftist tendencies of his friends in Greenwich Village and Paris. Now he did a political about-face. Communism under Stalin scared and horrified him. He hated what it did, and he hated its effect on the people forced to go along with it. For the rest of his life he would take the Communist threat seriously because of the terror and disruption he had seen in the eyes of Stalin's subjects. Communism had been an idea; now it became a devil. Later, when the rest of the world had changed its mind again, Cummings never forgot his trip to Russia, where he had seen for himself the price people can pay when their supposedly benevolent government goes out of control.

Cummings had left for Russia on May 10, 1931. By June 14 he was headed for New York, where his personal life was brewing the kind of disappointment on an intimate level that communism had turned out to be on a political level. Almost as soon as he left Paris, Anne discovered she was pregnant. Not just because he was traveling but because of Communist censorship, Cummings failed to get the letters she sent. She decided on an abortion and returned to New York to have the operation. In her hour of need, her husband was nowhere to be found; and so she turned to other friends, including the wealthy man who had been Cummings's rival for her affections all along. By the time Cummings got back to New York with Diana, whom he had picked up in Switzerland, his second marriage was beginning to fall apart.

Now his marriage became a nightmare. Anne's ex-husband, Ralph Barton, Diana's father, had killed himself on May 19, and the emotional fallout as she grieved for a man she had left was more than Cummings could handle. In retrospect, it seems clear that Anne was an alcoholic. At the same time, on the death of Edward Cummings, Rebecca Cummings had deeded Joy Farm to her son and, in an ill-advised fit of generosity, his wife. Rebecca loved children, and perhaps she had been moved by Diana's enjoyment of the country. Now, because of this legacy, Anne started threatening to take Joy Farm. She turned to other men. She got drunk and embarrassed Cummings in front of his friends, complaining that his penis was inadequate and bragging about men who were better lovers.

But Anne's infidelity would be her own undoing and Cummings's salvation when it came to the ownership of Joy Farm and his legal freedom. By the end of 1931, she had another steady lover, an assertive dental surgeon who, some thought, beat her. Soon she was pregnant with her lover's child. In June she went to Mexico for a divorce decree. She was still unwilling to part with her share of Joy Farm, and both she and Cummings hired lawyers. Negotiations ensued.

Cummings threatened to have the Mexican divorce nullified. After his first marriage, he had lost his innocence, his friend and patron Scofield Thayer, and his daily connection to his daughter. After his second marriage he balked at losing the place in the world where he felt most at home.

In May of 1932, Cummings got word that his friend Hart Crane had died. He had jumped overboard from a ship on the way home from Mexico, apparently a suicide.

8

Eimi and Marion Morehouse

Eimi, Cummings's second memoir, begins on Sunday, May 10, 1931, when he boards the train from Paris for Russia through Poland, and it ends 443 pages later on Sunday, June 14, when, again on a train, he crosses from Switzerland back into France. The title, Greek for "I am," is an assertion of identity provoked by Cummings's month-long visit.

After *his* visit to Russia in 1921, a decade earlier, journalist Lincoln Steffens famously exclaimed, "I have been over into the future, and it works." Many of Cummings's friends and colleagues agreed. But a July 1931 interview with a reporter from the Paris edition of the *Chicago Tribune,* just after he returned from Russia, shows the first hints of a controversial, surprising reaction to Cummings's own journey to Russia. His opinion of what was happening there would sharpen and get angrier over time as the situation under Stalin got worse.

The Russians, Cummings explained to *Tribune* reporter Don Brown, were very scared and very serious. Cummings liked the Russians, but he did not like Russia and, more amazingly, he did not like communism. "Are the Russian people happy? They struck me like this: they just love to suffer and they're suffering like hell, so they must be happy. You know Dostoevski . . . People talk about the strain and tension of life in the United States. It is nothing to that in Moscow," he said. "If you said 'boo' to some of these people they might drop dead . . . they are in a particularly nervous condition."

"Cummings went to the Soviet Union with his eyes open and without an agenda," writes Christopher Sawyer-Lauçanno. "But his experiences there, in which he witnessed first-hand the privation and sadness of the Stalinist state, certainly helped him develop an agenda."

By the time he sat down to write *Eimi,* using his Russian journals as a template, Cummings had become furious about the condition of Russia and what he saw as the failure of the great Communist idea. His natural perversity had added heat to his observations. Later he referred to Russia as the "subhuman communist superstate, where men are shadows & women are nonmen. This unworld is Hell."

Eimi describes a terrifying, hellish place where frightened people trudge along in their desperate, monotonous ruts, preyed upon by political tourists come to see the Great Experiment and kept in line by the menacing men of the GPU, who know everything about everyone. Perhaps as a relief from this oppression, there is a great deal of drinking in the *Eimi* story, even for Cummings, who was never stingy or reluctant when it came time to drink or smoke. Because of his questioning attitude and because he immediately started taking long, aimless walks in Moscow, the GPU seems to have concluded that Cummings was a spy. He was followed almost everywhere he went, which probably did not improve his impression of the place.

He also decided to write in a stream-of-consciousness style with experimental words and a completely original syntax like that of the better-known James Joyce's *Ulysses*. *Eimi* has been published as a novel and as a memoir, but whether he was writing nonfiction or fiction, Cummings remained at heart a poet and a visual artist. Like many of his poems, *Eimi* has a pattern of words that varies completely from page to page to suit the content. As a poet and painter, Cummings was continually trying to merge the two forms of creativity. His account of his first dinner with Joan London and her husband, for instance, is a typical descriptive sentence from the book. "next:in the very diningroom where vodkaful romp romped while the alarmed flowerbuyer fluttered and ex-sulked vodkaless, a pompously incoherent conversation fetters 9 tensely untogether—e.g. to my right, a 'Russian actor' who doesn't speak anything else."

Cummings is more famous for style than for substance. Even today, he is better known for abjuring uppercase letters than for his poems or books. Everyone makes the same joke about him. *Eimi* is a good example of Cummings's prose, which, with its pell-mell words and images and reinvented grammar, rewards careful study but is not easy to read. "He avoids the cliché first by avoiding the whole accepted modus of English," his friend William Carlos Williams wrote about Cummings's prose style.

"He does it, not to be 'popular,' God knows, nor to sell anything, but to lay bare the actual experience . . . He does it to reveal, to disclose, to free a man from habit. Habit is our continual enemy as artists and as men."

The book was published first as a novel—editors at Covici, Friede, which had published Cummings's two previous books, thought it worked best as a novel. Cummings created many different characters—versions of himself—as narrators, using a kind of pidgin Russian to name them: Kemminkz, Peesahtel (a scan of the Russian word for writer), Hoodozhnik (artist), and the "heroless" hero. Also, of course, he writes as the ubiquitous Cummings i. "i is small, usually inconspicuous, but nimble and resilient and completely committed to its liberty," writes Madison Smartt Bell. "It runs around inside the wainscots of Soviet Russia like the mouse in a *Tom and Jerry* cartoon."

Loosely based on Dante's visit to the underworld—Cummings calls Russia the "unworld"—the story features the silly, waspy Henry Wadsworth Longfellow Dana as the Virgil of the Metropol Hotel. A friendlier guide for Cummings was Joan London, who in *Eimi* becomes the author's Beatrice.

In New York City in the 1920s, in Cummings's community, there was a lot of dreaming about the beauties of Lenin's new government and the glorious revolution on the other side of the world. American capitalism seemed to be failing, especially after the stock-market crash of 1929. The great American ideal of freedom seemed to exist only for the rich, while working-class people and the poor were stranded in a backwater of democracy where scarcity and deprivation were the rule. With the wealthy, oblivious Herbert Hoover as president—a president who seemed to purposefully fail to understand what was happening—our country seemed to be sailing over the edge of the civilized world.

In Communist Russia, on the other hand, authority had been overthrown, and the dream of a workers' government had been realized. Writers like Malcolm Cowley, Sherwood Anderson, Alfred Kazin, and even Ernest Hemingway and Scott Fitzgerald eagerly embraced the idea that Russia had succeeded where America had failed.

Perhaps Cummings was just too late. By 1931, things had begun to turn sour in Russia. Lenin had died in 1924, and the resulting power struggle ended with Joseph Stalin, already paranoid when he ascended in 1928. Trotsky had been exiled a year later. The dream of the Soviet

Union was nine years old, and Cummings visited it at the beginning of its bloody, criminal end. No one was better suited to pick up on the fact that the government by the people had turned into a government against the people. Hoover was a bad president, but he was a bad president in the context of a democratic system that worked.

The year 1931 was a fascinating moment in world history, a moment when democracy and socialism passed each other, going in two different directions—one toward success and the other toward failure. When *Eimi* was first published, Cummings's account of Russia was shocking and deeply disturbing to his own friends and community in Greenwich Village, where many people still needed to believe that the Russian ideal was working. He lost friends, and people crossed the street to avoid him. Malcolm Cowley and Edmund Wilson were horrified at what seemed to them, accurately, to be a sudden veering into right-wing conservatism on the part of their erstwhile left-wing drinking buddy. George Jean Nathan called *Eimi* the worst book of the month. The poet Karl Shapiro wrote that it was "a four hundred page garland of bad fruit thrown at the Soviet Union, [which] missed the mark entirely." Other reviewers complained about the way the book was written. "If only Cummings would condescend to let his readers read him," wrote Lewis Gannett in the *Herald Tribune*.

Cummings's disgust for communism wasn't restricted to the pages of *Eimi*. In one poem he decried both the Russians' fear and their lack of hygiene:

> kumrads die because they're told)
> kumrads die before they're old
> (kumrads aren't afraid to die
> kumrads don't
> and kumrads won't
> believe in life)and death knows whie
>
> (all good kumrads you can tell
> by their altruistic smell
> moscow pipes good kumrads dance)
> kumrads enjoy
> s.freud knows whoy
> the hope that you may mess your pance

every kumrad is a bit
of quite unmitigated hate
(travelling in a futile groove
god knows why)
and so do i
(because they are afraid to love

Having little money had never bothered Cummings—in fact, it seemed to delight him. Cummings was thrilled at being able to act the part of a Yankee aristocrat who lived on crumbs and ate humble fare off ancestral china. He had grown up in a world where money didn't matter, and he embraced the shabby eccentricity of intellectual Cambridge where professors were too wrapped up in the world of ideas to care if their clothes were shabby or their roofs leaked.

Poverty was unbearable for Anne. She certainly did not have in mind riding out the Great Depression with a penniless artist who wasn't even interested in having a job. All around her, people seemed to have lost everything they had. Edmund Wilson was living in a furnished room. Cummings's friend Jim Light was so poor he slept on a doctor's operating table. Her own wealthy lover—the man who had caused Cummings so much jealous pain—had also lost his money. Where could she turn for security? By October she was having an affair with a dentist who, Cummings heard, regularly hit her. Soon she was pregnant, by the dentist. His second marriage was over.

Then, in the spring of 1932, an extraordinary thing happened. Anne had left him, and of course he was interested in meeting women. Cummings loved women. On June 23, 1932, Jim and Patti Light—he had directed *Him* at the Provincetown Playhouse—took him backstage after the performance of a play in which another friend of theirs, Marion Morehouse, had a small part. Marion was a woman with a murky past who had come to New York in the 1920s to make it as an actress, but who instead had already had phenomenal success as a model. Like Cummings, she adored the theater and longed to be part of it; also like Cummings, she didn't think much of the clothing industry that had become her career. The four went to dinner at Felix's restaurant. "As soon as you saw her," Cummings wrote much later in his journals, "something in yourself told you, 'she's too tall for me.' "

Indeed, the gorgeous young actress was twelve years younger than the thirty-seven-year-old Cummings and almost six feet tall. Long-legged, with huge eyes and a pretty face, she was sexually generous—a trait that would delight and torture Cummings in the years to come—and charmed by Cummings's animation, humor, and lack of pretension. Edmund Wilson found her stagy and "not spontaneous," but Cummings had enough spontaneity for the two of them.

Marion was not interested in reading or in the arts, except for the theater—and she was not interested in the intellectual part of the theater, either. She had probably not graduated from high school. She was not an intellectual, she was averse to becoming one, and she didn't like Cummings when he launched into his brilliant monologues—monologues that featured two Harvard degrees and one of the best minds of his generation. "During one of your early meals with her in a little wop speakeasy which she knew of, you were soaring along in your natural way—& she looked at you imploringly; as if to say 'please! Don't be intellectual with me: I'm just a woman!' " he wrote later. "whereupon you came down to earth . . . &have been there ever since."

Yet Marion was beautiful—officially, famously beautiful—and she was also obliging and charmed. In fact, his first night with Marion was the beginning of thirty years of love and friendship between them—the kind of love and friendship that had previously been impossible for him. Cummings was always a man who made lemonade out of lemons—writing about his problems with women, he described the way in which "the curse becomes a blessing, the disappearance an emergence, the agonizing departure an ecstatic arrival." Still, his history with women was as much a failure as it could possibly be, with its two failed marriages and its lost daughter, Nancy.

Cummings was an angry man, an anger that became more of an irritation with the entire world when he drank and as he aged. The anger was a problem with the women he had picked. Yet the story of his life is the story of a man who reaped the benefits of anger. He was able to turn defiance into creative force and to express for all of us his delight in the world and his fury at the world and the men and women in it.

Cummings's story, as his biographers tell it and as he told it, is hard to understand in our modern context. He had two of the most disastrous marriages imaginable—marriages that featured adultery, lies, deceit, the loss of a child, and constant heartbreak. The psychological wisdom of the twenty-first century is that we carry our problems within ourselves. Somehow, either Cummings just met the right person when he met Marion, or he had changed. He had been seeing a psychoanalyst, Fritz Wittels; he was older. Perhaps he was also wiser.

Marion was a very different woman from Elaine or Anne. She was a self-invention. Her story of being born in South Bend, Indiana, to Roman Catholic parents who moved to Hartford, Connecticut, where she was educated at a school called St. Ann's, turns out not to be true. Wherever she came from, she arrived in New York hoping to make it as an actress. Marion was an inspired chameleon. As Edward Steichen pointed out, when she put on a gown or a riding habit, she became the woman who would wear those clothes.

With Cummings, too, she was a chameleon. Far more successful on her own than either of his other wives, she was at the same time less stubbornly set in her identity. She was also less desperate. Elaine had been an aristocratic princess who had been rejected by her prince and was hungry for affection; Anne had been the mistress of a man who wouldn't marry her. Marion was fine without Cummings, and she decided sometime in that night at Felix's that she would also be fine with him. Marion brought him back to earth, and he found that earth had its benefits.

With Marion, Cummings became less pretentious and more appreciative of simpler pleasures—food, friends, and sex. Marion didn't have children, and this gave Cummings plenty of space in the relationship to be the mischievous boy he sometimes seemed to be. Of course, with his quicksilver mind, he also saw the problems with this, which eventually unfolded as the two of them grew old together. Cummings already had a child; he did not want another, not even with Marion. "When you refused to let her have a child (unless she 'do her share' in supporting it)," he wrote enigmatically, "you sealed your own doom: making yourself her child, her baby—and herself your all-protecting mother." In this mood, Cummings even saw Marion's learning to cook his favorite dishes as a manipulative ploy to control him.

Yet, by the time he met Marion, Cummings had also changed. His marriage to Anne had been precipitated by a realization he had had on

Fritz Wittels's couch—that it was time for him to stop being a boy and start being a man. With his complicated relationship to authority and the energy he got from being a rebel, this shift from boyhood to manhood was not as simple as it had seemed. His marriage to Anne Barton seemed a high price to pay for manhood. Marion didn't make demands the way Anne had, and she didn't cheat on him, either—at first.

Another difference between Marion and Anne and Elaine was that Cummings specifically chose to be with Marion. She was available and he courted her and won her. Elaine, on the other hand, had found him desperately in love with her and led him into their sexually unsatisfying affair. Anne, too, had needed someone and chosen him. His courtship of Marion, with flowers and love notes and drawings of elephants, was tender and two-sided. Their connection was less about neediness and more about affection; their love was free to grow and blossom.

And Marion provoked some of Cummings's most beautiful and intelligent love poems, including one sonnet that is almost a paraphrase of Shakespeare's Sonnet 116, "Let me not to the marriage of true minds / admit impediments."

love's function is to fabricate unknownness

(known being wishless;but love,all of wishing)
though life's lived wrongsideout,sameness chokes oneness
truth is confused with fact,fish boast of fishing

and men are caught by worms(love may not care
if time totters,light droops,all measures bend
nor marvel if a thought should weigh a star
—dreads dying least;and less,that death should end)

how lucky lovers are(whose selves abide
under whatever shall discovered be)
whose ignorant each breathing dares to hide
more than most fabulous wisdom fears to see

(who laugh and cry)who dream,create and kill
while the whole moves;and every part stands still:

Cummings's mother, Rebecca, having successively loved and cared for Elaine and Nancy and Anne and Diana, was now more than willing to love Marion. The difference was that Marion, not bedeviled by her own needs and unmet desires, loved Rebecca back with a warmth and genuine feeling that never turned to jealousy or anything like it. Marion played well with others. Marion didn't complain that Cummings had too little money, as Anne had complained, or that he didn't love her enough, as Elaine had. She seemed to have no complaints. So although in one way Cummings had changed through his treatment with Wittels and through the process of aging—he was approaching forty—and perhaps through the process of heartbreak, he had also finally met the right woman, a woman who could give him the space to work and the warmth he needed; a woman he was proud to be with.

That autumn, Cummings had applied for a Guggenheim Fellowship. Henry Allen Moe, the principal administrator of the Foundation, was an admirer. Cummings wasted no words on his application, writing that he would produce "a book of poems." His plan was that when he got the money, $1,500, in the spring, he would take Marion to Paris on a trip they had both longed for.

Marion had never been abroad; the closest she had come was seeing friends off on the glamorous, sleek ocean liners docked at the piers on the west side of Manhattan. She had always longed to travel. A week after Cummings officially got the award, he and Marion were headed for France. In Paris they were able to sublet near the Porte d'Orléans. Marion learned to cook, and Cummings bought their wine. When Marion dropped by the offices of French *Vogue* just to say hello, her looks caused a small sensation. Soon she became the talk of the Paris fashion world and the favorite model of the glamorous photographer Baron George Hoyningen-Huene. Marion's Paris career brought in extra money and an invitation to the baron's villa in Tunisia.

Cummings was always delighted by Marion's success, both when she worked as a model and later when she became a photographer herself. In fact, he was disappointed by her inability to succeed as an actress. This was part of his boyishness, an attractive aspect of his sometimes androgynous nature. Marion's successes never threatened him. He was not brittle and macho and insistent on some form of masculinity. He was thrilled to have the most beautiful woman in the world on his arm and thrilled

rie Werner . . .

. . . and Anne Barton:
two portraits by
E. E. Cummings

Rebecca Cummings at Joy Farm in old age

Marion Morehouse, early 1930s

Cummings photographed
in his studio at Patchin Place
by James Sibley Watson

The glamorous Marion Morehouse shot by George Hoyningen-Huene, 1933

Cummings's drawing of Marion Morehouse

…cy at Joy Farm, 1950

…mmings self-portrait from 1947

Marianne Moore drawn by
Hildegarde Watson

Ezra Pound after his stay at St. Elizabe[th]
in 1957

Marion Morehouse in the 1930s

E. E. Cummings before
World War II

Cummings with his own painting of Mount Chocorua in 1950

to have a playmate who brought her own connections and talents to the table. Marion did not care about literature, but she was an adoring and appreciative student when it came to all things Paris.

For Cummings, physical size had an almost metaphorical resonance. He had been teased for his smallness and had felt overwhelmed by his father's great, masculine bulk. He had small, delicate hands and feet. If Elaine's ephemeral, birdlike beauty had made him feel like a big man, Marion's masculine lankiness sometimes bothered him. Still, he was falling in love with a woman who literally leaned on him whenever she took his arm, because of her physical height. "The physical act is an expression of a spiritual attitude," Cummings worried, although Marion's ambition to be an actress made him think she would not be leaning on him emotionally as Elaine and Anne had.

He emerged from his marriage to Elaine feeling inadequate sexually as well as in every other way. He was too slight, too short, too indecisive. As a result, he had lost his wife and daughter. Being with Marion, a large-boned gazelle of a woman who sometimes seemed to tower over him—so much so that it disturbed Ben La Farge years later—was a way to challenge that old idea of himself. There was a sweetness to Marion, a willingness to love that he had never experienced before in a sexual partner. Her height seemed to vanish as the two became closer. The two of them together shattered the conventional image of a couple just because of their size, and although he had had his doubts about this, Cummings came to relish it.

Age also worked in their favor. Cummings was almost forty, a man with a great deal of success behind him and a lot of experience. It was easy for him to have a relaxed authority with the twenty-seven-year-old Marion, the kind of authority that transcends the problems of masculine and feminine. Cummings was already a distinguished and celebrated artist, and Marion, for all her accomplishments, was still a girl.

The two set up housekeeping in Paris and were happy. They entertained the Pounds and anyone else they could find. Marion cooked and modeled; Cummings wrote and painted. "Marion's my new pride and joy: as you've probably guessed," he wrote his mother from Paris almost a year after he and Marion met. "Coming to a new language or world she immediately took it by storm . . . The *Vogue* people are doting on her slightest whim, creeping the boulevards on hands and knees to buy her orangejuice (with just the necessary goût of champagne) etc—as for Baron Huene,photographer de luxe,he wants us to visit him in Africa whenever he can stop snapping 'the most beautiful woman and the most poised in Paris.' A nice fellow,by the way."

Paris during the twenties and early thirties was the center of the New York literary world. Although Ernest Hemingway and his first wife, Hadley, had already drunk themselves out of their marriage and Hemingway had married the second of his four wives and decamped for the United States, many of New York's most important artists and patrons were still there. Lincoln Kirstein was also in Paris that summer, and when Cummings lost his passport and letter of credit after a particularly wild evening, which involved a great deal of drinking and also some dancing on the tops of cars, Kirstein lent him money.

Kirstein is an odd figure hovering in the background of the twentieth century and its creative community. Born wealthy, he cultivated eccentricity and apparently worshipped the ability to make art. While still an undergraduate at Harvard he had started a new magazine, *The Hound and Horn,* in which Cummings and almost everyone else published. Later he was a founder with George Balanchine of the New York City Ballet and one of the founders of the Museum of Modern Art. Already fascinated by dance, Kirstein asked Cummings if he wanted to write a ballet. Marion suggested a ballet of *Uncle Tom's Cabin,* the novel by Harriet Beecher Stowe, and Kirstein wrote the check.

Elaine, now officially Mrs. Frank MacDermot, also happened to be in Paris that summer of 1933—and as usual she wanted something from Cummings. MacDermot had decided to run for a seat in the Irish parliament. He hoped to represent County Roscommon. Doing this required him to have been married in the Roman Catholic Church. Elaine, twice divorced, could only be married in the church if both of her previous marriages were officially annulled.

An annulment, unlike a divorce, is a document stating that the marriage in question never happened. The annulment cites circumstances that invalidated the marriage from the beginning. If the marriage is never sexually consummated, for instance, it can be annulled—this is how Henry VIII wangled a legal marriage to his first wife, Catherine of Aragon, formerly his brother's wife, from the Church of Rome—something he was unable to do for his subsequent marriages. If one or the other party to the marriage was mentally ill at the time, it can be argued that the marriage never happened; if one of them was unfit to decide that they should be married, it could be decreed by the church that they had never really been married even if there were children involved.

Annulment is a medieval concept that the modern church still embraces. Elaine had already managed her annulment from her marriage to Thayer by testifying that he was mentally unstable and therefore unable to make the decision to marry. Ipso facto they had never "really" been married in the eyes of the church. Annulling her marriage to Cummings was a more difficult problem. Elaine's argument was that since she and Cummings had verbally agreed to let each other out of the marriage if that was what either of them desired, they had never really had a marriage. It was a thread of an idea, but apparently she was desperate to please and accommodate her new husband. She had even found a Parisian priest who was willing to facilitate the annulment if Cummings would meet with him.

But Cummings wasn't interested in obliging Elaine, the woman who, after all, had heartlessly severed his connection to his only child. He refused to answer her messages. What did he want with her now? She coaxed and pressured and wheedled, using their mutual friends. Finally she caught up with him, running after him on the street and calling his name. Always the gentleman, he agreed to meet with her.

He brought Marion to their lunch at a small restaurant in the Rue de l'Echelle, inwardly crowing that he was with a woman so beautiful and loving that Elaine could eat her heart out. But it was Cummings whose heart had been continuously eaten out by the loss of his daughter. As always, Elaine had the upper hand. She didn't care that Cummings had moved on to taller and more beautiful things. She wanted what she wanted. Cummings once again seemed helpless in front of her onslaught. At least he got his first news of Nancy, who was now thirteen, in seven years. She was at school in Bexhill in England, Elaine said. But when Cummings said he would like to meet MacDermot as a way of seeing Nancy, Elaine burst into tears.

So for a minute or two, Cummings had the upper hand. Elaine and Frank needed something from him, and he needed something from them—visitation with his daughter for himself and his mother. But once again, in this negotiation, Cummings backed away from winning. Was it that his newfound happiness with Marion made the painful discon-nection from Nancy seem best left in the past? What did Marion think about Nancy? Cummings had made it clear to her that he wasn't willing to have more children, although at that point she certainly had plenty of time before making such an important decision. She was more beautiful than Elaine and younger than Elaine and a million times more loving than Elaine, but Elaine would always be the mother of Estlin's child. Cummings had drafted a telegram to Elaine saying there would be no annulment unless there was something definite about Nancy. Elaine appeared to relent, and Cummings wrote to MacDermot, who gave a friendly but noncommittal reply.

Cummings dutifully did his part. Still a Yankee at heart, he couldn't quite believe that there were people—the MacDermots, for instance—who could make promises and then break them. He seemed stunned, like prey before a strike, that Elaine could be so charming and so agree-able and then seem to forget what she had promised altogether as soon as she got what she wanted. Cummings visited the priest with Elaine and agreed that the marriage had always been provisional. Then Elaine, Marion, Cummings, and MacDermot all went out to dinner.

But no arrangements were made for Cummings to see his daughter. Rebecca Cummings, writing that she was delighted to hear that her son was happy to be in Paris with Marion, then wistfully added: "I only wish I might have a photograph of Nancy & know whether she has ever received my birthday gifts." The upshot of all this was pathetic. Once again Cummings's way of engaging with the world was cooperative and ineffectual—the opposite of his father's. Instead of seeing Nancy and get-ting to know her again, Cummings settled reluctantly for a few snapshots finally sent to his mother, and a few schoolgirl thank-you notes for gifts without any acknowledgment of the importance of the giver. Was this what he really wanted? Had the idea of Nancy become part of a painful past, while the present was all the adored Marion? At any rate, it's what he got.

By the end of the summer Marion and Cummings had accepted Hoyningen-Huene's offer and were ensconced in a Moorish palace by the sea. "There in Africa were flamingoes and fairies and burros with long warm strong thonglike ears and even an occasional scorpion," Cum-mings wrote to Hildegarde Watson. "Born under Libra, Estlin did not see the scorpion;which disappeared into a double you sea. Marion saw it,but she was not afraid and so their existence passed like a day in the night. Effrica . . ."

After this amazing year together, the couple left Tunisia for Italy—Estlin wanted Marion to see the Sistine Chapel—and finally in December sailed for New York on the *Bremen*. Their time abroad cemented the two as a couple, and they would be together for the rest of their lives—they always considered each other, wept and raged at each other's misfortunes, and supported each other through the many difficulties ahead. Later in their life together, as Cummings and then Marion became seriously ill, they took turns taking care of each other. As far as women were concerned, Cummings had found his soul mate. Cummings-and-Marion became a one-word way of describing them. Within a year of their return from Europe, Marion had found a small apartment to rent on the ground floor of 4 Patchin Place, downstairs from Cummings's studio.

9

No Thanks

By December of 1934, when Cummings and Marion returned to Greenwich Village from their year in France, Tunisia, and Italy, the United States had slid into the awful depths of the Great Depression. In November of 1932, Franklin Delano Roosevelt had beaten Herbert Hoover by a landslide. FDR was inaugurated in Washington, DC, in March of 1933, and in his inauguration speech, paraphrasing Thoreau, he told the American people that the only thing they had to fear was fear itself.

Like Cummings, Roosevelt was an aristocrat and a Harvard man, but he had been at Harvard under the liberal Charles Eliot rather than the conservative A. Lawrence Lowell, and perhaps this was what enabled him to work brilliantly within the political system. By this time Cummings had turned against all political systems. Unfortunately for him and his fellow writers, although Roosevelt had already introduced the federally funded job corps and public works projects that would begin to alleviate the Depression, the publishing industry was still in the doldrums.

It was true that President Roosevelt had changed the way government supports its people in the heady "Hundred Days," the early months of his administration, during which Congress and the Senate seemed to pass any law he wrote—creating the Civil Works Administration, the Gold Reserve Act, the Crop Loan Act, the Farm Relief Act, the Cotton Control Act, the Securities Exchange Act, the Communications Act, the National Housing Act—in the creation of what was essentially a new government called the New Deal, which Cummings called the "nude eel." All this did not bring significant help to the Greenwich Village community of writers and poets where Cummings had once been a star.

The New York City to which Cummings returned was a city hit hard by the Depression. What was worse than the poverty—Cummings was accustomed to scrounging for food money—was the change in attitude brought by poverty. The economic disaster that the country was living through had a powerful effect on the mood of critics and publishers and readers—men and women on whom Cummings in spite of himself was dependent for his audience and his livelihood.

For the first time in his career Cummings, the prodigy from "Hah-vahd," the young winner of the prestigious Dial Award, the friend of Marianne Moore and William Carlos Williams, had trouble getting a book published. For a man who had been eagerly sought after and published while he was still in college, this was infuriating and humiliating. Sales of his books in print—*Eimi, Is 5, W (ViVa),* and the mixed-media *CIOPW*—were unthinkably low; fewer than ten copies in 1935, for instance. His ballet, *Tom,* had been held up by Lincoln Kirstein because of problems with the music, problems that were beyond Cummings's control.

Cummings's new book of poems was apparently unpublishable. His agent at Brandt & Brandt couldn't find a willing editor, although the manuscript was sent out to more than a dozen houses. His friend S. A. Jacobs, of the tiny Golden Eagle Press, couldn't raise the few hundred dollars to pay the printing bills to publish it himself. As Richard Kennedy points out, this situation illustrates Cummings's struggle for recognition as a serious writer. It also illustrates the fate of many American writers whose careers and incomes rise and fall dramatically depending on the public mood and the whims of cranky critics. "In the previous dozen years, he had published five volumes of poetry, a play, a collection of his art work, and two remarkable prose narratives," writes Kennedy, "but now fourteen publishers had refused to undertake the publication of one of his most important collections of poems."

As Cummings's personal life seemed to magically fall into place with his union with Marion, his professional life seemed to have fallen out of the benevolent stream of progress that had been his career path since Harvard. This began a slow deterioration of Cummings's already frayed connection to those in authority—anyone in authority—and the American critical establishment.

Looking back from the vantage point of the twenty-first century, more than fifty years after his death, Cummings seems like a man with an enviably successful career; but like many American writers he had years of anxiety and hardship, of being sniped at and attacked, of struggling to make a living, to buy food and pay the rent. This kind of rejection is part of being a writer. Men and women who are somehow constituted to get energy from rejection—no matter how painful that might be—are the ones who survive as writers. Cummings was already angry, and this anger at the corrupt establishment—in Cambridge and on the Western Front and wherever he encountered it—had been a furnace in which he forged the wild, rule-breaking originality of his work.

One bright spot in April of 1935 stood out both as a pleasant surprise and, although Cummings didn't know it then, ultimately as the start of a new and more fruitful and stable career. Cummings had met a young woman named Helen Stewart at a party in New York in 1934; it was one of those nights when he was relaxed, funny, and brilliant. He sat on the floor and told stories, and Stewart, who lived at the Prasada, a ritzy building on Central Park West and who was a student at Bennington College in Vermont, was enchanted. As it happened, Stewart was the literary representative of the Bennington Student Educational Policies Committee, and she and her classmate Dorothy Case, another Cummings fan, decided to invite Cummings to speak there.

Bennington, a progressive women's college founded in 1932, was built around a U-shaped red barn in a classic New England campus style. Its white-columned, three-story brick Commons building, topped by a bell tower, looked west over a vast lawn enclosed by picturesque green-shuttered clapboard dormitories and ending in a sheer drop that students called "the end of the world," as in "let's go read in the Adirondack chairs down at the end of the world." Vermont seems to conspire with Bennington's architecture. On an early May day, lilacs hang heavily against the white frame dorms, the birds swoop and sing in the eaves, and the world smells of spring.

A jewel in the crown of the American progressive-education movement, Bennington had attracted a new kind of girl, a girl who was often wealthy, often opinionated, and dedicated to the development of the individual mind and spirit in a way that many colleges—think of Harvard under Lowell—actively discouraged. "We have been able to avoid the rather deadly virginal and old-maid atmosphere of some of the women's colleges," Bennington president Robert Devore Leigh wrote proudly to a colleague. Had they ever! Bennington students were famous for their beauty and their pursuit of some kind of airy-fairy self, what Joseph Campbell, at another women's college—Sarah Lawrence—would later call "bliss."

Then as now, Bennington was as much a state of mind as it was a place in southern Vermont. There is magic to the place; connections and events happen there that seem to be larger than life, and Cummings's visit was no exception. Cummings, the aristocratic seeker, the rebel, the questioner, was tailor-made for Bennington, which was an aristocratic experiment in overthrowing the rules and the rulers—an experiment financed by those rulers themselves, the Bennington parents, who paid one of the highest tuitions in the country.

"After discussing the whole question of rules," wrote Janet Summers in minutes of a meeting of the first class at the college, "we felt that here we had the opportunity to try a more ideal system—one based on the theory that most of us had learned to govern ourselves." This was a revolutionary sentiment in the 1930s, when education for women was still controversial, but Cummings himself could hardly have said it better. Furthermore, although it was a time when the country had little interest in literature, things were different at Bennington, where the brand-new English Department was being run by the scintillating, beautiful poet Genevieve Taggard, a friend of Bennington's neighbor and reigning poetic spirit, Robert Frost.

Bennington paid attention to its students. Evenings were usually devoted to readings attended by the students, the staff, and interested townspeople, often delivered by people brought in by the students. In its early years the college hosted Frost, Buckminster Fuller, and Efrem Zimbalist. Stewart was able to persuade the administration to invite Cummings to come to the college to read on April 24 for travel expenses and a $25 speaking fee. Cummings spent the night at an inn in Old Bennington, across from a white church surrounded by a village green right out of a Currier and Ives print.

"I too was at Bennington College, the Higher Education, meaning que les demoiselles—of all dimensions and costumes—sit around each other's rooms quaffing applejack neat," he wrote to his friend Pound. The girls delighted Cummings with a story about marauding Williams boys, who had caused the administration to hire a nightwatchman—but in true Bennington style, the first intruder to the women's dorms arrested turned out to be a distinguished professor of physics.

Bennington considered itself the center of the New England literary world, and its faculty and students dedicated themselves to proving that assertion. "Three or four times a week everyone climbed the Commons stairs to the theater to hear a lecture or to find out what the dancers, actors or musicians had been up to," writes Thomas Brockway in *Bennington College: In the Beginning.* Workshops and formal productions acquainted the community with its most talented students. But Bennington also had its eyes on the larger world—one of the curricular innovations it offered, and still offers, was a work-study semester in which every student took some kind of job off campus.

At 7:30 at night, Cummings read in a high-ceilinged new space at the top of the Commons building with moonlit, sweeping views of the surrounding meadows. The girls crowded into the rows of seats to hear him. The scene seemed to fluster him—it was his first reading of this kind. Stewart was even more nervous, as was her friend Dorothy Case. She stammered as she started her introduction, she told Richard Kennedy in an interview for his biography, and as she faltered the room spontaneously exploded in a chorus of voices reciting Cummings's "Buffalo Bill's defunct." In the official Bennington version, the students were reciting the poem before Cummings and Stewart appeared; at the moment Cummings stepped onto the stage, they happened to be roaring out the penultimate phrase—"Jesus he was a handsome man."

Cummings finally stood up at the lectern and the girls calmed down just enough to let him talk. This was his first reading, and he took it seriously. His readings were timed and practiced and they were extraordinary events—so extraordinary that a decade after his appearance at Bennington, reading poetry was to become the career that would make Cummings famous. For now, it was wonderful to be adored in a setting where poets mattered.

"E. E. Cummings, distinguished modern painter and poet, gave a reading of his poetry at one of the regular evening meetings at Bennington College this week," the *Bennington Banner* announced a few days later.

Mr. Cummings' poetry has been widely read and studied at Bennington and has aroused much interest and appreciation on the part of the students. His audience, therefore, was large and enthusiastic, and he responded to it with friendly goodwill.

Evening meetings are an important part of the Bennington system. Through them an attempt is made to tie together subject matter of the different divisions of the curriculum. At each meeting, of the which there are two or three a week, an expert in his field, either a member of the faculty or an outside speaker, lectures to an audience of students and faculty who attend because of their interest in that or a related subject. The lecture is followed by an informal question period which usually results in animated discussion.

The fakirs of the literary establishment might have been turning on him; publishers might have decided he was not worth the price of printing. But Helen Stewart and Dot Case adored him, and at Bennington he was a star.

Back in New York City, the Depression was still deadening hopes and interest in literature. There still were no publishers for Cummings's book. Brandt & Brandt admitted defeat. When Rebecca Cummings put up the three hundred dollars to pay the printing bill, and S. A. Jacobs ran the presses, Cummings angrily titled the book *No Thanks* and dedicated it to the fourteen publishers who had turned it down: Farrar & Rinehart; Simon & Schuster; Coward-McCann; Limited Editions; Harcourt Brace; Random House; Equinox Press; Smith & Haas; Viking Press; Knopf; Dutton; Harper & Brothers; Scribner's; and Covici, Friede.

The publication of *No Thanks* elicited more criticism. "E. E. Cummings is far more incomprehensible than his poetry," wrote Louis Untermeyer, then the reigning anthologist of formal poetry. "He cannot make up his mind who or what he wants to be . . . there is in him a sensitive commentator and an ornery boy, a skillful draftsman and a leg-pulling cheapjack, a subtle musician . . . and a clown." The Depression had changed even the mood in the Village. Cummings, who had once, in the twenties, seemed a brilliant voice raised against corrupt authority, an inspired bad boy, began to seem superfluous at a time when railing against the rules was less important than getting enough to eat.

In the thirties, this country wasn't as amused by naughtiness that railed against all things parental and tweaked their preconceptions. In the thirties, everyone was as serious as a revolution. Politics was king, and old friends who had become disenchanted with Cummings's lighthearted work also broke with him over his anticommunist and increasingly conservative politics. A writer without a publisher, Cummings saw his reputation begin to wane. He had failed. Other writers began to toll his death knell. "Once with *The Enormous Room,* he swam for the moment to the surface," wrote Ford Madox Ford in *The Forum.* "Today as far as I know he supports himself by painting portraits."

> Jehovah buried,Satan dead,
> do fearers worship Much and Quick;
> badness not being felt as bad,
> itself thinks goodness what is meek;
> obey says toc,submit says tic,
> Eternity's a Five Year Plan:
> if Joy with Pain shall hang in hock
> who dares to call himself a man?
> . . . .
> King Christ,this world is all aleak;
> and lifepreservers there are none:
> and waves which only He may walk
> Who dares to call Himself a man.

So Cummings wrote in this bleak year.

Sometimes his anger seemed to weigh the poetry down, but at other times its blistering energy raised the words to a new level. One of his best-known and most triumphant poems comes from this well of disappointment and fury in *No Thanks:*

> the boys i mean are not refined
> they go with girls who buck and bite
> they do not give a fuck for luck
> they hump them thirteen times a night

one hangs a hat upon her tit
one carves a cross in her behind
they do not give a shit for wit
the boys i mean are not refined

they come with girls who bite and buck
who cannot read and cannot write
who laugh like they would fall apart
and masturbate with dynamite

the boys i mean are not refined
they cannot chat of that and this
they do not give a fart for art
they kill like you would take a piss

they speak whatever's on their mind
they do whatever's in their pants
the boys i mean are not refined
they shake the mountains when they dance

At last he had found the right woman with whom to share his life, Marion Morehouse, but everything else seemed to be falling apart. If his trip to Bennington was an experiment that ended up being a brilliant, inspired day and night, Cummings's other 1935 adventure was also an experiment—one that ended in an almost farcical and personally bruising disaster for both him and Marion.

In the winter of 1935, Cummings did what many New York writers did in the 1930s, '40s, '50s, and '60s when they had severe economic problems—he went to Hollywood. Although F. Scott Fitzgerald and William Faulkner had gone before him, it is hard to believe that anyone thought this was a good idea. It was true that Cummings vaguely believed that he wanted to write a screenplay. He meant, however, to experiment with the form, not to obey it. His ability to write to order, to obey anyone else's guidelines, was almost nonexistent. He had no experience of writing screenplays and no desire to do anything but continue with poetry and painting. Were they going to make a movie out of *Eimi*? At this point in his life, even Cummings's letters to friends are so playful and modernist as to be almost incomprehensible.

Nevertheless, a lawyer friend, Maurice Speiser, had arranged for Paramount to offer Cummings a scriptwriting job. He turned that down, still in his right mind and not inclined to honor what was referred to as the Golden Age of Hollywood. Cummings had always favored the freedom and improvisational nature of the theater, and movies didn't interest him much. But when another offer came from his old friend Eric Knight, the eccentric Yorkshireman who had written *Lassie Come Home,* his resistance was down.

Knight and his wife were friends of Cummings and Marion, and Knight urged Cummings to try Hollywood, where, he bragged, he was making a silly amount of money. Knight and Cummings had a further bond: Knight, too, had been separated from his children by his former wife, and the two men spent hours talking about this. Hollywood was the ticket! Everyone agreed that Marion could find work acting or modeling in the City of Angels in the Golden State. It wasn't just the Okies and those down and out from the Depression who were packing up to seek their fortunes in Hollywood; it was also writers and actresses. Marion's old friend Aline MacMahon was already doing well there.

The final persuasive push, after a winter that had been the hardest Cummings had yet lived through, came when he ran into a young man, Edward Titus, whose father he had known in Paris. Titus was a huge Cummings fan—an oasis in a desert—and urged Cummings and Marion to accompany him and his wife in their commodious Packard on a trip to Los Angeles via Mexico City.

The two couples started out amicably and stopped to see the sights in Washington, DC, and New Orleans. They were off on a great adventure. In the close quarters of a car, even a Packard, Titus's hero worship became cloying and tinged with jealousy. Cummings found it hard to put up with the young man's judgments and criticisms, delivered as if he knew what he was talking about. Marion couldn't stand Mrs. Titus. Predictably, by the time the two couples reached Mexico City they were no longer speaking. Cummings and Marion, with five dollars to their name—a bill Cummings had found in the pocket of some old pants at the bottom of his suitcase—checked in to the cheapest pension they could find and wired Rebecca asking for money.

As always, the Bank of Mom was open for business and ready to lend. She wired a hundred dollars and forwarded another five hundred from

Cummings's aunt Jane, with whom she was now living back in Cambridge on Irving Street. After two weeks of fun in Mexico City—when Cummings had money, he spent it—the Cummingses took their first airplane flight, up to Los Angeles, where they were welcomed by the Knights. They quickly rented a cheap apartment on Eleventh Street in Santa Monica, near their friends. The Knights and Aline MacMahon lent cars, and a round of meetings was scheduled.

If New York had seemed hard, Hollywood was even more unyielding. The place was booming, that was true. The talkies had swept in, and actresses like Greta Garbo and Katharine Hepburn were starring, and actors like Clark Gable. This did not translate into interest in a New York poet with an attitude problem. Knight's friend the Austrian-American director Josef von Sternberg did not want to meet with Cummings. He did meet Irving Thalberg at Metro-Goldwyn-Mayer, but Thalberg took a pass. Cummings could not manage to be earnest enough for the movie culture; he insisted, for instance, on calling Thalberg's studio "Metro Goldfish and Mayer." Los Angeles did not seem the place for saying whatever was on your mind and doing whatever was in your pants. In his boyish, aristocratic way he was trying to be amusing. The Hollywood moguls did not get the joke. Disney had just released the first short featuring a bumbling star named Donald Duck, and their *Three Little Pigs* was also a hit, but it was not interested in hiring the forty-year-old cutup from New York. This bitter experience, which piled failure on top of failure, had the awful result of deepening Cummings's verbal anti-Semitism, and this too may have hurt his chances in Hollywood.

Marion, who had been the toast of New York and Paris, didn't do well, either. For one thing, suddenly she was over thirty in a town where, for a woman, being over thirty was like being dead. Hollywood was all about acting and not at all about fashion. Marion's ability to combine the two was apparently not attractive to prospective employers. No one cared if she could become the woman who would wear the clothes. No one cared about clothes at all. Fashion magazines were regarded as an East Coast affectation. Desperately, Marion sought out the great western photographer Edward Weston, hoping that like his colleagues Steichen and Hoyningen-Huene he would want to pay to photograph her. Weston was not interested. He asked Marion if Cummings would be willing to sit for a few portraits. No money, of course.

Rejected all over again in a place they had hoped would give them a new lease on life—or at least a new lease on their faltering finances—the Cummingses became increasingly homesick. By September, they were ready to admit defeat and go east again, but they couldn't afford to leave. Desperate, they hitched a ride as far as the Mexico/Texas border with Isamu Noguchi, whom they had met through MacMahon. Out of money again, they wired Rebecca, who obliged by sending the train fare back to New York. As soon as possible they headed for the healing hills of New Hampshire.

Autumn in New Hampshire is one of the most extraordinary experiences the natural world has to offer. Because the state is built on rock, with dozens of lakes carved out by ancient glaciers, the radiant, astonishing colors of the maples and oaks when they begin to flame out for the winter seem more vivid than anywhere else. Bright red and orange, impossible vermilion and deep sienna create a lacy screen against the bluest imaginable sky. The forest creatures, the deer and squirrel and chipmunks, are actively preparing for one of the longest and bitterest winters in the country, and there is a sharpness to the air, a sharpness laced with the smell of apples, that signifies the change of season. The sound of wood being chopped and split echoes everywhere, and woodpiles grow until they take over porches and driveways. Night falls fast, the late afternoon casting long shadows on the meadows and on the lakes; and as the sun sets behind the mountains, it creates a shining path across each body of water. Cummings took long walks and tried to find a direction for his life and his work. At night he read and reread and annotated Thomas Mann's *Joseph and His Brothers*.

Cummings continued to publish sporadically. His career seemed to be over. A slim book of poems came out in England. Lincoln Kirstein came out with a small edition of the scenario for the ballet *Tom*. But in October, while Cummings and Marion had been crunching through the New Hampshire leaves and building fires for warmth in the evenings and ogling the carpet of stars over Silver Lake, Cummings's oldest and closest Village friend, Gaston Lachaise, died of leukemia at the age of fifty-three. Cummings and Marion headed south for the sad funeral.

The handsome, adventurous Lachaise had been at the center of a group of writers and artists who surrounded Cummings in the Village. Cummings had always had a gift for friendship—he was charming, funny, and generous. Beginning at Harvard, his connections had catapulted his work into the public eye, gotten him to the Western Front and back again, and launched his career as a poet. Cummings was an infinitely social animal, a man who could come alive at a good party no matter what discouragements and financial problems were taking place in his life outside the party. During the years he had known Lachaise, he had also been close friends with Hart Crane and their mutual editor, Malcolm Cowley. His friend Marianne Moore had sponsored his work at *The Dial,* which was paid for by his friend Scofield Thayer. Now, even at his close friend's funeral, Cummings experienced the humiliation of the has-been. He was not asked to give a eulogy; few people seemed to recognize him. In one account of the funeral, Cummings was described as being "so slightly acknowledged as to be practically of no use." Cummings was forty-one now, and his best years seemed to be behind him.

Even in these hard years, Cummings kept writing. He would retire upstairs to his studio at Patchin Place or Joy Farm and, in his choppy, slanted handwriting, with a pen on paper transform his thoughts, feelings, and observations into perfectly formal lines that broke all the rules. Nothing stopped him from producing poems, even if no one seemed to want to read them. Marion was a mainstay, as was his mother. Cummings had a combination of confidence and perversity that forced him forward toward an audience that no one could locate.

The first good news in a long time came in 1937, when Cummings was forty-two, and his agent Bernice Baumgarten of Brandt & Brandt had lunch with Charles Pearce, a young editor at Harcourt, Brace, and the conversation turned to Cummings's work. Both agent and editor were disturbed that most of Cummings's work was out of print and unobtainable. Although Harcourt, Brace had turned down *No Thanks* and been duly thanked in the dedication, and although many editors there were not Cummings fans, Pearce's energy and enthusiasm prevailed. He would edit, and Harcourt, Brace would publish, a new volume of Cummings's titled *Collected Poems,* which would serve to make his poetry once again available. "If most people were to be born twice they'd probably call it dying," Cummings wrote in the book's introduction. Indeed, he was being reborn, whether he knew it or not.

Collected Poems, published in February of 1938, was the beginning of Cummings's career as a major American poet, a metamorphosis from his previous incarnation as a precocious bad boy. Cummings and Pearce chose poems from the hundreds he had written in the past decades, starting with poems from *Tulips & Chimneys* and adding twenty-two that were brand new. "My poems are essentially pictures," Cummings told Pearce as they worked together.

In his introduction to the elegant volume, Cummings wrote directly to his readers, exhorting them to share in his transcendent view of human experience. "The poems to come are for you and me and are not for mostpeople," he wrote, "—it's no use trying to pretend that mostpeople and ourselves are alike. Mostpeople have less in common with ourselves than the squarerootofminusone. You and I are human beings; mostpeople are snobs." Once again he was the mischievous, blindly optimistic man and loving observer who had written the early poems and *The Enormous Room*. "With you I leave a remembrance of miracles:they are by somebody who can love and who shall continually be reborn."

In selecting poetry for the collection, Cummings axed some of the angrier poems—neither "Jehovah buried" nor "the boys I mean" is there—and included his most playful. *No Thanks* is partially represented by one of his most lighthearted poems about men and women, written in nursery-rhyme iambic dimeter:

may i feel said he
(i'll squeal said she
just once said he)
it's fun said she

(may i touch said he
how much said she
a lot said he)
why not said she

(let's go said he
not too far said she
what's too far said he
where you are said she)

may i stay said he
(which way said she
like this said he
if you kiss said she

may i move said he
is it love said she)
if you're willing said he
(but you're killing said she

but it's life said he
but your wife said she
now said he)
ow said she

(tiptop said he
don't stop said she
oh no said he)
go slow said she

(cccome?said he
ummm said she)
you're divine!said he
(you are Mine said she)

With the four-hundred-dollar advance from Harcourt, Brace, Cummings and Marion headed back to Paris via London, where they were to visit the zoologist Solly Zuckerman. The summer of 1937 was a strange time to be in Europe. The Spanish Civil War was on, and Mussolini had joined forces with Adolf Hitler. At a dinner given by Zuckerman, Cummings and Marion met the famous philosopher and womanizer A. J. "Freddie" Ayer. "Some men play golf, Freddie played women," said one of Ayer's three wives, Dee Wells.

Ayer's most famous book, *Language, Truth, and Logic,* had just been published, a fierce argument on the subject of argument about the existence of God. Ayer, who was on his way to Oxford via a wartime stint in the British Secret Service, got Marion in his sights. She was a famous beauty whose beauty of late had not been much appreciated. After a secret two-day courtship he finally succeeded in sleeping with her. For him, it seems, she was no more than a conquest. For her, he was a mistake. The day afterward, Marion confessed all to Cummings. He was distraught, although the two did not expect monogamy from each other. This time, she succeeded in reassuring him that he was the only man she loved, and their life together went on as usual.

In Paris Marion and Cummings had tea with an aging Elaine—no longer a delicate, dewy beauty—and her now one and only husband, Frank MacDermot. Although Cummings asked about his daughter, and was told she was at school in Vienna, he had seemingly given up hope of ever having a parental relationship with her. She was seventeen, a young girl who had been ferried from one school to another in Ireland, Switzerland, and Austria and who was already reading and writing poetry.

Unbeknownst to Cummings, Nancy had read his poems and been moved and excited by them. Of course she had no idea that he was her father. Elaine had kept her secrets, an easier job because Nancy was usually at boarding school. Nancy asked about her father, but she never got answers. Occasionally Elaine would refer to her time in New York, or her time with Nancy's official father, Scofield Thayer. Once, Elaine let slip that she had been married to Cummings—was she trying to impress her adolescent daughter? When Nancy excitedly asked for more information, Elaine refused to elaborate. Nancy glossed the comment over as one of her mother's fantasies about her romantic youth in a faraway place. Talking with Elaine about Nancy was painful for Cummings. It was clear that even if he longed to see her, even if he did get to see her, she would have no idea who he was. Time and Elaine had done their work well. Dependent on Marion, concerned about his ability to write, constantly worrying about money, Cummings once again gave up the idea of ever seeing his daughter.

When the Cummingses returned to New York, it was to find that *Collected Poems* had done its work. Cummings was hailed as an important poet—the first real encouragement for his writing in a long, long time. "This is the poetry of a man of complete artistic integrity," wrote one reviewer.

Other reviewers, from Paul Rosenfeld to S. I. Hayakawa, praised the book, and John Peale Bishop in a long essay in the *Southern Review* treated him as an important poet and considered all his work in the context of twentieth-century literature. Marianne Moore had nothing but praise; he got a fan letter from Carl Sandburg; Robert Penn Warren included "Buffalo Bill" in his seminal *Understanding Poetry*, which was used as a textbook in many colleges; and *Collected Poems* was nominated for the year's Pulitzer Prize. "When Cummings writes, 'Birds sing sweeter than books tell how,' he is singing his theme song," Harry Levin wrote in a later evaluation of Cummings's work. "Poetry might be described in his terms, as the vain attempt of books to emulate birds." Cummings's natural lyric affirmation, Levin wrote, had turned brilliantly under the stress of modern circumstances into satirical negation. "The daughters of Greenwich Village are caught, as it were, on the rebound from the dowagers of Brattle Street."

Yet the twenty-two new poems included in *Collected Poems* sizzle, fizz, and snap with Cummings's joy in life, his respect for the unconventional, and his delight in all things strange and unusual and humble. The best of the poems, which ends the book, begins with an invocation,

> you shall above all things be glad and young.

and ends with one of his most powerful, thrilling couplets:

> I'd rather learn from one bird how to sing
> than teach ten thousand stars how not to dance

Cummings and Marion had been together five years, and their ménage at 4 Patchin Place was taking on a conventional domestic flavor. Although Cummings kept a separate studio, they were really living together as man and wife, although they were not married.

Now, once again Marion took up with another man, English director Paul Rotha. A young, unmarried filmmaker, Rotha would later win two Academy Award nominations for his documentaries. He was smitten by Marion, and she gave in for a while. Then, as always, she confessed all to Cummings. He didn't want to marry Marion. He couldn't bear to have another child with her or with anyone else. He didn't want to tell her what to do, because he did not want to be told what to do—but he did not want her to cheat on him, either. After many talks with his contrite lover, and a few consultations with Dr. Wittels, Cummings decided to patch it up with Marion, accept her apologies, and move on.

IO

Ezra Pound and *Santa Claus*

B iography is an exercise in context. In writing a life, biographers must create the time in which that life was lived. Sometimes, biography looks back in judgment, condemning a subject's actions with the advantages of modern knowledge and customs. Sometimes, a biographer will try to re-create circumstances in which a subject's actions may be understood in a way in which they could not be understood at the time of writing.

Behavior that was considered normal in the 1920s, '30s, and '40s when Cummings was alive is now thought to be addictive, self-destructive, racist, or perverted. Behavior that is now considered normal—in sexual orientation, in marital status—was then considered addictive, self-destructive, and perverted. For instance, for most of Cummings's life almost everyone gleefully chain-smoked. No one thought twice about the damage smoking might be doing to lungs and heart. On top of that, most of the writers he knew and most of his friends drank huge amounts of liquor without thinking twice about it. The middle of the twentieth century was the age of literary drunkenness—a drunkenness so prevalent that even now, when most writers do not drink to excess, many people still link creativity and alcohol. Cummings and his friends and colleagues were almost always drunk or hungover or in that uncomfortable place in between.

Beginning in the 1940s the discovery of prescription drugs and many doctors' willingness to prescribe them added another layer of physical change to an already toxic cocktail. Cummings took Miltown, Librium, and Nembutal, and this was never considered a medical problem. He was not alone. The concept of side effects doesn't seem to have entered the public mind until the end of the twentieth century.

Furthermore, in those days very few people did any kind of routine exercise. When the highly respected University of Chicago president Robert Hutchins was asked about exercise, he said that when he had the urge to exercise he lay down and waited until it passed. Everyone thought this was very funny. The now proven benefits of exercise—for the body, for the brain, for mental health—were unknown. People imagined that exercise would kill them rather than make them stronger. Although they ate less processed food than we do, few people except kooks thought twice about the effect of certain foods on the body. There were few gyms, few health-food stores, and although there were some food faddists, they were marginalized and often mocked.

In terms of racial, sexual, and religious tolerance, the men and women of the 1940s and '50s might as well have been in the Dark Ages. Jim Crow laws dominated the South. Although women had had the vote for twenty years, few of them had their own political opinions; they deferred to their breadwinning husbands. There were no women in the Senate or the House. Few women had jobs except as homemakers and mothers. Casual anti-Semitism was common. Professional anti-Semitism was expected. A letter from the Yale admissions committee about an applicant referred to the dark coloring and low brow of the applicant's "Hebrew race."

In the world in which Cummings lived, homosexuality was almost entirely unacceptable and unheard of. President Lowell had mounted a campaign against homosexuality at Harvard, but he was not alone. Although Harvard boys sometimes horsed around, and although Cummings had lusted after Jim Watson and William Slater Brown and had all but ogled the other inmates at La Ferté-Macé in *The Enormous Room,* it seemed not to occur to anyone that he might be legitimately bisexual—perhaps because in his world there was no such thing as legitimate bisexuality. A man was either a man or an illegal freak.

As late as 1960, the critic and professor Newton Arvin was arrested by federal agents in a dawn raid on his apartment—he had made the mistake of sending photographs of partially naked young men through the U.S. Mail. The federal government decided that these photographs were illegal. Arvin, once a well-respected member of the literary

community—"Newton was my Harvard," Truman Capote famously
said—was fired, jailed, and died three years later. His trial was a scandal
that terrified anyone who was even thinking of ever acting on being gay.
Testimony detailed the men he had slept with, and these men were also
fired and hounded out of their communities. Yaddo, the writers' colony
where Arvin had done much of his work, asked him to resign.

For Cummings, these signs of intolerance were all disasters, occasions
for the forces of conventional evil to shut down the freedoms he celebrated. Cummings always identified with children—his favorite poem
was Wordsworth's child-worshipping "Intimations of Immortality." In
the poem, children come innocent and whole from heaven, "trailing
clouds of glory," very much like Adam and Eve in the Garden of Eden
before the Fall. As they age, children are corrupted by our dark, pun-
ishing civilization. "Shades of the prison-house begin to close/Upon the
growing Boy," Wordsworth writes.

In poem after poem Cummings, like Wordsworth, his spiritual fore-
bear, idolized both youth and the natural world. The young were wiser
and purer, more innocent and more beautiful than the self-appointed
elders of the world. Nature with its indecipherable glories was where true
enlightenment could be found.

> may my heart always be open to little
> birds who are the secrets of living
> whatever they sing is better than to know
> and if men should not hear them men are old
>
> may my mind stroll about hungry
> and fearless and thirsty and supple
> and even if it's sunday may i be wrong
> for whenever men are right they are not young
>
> and may myself do nothing usefully
> and love yourself so more than truly
> there's never been quite such a fool who could fail
> pulling all the sky over him with one smile

In Eden and in our species and implicitly in Wordsworth the "shades
of the prison-house" are sexual. Children and animals and birds have a

joyful apprehension of the erotic world not tethered to a particular gender. It's only with puberty that a boy becomes a heterosexual or a homosexual man or a little bit of both. For a boy growing up in a household with an overbearing masculine father, in a town and a time when there was no such thing as homosexuality, any attraction to men must have been deeply confusing and painful.

An analysis of his own various dependencies—on his father, on Scofield Thayer, on Elaine—written in Cummings's journals, notes that when Thayer was in analysis with Freud, Freud urged him to make Cummings marry Elaine. In doing so, he was "relinquishing self-expression for morality and returning to my childhood," he wrote. Clearly defining his own desires was a struggle. Whatever ambivalence Cummings may have had was safely hidden in his alliance with one of the most beautiful women in the world. Cummings and Marion were tied together by love, possessiveness, and perhaps a few unexplored secrets.

As the Depression eased and the war approached, and with the publication of *Collected Poems*, Cummings's reputation was slowly reestablished. Yet the advent of World War II was cataclysmic and dreadful for Cummings and Marion. As a man and as part of a couple, traveling had been one of Cummings's greatest delights. He was a citizen of the world. Now that world seemed to be coming apart. Cummings and Marion had traveled to England and France in 1937, starting off with the advance for *Collected Poems* and continuing with two checks cabled by the ever-willing Rebecca and a third check from her with money that her son had instructed her to borrow from their friends. England seemed sad.

As he aged into his forties Cummings became increasingly frail, and Marion also began to suffer from severe arthritis. His back hurt almost all the time, and this chronic pain eroded his good humor and his delight in the small things in his world—the slant of afternoon light, the pleasures of a dinner at Khoury's or a stiff drink at the end of the day, the look of absorption on a the face of a young woman who had come to understand him through his work.

By the early 1940s the pain in his back and legs had sent him for a variety of cures that finally led him to Dr. Frank Ober in Boston. Ober X-rayed him and diagnosed him with osteoarthritis of the spine. Cummings was a man whose body had been subjected to many hardships. He had spent three months in France sick and close to starvation, and he had smoked cigarettes since he could remember. He despised exercise and drank a lot. He took Nembutal to sleep, and when it didn't work, he took more Nembutal. Still, it's hard not to think that this back and leg pain had some kind of psychological basis. Cummings's beloved world seemed to be ending, as his colleague T. S. Eliot wrote, "not with a bang but a whimper."

Ober told him to baby himself and change his way of living, and he created an elastic corset for Cummings to wear that would stabilize his back. "It resembles armour; but I feel like somebody living in a drain Pipe . . . rather than like any ancient Roman, though stoicism comes in mighty handy these days," he wrote his mother. Dr. Ober also told Cummings to try to cheer up.

Stoicism is not a recipe for good moods, and Cummings's seemed to sink as the war progressed. He was against it, but then he was against almost everything. "His feelings were so bitter that the word pacifist does not seem quite suitable," Richard Kennedy wrote. In letters to Pound he quoted Thoreau and then wondered angrily, "Dew yew figger Mr. Thoreau wuz a onanist or an eunuch?"

Although the old music would sometimes float up from inside him and fix itself on the page, the poems written during the war and collected in 1944 in *1 × 1 (One Times One)*, published by Henry Holt, are even angrier and uncharacteristically bitter:

> of all the blessings which to man
> kind progress doth impart
> one stands supreme I mean the an
> imal without a heart.

When Pound let him know that the National Institute of Arts and Letters had turned him down, in spite of repeated nominations from Archibald MacLeish, Cummings made fun of the august body of literary lights that Pound called the "Insteroot (ov Awts n Lers)." Nothing seemed to please Cummings, and the world spinning toward an apocalypse of hatred was reflected in his own anger. Pound had sent a friend, the artist and writer Wyndham Lewis, to visit him. "I saw him in New York," Lewis wrote Pound later. "But he was such a jumpy and peppery little creature it was impossible to talk to him much."

Cummings's anger, which had once flamed into brilliant, gorgeous cascades of words, seemed to turn inward. The educated antiformalism that had led to the brilliant, revolutionary poems of his youth—"Buffalo Bill's," "All in green," "the Cambridge ladies"—became more anti- and less poetic. Everything always seemed to go wrong on a personal and on a cosmic scale. Cummings was an equal-opportunity hater. He hated Hitler and he hated the Jews. He hated Roosevelt and he hated Stalin—he especially hated Stalin. He hated the critical establishment and he didn't like the new restaurants on Tenth Street. He made fun of other poets who had once been his friends, William Carlos "Doc" Williams among them.

In the spring of 1939, Pound sailed to New York on the *Rex* partly to visit Cummings, who welcomed him with a telegram. Pound's visit was something Cummings had anticipated with some gladness, but Pound's large, cranky presence in the cramped rooms at 4 Patchin Place was more than Cummings or Marion could bear. Everyone wanted to meet the Great Man. At a dinner at Robert's on Fifty-fifth Street, Max Eastman thought Pound was "attractively curly-headed, almost rolly-polly, and with lots of laughter in the corners of his eyes—nervously restless, however, with the insatiable thirst of the self-infatuated 'great man' . . . I found him sweet and likeable withal." Pound lectured the group—Cummings, Marion, Eastman, and a reporter, Guy Hickock—on eating habits, exhorted them to eat lightly, and then ordered the most expensive thing on the menu—"a thick and sanguinary steak and exquisite red wine."

Cummings was disturbed by Pound's burgeoning anti-Semitism. "We don't know if he's a spy or simply schizo, but we do feel he's incredibly lonesome," he wrote to his old friend Jim Watson. "Gargling antisemitism from morning till morning doesn't (apparently) help a human throat to sing." Everyone wanted to see Pound while he was in New York, but the Great Man couldn't be bothered to answer phone calls from the likes of Williams or Ford Madox Ford. "I find poor Pound on his back on the frontroomcouch looking like a derailed fast freight & gasping it was too hot to telephone, but when I offered to invite Williams over here the patient weakly said no," Cummings wrote Watson. June in New Hampshire is black fly season, but on the first warm day, Cummings and Marion decamped for Joy Farm, leaving Pound in possession.

During this time the one person close to him, the one he didn't mock, was Marion. Cummings's frailty made him extremely dependent on her, as later her illness would make her dependent on him. The two grew so close that anyone from the outside seemed like an intruder. Marion became more and more protective, as if shielding Cummings from his admirers and the rest of the world would make him less angry or less sick. This put a huge strain on her—she was essentially the nanny to a cranky, aging boy. It also set up a kind of isolation for the two of them that later caused a lot of heartbreak. For the moment, under the stress of aging and illness, Marion and Estlin could only thank God that they had each other—no one else could tolerate them.

As the war wound up to its dreadful climaxes, Pound also seemed angrier and angrier, crazier and crazier. Back home in Rapallo in 1940, he wrote to Cummings that the U.S. was governed by "foreign jew agents." The letter is an almost incomprehensible jumble of anger and confusion, mixing praise for Hitler's farm program, a reference to Cummings's poem "the boys i mean are not refined," and paragraphs of anti-Semitic, anti-American ranting. Cummings answered with his sweetest, most lighthearted self. "Spring is coming. Two penguins salute you from our mantelpiece. The lady sends love and the elephant wishes bonne chance . . ."

By 1942 Pound was ranting on paper from Rapallo about setting up a provisional government of the U.S.A. Cummings responded with his mother's favorite slogan, "health and a senseofhumor." But health and a sense of humor seemed to have deserted Pound along with everything else. Attracted by his anti-Semitism and his hero worship of Italian fascist dictator Benito Mussolini, the Italian government paid him to make a series of repulsive radio broadcasts in favor of Nazi Germany and its leaders. The war was the end of Ezra Pound as a respected poet, critic, and friend.

Cummings, however, had more lives left to live, although the hardships of the late 1930s and early '40s made changes in his character and in his hermetically sealed relationship with Marion that would affect the rest of his life. Cummings's health was never again robust, but with the help of Dr. Ober, a variety of pharmaceutical painkillers, and judicious amounts of alcohol he was able to go on. His sweetness and his delight in the natural world saved him from the bitterness and insanity of some of his friends—Hart Crane, Joe Gould, and now Pound. Also, he found the buoyancy and support of another a less lonely career than writing poems.

The fury against all rules and authority that seemed to take hold of Cummings in his late teenage years and when he was at Harvard was tremendous fuel for a writer and painter. Oh, there were so many rules to break! There were so many phonies. There were so many men in authority who didn't know what they were doing, or who used their power to hurt. From A. Lawrence Lowell to the moronic United States officers who hated the French army they had gone to the Western Front to help, Cummings's life was a great feast of bogus authority just waiting to be consumed. A generation before L. Frank Baum wrote the great parable of phoniness, *The Wonderful Wizard of Oz,* Cummings was already at it, drawing back the curtain to reveal anything he could that was fake or pretentious or unnecessarily rigid.

Anger doesn't age well. Angry young men are sexy; angry old men are less appealing. The progression from heralded poetic prodigy in the 1920s to sharply criticized loner in the 1930s had taken its toll. Cummings didn't care about the fakirs of the establishment, but he was tired. As the war came to its dreadful and victorious endings with D-day and the bombing of Hiroshima and Nagasaki, there was little celebration at 4 Patchin Place. Although he was hardly involved, Cummings agreed with his friend Pound in thinking that the war was a campaign to save capitalism, a kind of conspiracy by the superior forces he hated so much.

News of Pound's fate after 1945 trickled in to Patchin Place in horrifying detail. In the past, when Cummings had been the naughty boy, Pound had often played his forgiving father. Cummings's real father was ill equipped to understand what his son was up to; Pound understood perfectly. For four years, from November 1941 to December 1945, Cummings's letters to Pound's address in Rapallo went unanswered.

During World War II Pound had come unhinged and been politically transformed into one of the most active and most self-destructive writers in the history of literature. He had sent off thousands of increasingly loony letters and visited the United States to see anyone in Washington, DC, who would let him in to rant. In 1943, because of his radio broadcasts against the United States in general and against Jews in particular, he had been charged in absentia with treason. During the liberation of Italy, Allied partisans took Pound from his house in Rapallo. As he left home for the last time, he stuffed a copy of Confucius in his pocket.

Pound was far from contrite. He wanted to telegram President Truman and deliver a final broadcast. He told a reporter that Hitler was a saint like Joan of Arc and that Mussolini was a good man who had gone astray. Pound's mug shot from his 1945 arrest shows a handsome man with a lined, intelligent face and wild, crazy eyes. On May 24 he was transferred to a training center north of Pisa, where he apparently made more enemies.

In Pisa, a temporary U.S. commander had him detained in a six-by-six-foot steel cage lit up at night by floodlights. With no exercise, eyes inflamed by dust, no bed, no belt or shoelaces and no communication with other human beings, Pound slowly went mad. Whatever vestiges of his former brilliance remained in him were wiped out by the three weeks he spent like a caged animal in American custody. He had not yet been tried. Confinement in a floodlit cage is torture, against the law, cruelty beyond imagining. Pound was sixty years old. Later, he recorded some of what happened in *The Pisan Cantos,* Canto 80, when Odysseus drowns "when the raft broke and the waters went over me." In July he was finally diagnosed with a mental breakdown and transferred to a tent and given reading material.

Pound's fate, in spite of his own erratic attacks on his own country and especially on Jewish people and institutions, as well as the brutal, illegal punishment for that, certainly underlined many of Cummings's worst fears about the dark forces behind the news and the political scene. By December of 1945, when Pound ended up in a Washington, DC, mental hospital, Cummings brightly wrote him: "Welcome home!" the letter began. He had met with Pound's lawyer, Julien Cornell, who had filled him in on some of the circumstances of Pound's arrest and hospitalization; and he had sent his friend, via Cornell, a book by Charles Norman in Pound's defense. The rest of the letter is the kind of chatter that hopes to alleviate unbearable circumstances. "Marion's been in the hospital a year with one kind of arthritis: I've entertained(off & on)another kind . . . Now we're both of us much better, and shall leave for Arizona . . . whenever a train will take us. If,in the meantime,our mutual state of health permits,we'll naturally stagger down to Washington & say hello to you & stagger back again. But if not,here's our love."

But Pound was a different man, broken by the brutality of the Allied forces, his own government, the so-called good guys. The first note he sent Cummings from St. Elizabeths, the mental hospital where he would be incarcerated until 1958, was a pathetic, un-Poundian one-liner post-marked January 25, 1946: "I like getting letters." Cummings wrote back, but it's hard to measure the effect Pound's experience had on him. The bitterness of the war, the isolation within his marriage, the fury at all those in authority who claimed to have right on their side but thought it was fine to torture an old man—these came together in a cumulative paranoia that scarred Cummings for the rest of his life.

Some days everything seemed to test their courage. One spring after-noon Marion, standing in the rain waiting to cross Sixth Avenue, was hit by a car pulling out of a parking space. Nobody knocked down Marion Morehouse. She got into the car that had hit her and made the driver take her to Patchin Place, meanwhile taking his number. Once home, she "changed her clothes, lay down for a few minutes, then arose, made tea for me an a couple of guests, and rang the big elephant-bell," Cummings wrote to Hildegarde Watson. "I hereupon descended from my pied-a-ciel to find her radiantly entertaining the company."

During those awful years, Marion, who had been Cummings's main-stay and protector, suddenly had her own, intensely painful bout with arthritis, as he had written to Pound. She was hospitalized and rehospi-talized. Cummings was thrust into the role of caretaker, which he tried to fulfill but which did not come naturally to him. Finally the couple, at the urging of friends, decided to spend a few months in Arizona, where the dry air was thought to be a cure for many things, including arthritis. Cummings's friend James Angleton's wife, Cicely d'Autremont, had par-ents with a big place in Tucson who invited both Marion and Cummings to stay. Whether this actually helped the situation, or whether changing everything was the cure—as it often is—they both felt better by the time they returned to New York.

Nancy had never been far offstage in Cummings's life, although he hadn't seen her for more than a decade. She was a young woman now, he knew that much. He had missed most of her childhood. Cummings was always on the side of children, and in those awful years he began writing another play, *Santa Claus,* in which he once again debunked the blatant warmongering of American culture. In the play, which is about a reunion between a parent and a child, Death tries to masquerade as Santa Claus, and the only person who can see through the mask is a child.

Like the little boy who pointed out that the emperor had no clothes,

Cummings's children were all both innocent and profoundly sophisticated. Since the invention of childhood at the beginning of the nineteenth century, conventional views of children had shifted from the idea that they were evil beings who had to be civilized by adults—the preacher and educator Jonathan Edwards called them "vipers"—to the idea that children were angelic beings who were corrupted by adults and adult civilization.

To Cummings, the child was the salvation of the adult world, and he aimed to preserve his own childlike qualities not just because that made life more fun but also because that was, he thought, the way for our world to survive. Cummings loved his father, that consummate adult; but it was his mother's playfulness and his uncle's rebelliousness and his own boyishness that he embraced. For Cummings, remaining a child was a sacred trust. Perhaps he didn't want children because of the heartbreak of watching them grow up. Far from the act of irresponsibility that critics accused him of, he believed that remaining a child was the only way to save the world. Psychiatrists might say that the painful loss of two childhoods—Nancy's and, earlier, his own, in the cold waters of Silver Lake—made his beliefs stronger; but it was with an intellectual as well as an emotional force that he refused to become one of the pompous, phony, warmongering, wisdom-spouting fakirs who seemed to be ruling the world. His poetry got sadder:

> let it go—the
> smashed word broken
> open vow or
> the oath cracked length
> wise—let it go it
> was sworn to
>
>   go

> let them go—the
> truthful liars and
> the false fair friends
> and the boths and
> neithers—you must let them go they
> were born
>
>   to go

let all go—the
big small middling
tall bigger really
the biggest and all
things—let all go
dear
        so comes love

No one was more serious about lack of seriousness than Cummings. United States history, after all, begins with a rebellion—the colonies were the naughty children of their English father, the king. Even at its most pretentious, our country has a quality of playfulness and contrariness not found elsewhere. During the Great Depression and World War II, these qualities were scarcer than at any other time in our history. But as the war faded in memory, leaving a wake of prosperity, the country began to lighten up and realign itself in a way that was more bearable for Cummings. Once again he began to sketch and sing.

Cummings dedicated *Santa Claus* to Fritz Wittels, the psychiatrist who had been his emotional mainstay and friend. As Cummings turned fifty, his life was getting better. In 1945, he won his first prize in a long time, the $670 Shelley Memorial Award from the Poetry Society of America. Yet the scars of the awful years when his own audience turned against him, when a close friend was locked in a cage, when illness and chronic pain seemed to infect him like a virus, were not so easily healed.

II

Rebecca and Nancy

Cummings's mother, Rebecca, was a Massachusetts Yankee in the best sense of the word; she was a descendant of the Pilgrims who believed in the twin Yankee gods of reform and good sense. She was, as Cummings wrote, "the genuine 101% New Englander!" For him she was a kind of hero, a woman who based her life on the innate goodness of human nature in general and on her son's talents in particular.

In the last years of her life, she lived with Cummings's sister, Elizabeth Cummings Qualey, and her husband, Carlton Qualey, an itinerant history professor who studied Norwegian-American communities, and their two children, John and Mary, whom she adored. It was for those children that Elizabeth Qualey wrote her memoir of growing up in Cambridge at the turn of the century, *When I Was a Little Girl*. Although the Qualey family moved around—from New York, where Qualey taught at Columbia, to Pennsylvania, where he taught at Swarthmore, to Michigan, where he taught at the University of Michigan—Rebecca Cummings seemed to adjust to being the peripatetic old person in their academic entourage. In the summer of 1946, on a visit to his sister's household, Cummings saw his mother for the last time.

Both Cummings parents had always used the romantic notion of the moon in the night sky all over the world as a means of communicating with each other and with their children. For instance, when Cummings was in prison at La Ferté-Macé during World War I—the three months of incarceration that would become *The Enormous Room*—his father wrote to him telling him to look at the moon through the prison windows at night. His father, standing outdoors at 104 Irving Street in Cambridge on the other side of the world, would also look at the moon, and in some way the two men would connect. Now Cummings would look at the moon and think of his mother far away. As Rebecca's influence waned, as she eventually turned the Cummings house on Irving Street over to Edward Cummings's sister Jane, Marion's influence waxed.

Always honest in his own journals, after his last visit with his mother Cummings wrote that he was shocked by her appearance. How could this old, deaf person be the mythical being who was his mother? His last letter to her, in January 1947, tells a funny story passed on by his friend Cyril Connolly, the British editor of *Horizon*. When interviewed on American radio and asked about his religion, Connolly had answered that his religion was Cummingsism. The interviewer was horrified and asked, "Don't you know he is a traitor?" When Connolly pointed out that she had confused Cummings with Pound, the interviewer shrugged: "It was one of those three—Eliot or Pound or Cummings." Rebecca Cummings was always her son's best and most appreciative audience.

Her death that same month released him into remembering her dearness and her unconditional love. "an extraordinary human being, someone gifted with strictly indomitable courage, died some days ago," he wrote to his friend Hildegarde Watson. "she was eighty-seven, very deaf and partially paralyzed; young of heart and whole of spirit." In her will, Rebecca left her eyes to be given to the blind.

Rebecca Cummings, a woman who delighted in children, had not seen her granddaughter Nancy in more than twenty years, but her death in 1947, a year in which the adult Nancy was closer geographically than she could have imagined, seems to be part of the puzzle of the three most important women in Cummings's life: Rebecca Clarke Cummings, Nancy Thayer Cummings Roosevelt, and Marion Morehouse.

While Cummings had been succeeding as a poet and plunging into career doldrums and floating out again, while he had been marrying and divorcing and finally finding and making a home with Marion, while he had been visiting Paris and befriending Ezra Pound and winning prizes for his work, in another part of the world his daughter, Nancy, had been living the pampered but lonely childhood of an expat daughter whose mother was married to an Irish politician. Her life got even worse when her mother had a son—Frank MacDermot's son—when Nancy was eleven. Raised by governesses as she went from country to country with her mother and the tyrannical MacDermot, "Nancy was early treated as a doll," writes Richard Kennedy, "something to dress up and show off to guests." In a poem titled "deb delights, London 1938," the eighteen-year-old Nancy wrote in an echo of the father she didn't know about:

> There is a very rich disgust in this
> in going dancing nightly at eighteen
> because eighteen
> and the system is corrupt which is
> generally recognized which changes nothing;
> give me back my ignorance
> it was never bliss but better far
> than this contemptuous cacophony.

There was plenty of money—Elaine's inheritance—but very little love or affection. There was no honesty between Nancy and her mother. Enrolled in a series of boarding schools, Nancy came to despise her stepfather, and he and her mother did everything they could to erase her childhood memories of another family.

The puny plans of human beings, especially those who hope to obscure the truth, look especially puny in Nancy's story. An artistic girl from the beginning, she started painting and was drawn to impressionism during her early school years. Her mother told her to stop, because painting was too messy. Was Elaine also afraid that Nancy's heritage as the daughter of a painter was going to assert itself? Nancy then started reading and writing poetry—poetry almost spookily like that of her father on the other side of the Atlantic Ocean.

During World War II, Elaine and Frank MacDermot and Nancy headed for England to enroll in Oxford. In May of 1940, the hawkish Winston Churchill became prime minister of England, replacing the discredited Neville Chamberlain. As Germany invaded Belgium, the German army began to push British and French troops west, and at the end of May the British staged a full-scale evacuation from Dunkirk. On June 4, Prime Minister Churchill famously told his embattled countrymen: "We shall fight on the beaches, we shall fight on the landing grounds, we shall fight in the fields and in the streets . . . we shall never surrender."

Nancy traveled to Dublin to see her mother that June, only to find that she could not return to England—the borders had been closed because of the war. Faced with staying in Ireland with the MacDermots or heading west for the unknown—the United States, where she could live with Elaine's sister Alexis—Nancy chose the unknown. In spite of the danger of an Atlantic crossing at a time when German U-boats were sinking ships at will, Nancy was determined to leave. She sailed in June 1940 on the USS *United States* from Galway, the last passenger ship to leave for New York from Great Britain during the war.

Appalled and upset at her daughter's choice, and seemingly terrified at what might happen to her in New York City, Elaine repeatedly warned Nancy against her "father"—Scofield Thayer. For reasons of her own, even twenty years later, she did everything she could to conceal the truth. Sometimes she had told Nancy that her father was dead. Now she confessed that he was alive in New York, but said that Nancy should avoid him because he had had a serious mental breakdown. Thayer had put money in trust for Nancy, and the prospect of Nancy meeting with Thayer's lawyer may have disturbed Elaine, although the lawyer would certainly not have revealed the kind of personal details Nancy hungered for. Perhaps she hoped that by setting up a "father" whom she was not supposed to see, Elaine would prevent her daughter from finding her actual father.

Nancy was already a passionate poet and a painter in spite of her mother's opposition. She was her father's daughter. "If, as has been asserted, imagination is the beginning of art, surely dreams are in the beginning of imagination or imagery; where then is the source of dreams, and which came first, the image or the experience," she wrote in *Charon's Daughter*, her collection of poetry and memoir.

Cummings's connection to his only child is one of the most illuminating, heartbreaking, and startling passages in his life. It is worth a book on its own. Its outlines, of a beloved and lost child who is finally restored through the whimsical forgiveness of the gods—or whatever power arranges our world—is the outline of a metaphor, a myth, a story from a storyteller. Was there an evil fairy presiding on the night of Nancy's conception, in a bed paid for by another man with a woman married to another man? Was Nancy under a spell that was finally, belatedly, broken?

When Nancy was a child, Cummings was still a young man. He

would always be famous for his affinity to children, for his own child-ishness, for his inability to grow up and his contempt for the structures and hierarchies of the so-called adult world. When it came to Nancy, Cummings behaved in an admirably adult way, although he was clearly under tremendous mental stress. Yet, for all of his good intentions—he legally adopted her and married her mother—his connection to her went terribly wrong, pushed by forces he could not control. The abduction of a child—and that's what Frank and Elaine MacDermot did, whatever prettier names they may have called it—is a great crime. It damages all concerned, and it certainly did in this case.

Fathers and daughters have bonds that no one else can understand. The unseen forces that drew a young girl raised in Ireland and Europe inexorably toward a shabby apartment in a tenement mews off Tenth Street in Greenwich Village, first guiding her toward a remote part of New Hampshire's Ossipee mountain range, seems just too fantastic to be coincidence. But whether it was fate or some kind of astonishing series of events coming together, the young Nancy Thayer—she refused to take the name MacDermot—was headed for a destiny that would change her world.

In New York City, living with her aunt Alexis, Nancy looked for work. Multilingual and as skilled with language as her father was, she found work as a translator, and she also trained in Morse Code and earned a radio operator's license. Eventually she found a job as a typist at an agency called Your Secretary Incorporated. She kept painting and writing poetry:

New York 1943
To the whimsical metallic moods
of drawing-rooms that face the park in a hush of green and
    silver
dusk is a delicate wrinkle over-
folded until
fills spills into the room fantastic power
of carved and clotted colour;
the green-and-silver sentence is embroidered with laughter
we have fashioned a velvet contented virtue
against the tangled dark.

Your Secretary Incorporated was a wartime agency run by Mrs. Kermit Roosevelt, the former society beauty Belle Willard, an extraordinary woman with a glamorous and tangled history of her own. Her husband, a great explorer who had famously traveled in the Amazon basin with his father, Theodore Roosevelt, and discovered its source at the River of Doubt, had served in the British army during World War I, enlisting even before there was American involvement.

By all accounts, Kermit Roosevelt was a hero. He had saved his father's life while they were stranded on the Amazon, refusing to let the older man be left behind and carrying him for miles through the dense jungle. He was handsome and distinguished and brave, but as he got older he also suffered from depression and alcoholism. By 1943, when Nancy went to work for Mrs. Roosevelt, her husband had lost many jobs and finally been exiled to Alaska, where, it was hoped, he would find a way to get sober.

Instead, in June 1943 Kermit Roosevelt committed suicide, although this was immediately covered up. His wife and children were told he had died of a heart attack, and the truth wasn't revealed until years later. Nancy, with her own secrets—revealed and not revealed—was drawn to this family, which knew a lot about secrets. The Roosevelts had four children, and Willard, his mother's favorite, lived in New York. He had enlisted in the navy but had not yet shipped out to the Pacific, where he would command the battleship USS *Greene.* He was a pianist and a musician who had already been to Paris and studied with the great Nadia Boulanger. Sometimes he stopped by the Roosevelt house to visit his mother and play the family piano to keep it in tune.

Mrs. Roosevelt was naturally an Anglophile, and Nancy Thayer, a sophisticated, beautiful, and confused young woman with no real family, soon came to her attention. Nancy began being invited to the Roosevelt house, and there she met and began to fall in love with her boss's musical son, Willard. This love affair was one of the linchpins in the eventual reunion of Nancy and her father.

Willard was a young man on the brink of going to war. He had been to Groton and Harvard, and he had an aura of aristocracy and secrecy that drew in the young girl whose own family life was built on secrets and protected with money and elite connections. Kermit's suicide was still a secret, but Nancy felt a bond with Willard, whose father, like the man she thought was hers, was distinguished, wealthy, Harvard educated, and mentally ill.

Mrs. Roosevelt adored Nancy, and this too was a powerful force. Mothers are often irresistible and unseen forces when it comes to their children's attractions. Remember that Anna Karenina's love affair with Vronsky begins when she meets his mother on the train. At any rate, the romance of the moment, the war in the background and the music in the foreground, swept the two young people forward. On December 23, 1943, while Willard was home from Pacific duty for a leave, they were married in New York, and Nancy went from being Mrs. Roosevelt's employee to being Mrs. Roosevelt's daughter-in-law.

Then, in 1945, in order to get out of the city during the hot weather, Mrs. Roosevelt happened to rent a summer place near Silver Lake, New Hampshire, close to the Cummings family's Joy Farm. The Roosevelt family and the James family were friends, and the Jameses had often urged her to try the beautiful corner of New Hampshire near Mount Chocorua. Nancy, whose husband was still in the Pacific and who was pregnant with their first child, decided to spend the summer in the coolness of the New Hampshire lake country with her mother-in-law. Of course Cummings, just a few miles down the road from his daughter, had heard about Nancy's visit to New Hampshire. Information about her marriage and her adult life had filtered through the grapevine. Some of his old friends had seen her, and it was his friend Billy James, his neighbor in both Cambridge and New Hampshire, who told him in September of 1945 that he had become a grandfather with the birth of Nancy's son, Simon.

Somehow, after all the years of being unable to see Nancy, having her nearby seemed to paralyze Cummings. Richard Kennedy suggests that Marion was a factor. "Marion, for whatever reasons, urged him not to reveal himself to her or to have any contact with her because she said it would upset him and 'interfere with his work.' " When it came to Nancy, Marion, who had always been extraordinarily loving and generous with Cummings's friends and family, seemed to become a different woman. A lot of time had passed. Both Marion and Cummings had been very sick. Marion had not had a child of her own. If she wasn't jealous of Elaine for having Cummings's child, she was certainly jealous of Cummings's time and energy.

Instead of arranging a visit with Nancy during the summer, Cummings and Marion lay doggo. They avoided the Jameses. Then, in the winter of 1945–46, Cummings wrote *Santa Claus,* his play about the reunion of a child and parent. First published in the Cummings issue of a Harvard magazine, the *Harvard Wake,* it is a morality play in five scenes. It begins when Santa, feeling obsolete, agrees to trade faces with the devil. The devil rallies the crowd behind abuses in a fictional factorylike place called a wheelmine. Santa and the devil are chummy; the devil points out to Santa that "children are your specialty." The crowd then turns on Santa Claus, but a child is able to see through the disguises. Both the child and Santa say that they are looking for something they have lost. "And I am looking for somebody too," the child says. "Knowledge has taken love out of the world / and all the world is empty empty empty," the Woman mourns. The play ends happily, however. The child rushes into the Woman's arms. There is also a reunion between the real Santa, the child, and the child's mother. The Woman kneels to Santa Claus.

As the vision of reunion was enchanting for Cummings, perhaps it was overpowering for Marion. She had saved Cummings from the agony inflicted on him by Elaine and, by association, Nancy. On his behalf, she hated Elaine. On his behalf, she had mourned Nancy. When she met him, he had been an emotional wreck. Now it seemed impossible for her to see or understand the importance of his daughter to him or, even more, the importance a father might have to his daughter. If Nancy reappeared, Cummings would certainly be upset and probably be emotionally taken up. Marion didn't want that.

Marion's plan was to keep the reunion between Cummings and Nancy from happening. When Cummings consulted with Dr. Wittels, he was told to relax and let events take their course. He would see Nancy when he was meant to see her, Wittels said.

Cummings had not spent time with Nancy, who was now twenty-seven years old, married, and soon to be pregnant with her second child, since the days when she was his adorable Mopsy in that dreadful year when he had married Elaine in Cambridge and finally was divorced by her ten months later in Paris. Did he know then that he wouldn't see his daughter again for more than a circumscribed visit until she was an adult?

The last times he had seen her were long past. In September of 1923, Cummings had casually written to his sister, Elizabeth, who was living in New York, that Elaine and Mopsy might drop in on her "just to make sure the social side is taken care of." Then, sometime in the winter of 1924, Cummings was granted three visits with Nancy in Central Park, supervised by her nanny. By this time he was heartbreakingly aware that his daughter was being slowly taken away from him. They played. He asked her to draw a picture for him. The nanny glowered. On their last of these three visits, as Cummings wrote, "he pushed all the tears of his love carefully into one corner of his mind and lifted an absurd hat to the huddled nurse who bowed and smiled." In March of 1927, Cummings had been allowed another visit with his daughter. "Nancy and I had a wonderful time walking up and down the room, joking, imitating each other, and making fun of things in general. Then we drew pictures for each other," Cummings wrote to his mother.

Soon after that visit, Elaine and MacDermot had permanently moved to Ireland with Nancy, and Cummings had not seen her since. Now, as she slowly resurfaced, as his friends began to describe her as the lovely wife of Willard Roosevelt and doting mother of her own son, Simon, Cummings's feelings for his daughter, which had been brutally repressed, began painfully to resurface, like the thawing-out of flesh that has been frozen for a long time. As feeling returned, pain returned.

Once again in the summer of 1946, Mrs. Roosevelt decided to rent the same house on Silver Lake, where Nancy and her baby son and her husband when he was off duty could spend the summer in the cool mountain air. Cummings heard through the New Hampshire grapevine that Nancy and her family were staying just up the road. Nancy, of course, had no idea that the man who was her real father, a man she thought of as a famous poet who had been a friend of her father's, was so close.

If Marion was afraid that Nancy would explode like an enemy mortar into the relatively predictable life she had built around Cummings's work, she had reason to fear. During the war years Cummings and Marion had become quiet, calmed-down older people. She had lost her astonishing looks. His satire had become more bitter, and at the same time his childlike sense of wonder continued to bubble up through his anger at the way the world was turning. He still thought about cheating on Marion and taking advantage of their so-called open marriage, but this happened more in fantasy than in reality. Sitting upstairs in his New Hampshire study, or his third-floor room at 4 Patchin Place, looking west over the low roofs of Greenwich Village and the small yards at the back of the block, he kept on working no matter what else was going on in his life. Once again his work life was thriving.

In 1940, after the success of *Collected Poems* in 1938, he published *50 Poems* with Duell, Sloan and Pearce, including the playful "anyone lived in a pretty how town" and the poem that is one of his longest, most famous, and most powerful. More than a decade after his father's death, Cummings found a way in language to understand death.

> my father moved through dooms of love
> through sames of am through haves of give,
> singing each morning out of each night
> my father moved through depths of height
>
> this motionless forgetful where
> turned at his glance to shining here;
> that if(so timid air is firm)
> under his eyes would stir and squirm
>
> newly as from unburied which
> floats the first who,his april touch
> drove sleeping selves to swarm their fates
> woke dreamers to their ghostly roots
>
> and should some why completely weep
> my father's fingers brought her sleep:
> vainly no smallest voice might cry
> for he could feel the mountains grow.
>
> Lifting the valleys of the sea
> my father moved through griefs of joy;
> praising a forehead called the moon
> singing desire into begin
>
> joy was his song and joy so pure
> a heart of star by him could steer
> and pure so now and now so yes
> the wrists of twilight would rejoice

keen as midsummer's keen beyond
conceiving mind of sun will stand,
so strictly(over utmost him
so hugely)stood my father's dream

his flesh was flesh his blood was blood:
no hungry man but wished him food;
no cripple wouldn't creep one mile
uphill to only see him smile.

Scorning the pomp of must and shall
my father moved through dooms of feel;
his anger was as right as rain
his pity was as green as grain

septembering arms of year extend
less humbly wealth to foe and friend
than he to foolish and to wise
offered immeasurable is

proudly and(by octobering flame
beckoned)as earth will downward climb,
so naked for immortal work
his shoulders marched against the dark

his sorrow was as true as bread:
no liar looked him in the head;
if every friend became his foe
he'd laugh and build a world with snow.

My father moved through theys of we,
singing each new leaf out of each tree
(and every child was sure that spring
danced when she heard my father sing)

then let men kill which cannot share,
let blood and flesh be mud and mire,

scheming imagine,passion willed,
freedom a drug that's bought and sold

giving to steal and cruel kind,
a heart to fear,to doubt a mind,
to differ a disease of same,
conform the pinnacle of am

though dull were all we taste as bright,
bitter all utterly things sweet,
maggoty minus and dumb death
all we inherit,all bequeath

and nothing quite so least as truth
—i say though hate were why man breathe—
because my father lived his soul
love is the whole and more than all

Then, in 1944, Henry Holt and Company published his next collection, *1 × 1*. The Cummings issue of the *Harvard Wake* in spring
1946 added kudos to his growing reputation from everyone in poetry
from William Carlos Williams to Wallace Stevens to Conrad Aiken.
By 1950, after the production of *Santa Claus,* his next collection, *Xaipe,*
was ready. Here, although satire and dark humor take over a great deal
of his voice, and his bitterness in one particular anti-Semitic poem has
shadowed his reputation to this day, Cummings was still one of the
most lyrical poets of his generation with a masterpiece like this one
which mixes formal perfection of the sonnet with a wild, expressive
syntax:

i thank You God for most this amazing
day:for the leaping greenly spirits of trees
and a blue true dream of sky;and for everything
which is natural which is infinite which is yes

(i who have died am alive again today,
and this is the sun's birthday;this is the birth

day of life and of love and wings:and of the gay
great happening illimitably earth)

how should a tasting touching hearing seeing
breathing any—lifted from the no
of all nothing—human merely being
doubt unimaginable You?

(now the ears of my eyes awake and
now the eyes of my eyes are opened)

The poet and literary critic John Malcolm Brinnin was drinking with Dylan Thomas one night, and when Thomas mentioned that he had always wanted to meet Cummings, Brinnin marched him right around the corner to Patchin Place. Cummings and Thomas stayed up most of the night drinking and talking. They became great friends—a friendship tragically interrupted by Thomas's death in November of 1953 at St. Vincent's Hospital, down the street from Patchin Place, after another long night of drinking.

Cummings was baffled by the deaths of his friends who could not control their drinking as he had—for the last decade of his life he kept to a three-drinks-a-day rule with a lot of success. No one understood that alcohol is a serious depressant, nor did we have the medical knowledge of brain chemistry that now shows us the mechanics of addiction. Later, talking to his biographer Charles Norman, Cummings described alcoholism as strangely and as well as anyone ever has. "I knew a couple of lemmings once," he said. "Nobody could stop them. On they rushed—straight ahead—and plunged in. Hart Crane and Dylan Thomas."

12

"I think I am falling in love with you"

Summer's end in the New Hampshire mountains is a beautiful and poignant time. The short green-growing season is over, and the apples are ripening in the orchards above Silver Lake. Great sunsets flame across the sky as if there were huge fires being banked at the edge of the world. The days grow short and the nights become cold enough for the warmth of a fire. The furnaces belch to life. The leaves have not yet begun to turn their glorious colors, the wildflowers are scarce, the lake water suddenly freezing, and it is very hard to get out from under the covers into the cold, cold morning air. The bite of deadly winter with its blizzards and howling winds, its ice storms and freezes, is now just a nip in the air. It's a time when you can literally imagine the earth slowly shifting on its axis away from the warmth of the sun, a time of reassessment and longing.

Finally, at the end of the summer of 1946, Cummings and Marion relented toward the woman who did not know that she was his daughter. Cummings asked his friend Billy James to bring Nancy Thayer Cummings Roosevelt and her husband, Willard, to Joy Farm for tea. Truman was in office, and the United States was a world power. Dr. Benjamin Spock had just published *The Common Sense Book of Baby and Child Care,* the seminal parenting book that told mothers that they knew more than they realized. Cummings had finished writing *Santa Claus,* and he wrote to Allen Tate, then an editor at Henry Holt and Company, about illustrations. Even in this good time for his career and his country, Cummings kept up his questioning attitude. In another perfect English sonnet he wrote:

when serpents bargain for the right to squirm
and the sun strikes to gain a living wage—
when thorns regard their roses with alarm
and rainbows are insured against old age

when every thrush may sing no new moon in
if all screech-owls have not okayed his voice
—and any wave signs on the dotted line
or else an ocean is compelled to close

when the oak begs permission of the birch
to make an acorn—valleys accuse their
mountains of having altitude—and march
denounces april as a saboteur

then we'll believe in that incredible
unanimal mankind(and not until)

The Jameses had been Cummings's neighbors his whole life. In Cambridge they lived at 95 Irving Street, just across from the Cummings house; in New Hampshire they lived five miles away in the house where the James family had spent the summer for generations; the James presence at Chocorua was one of the reasons Edward Cummings had been originally drawn to Silver Lake.

The second son of the great philosopher William James, Billy James was two years older than Estlin Cummings and had always served Cummings as a kind of spiritual older brother. A few years after the death of Rebecca Cummings, when the Cummings house on Irving Street had been sold to another family, James wrote Cummings about his feelings on what was going on across the street. "There are three roofers on the roof of your house, and now there is a large black poodle barking below. I don't like to think that there are Wagners across the way instead of Cummingses—particularly when I reflect that you were, in a sense, conceived in this room when Dad introduced your parents to each other."

For the moment at least, Marion's objections about Nancy had been overcome. Nancy was delighted at the prospect of meeting the poet she admired, one who possibly had been married to her mother at one time.

She hoped he would be more open about the past than Elaine had been. When the guests arrived at Joy Farm, Marion and the Jameses—all of whom knew that Cummings was Nancy's father—stayed outside, and father and daughter walked into the cool, deepening shadows of the house together.

Nancy was enchanted. Something was happening to her that she did not understand, but she sensed its tremendous importance. Cummings's voice, which others had compared to the sound of an organ or a magnetic and masculine siren song, was superbly resonant to the woman who was his daughter and who had heard that voice throughout her childhood. She didn't remember consciously, but she seemed to remember all the same. That afternoon in New Hampshire, she later told the biographer Richard Kennedy, Cummings's voice "seemed extraordinary, like a bell, like something come from afar, almost echoing." Little did she know that Cummings's extraordinary voice, both whispery and powerful, was indeed something echoing—an echo from her own childhood.

The tea at Joy Farm went well. Nancy and Willard were an attractive young couple. Marion seemed to have been soothed by the meeting, in which nothing was revealed except Nancy's admiration of Cummings as a poet. The two families—the Roosevelts and the Cummingses—began a low-key literary friendship. The next summer, the Roosevelts did not rent a house near Joy Farm; but when Nancy gave birth to her daughter Elizabeth, she wrote a note to Cummings announcing it. No one had told Nancy that Cummings was her father. The Jameses didn't think it was their job, and although Cummings knew that Nancy would eventually find out, there never seemed a right time to tell her. Without understanding what she was doing, she brought his painful past right into the present.

Almost thirty years earlier, when Cummings was estranged from Elaine but still deeply attached to Nancy, when he was in the early stages of the heartbreak of being separated from his daughter, he had written about a visit with her in his journal: "goodbye dear & next time when I feel a little better we'll ride on the donkeys and next time on the pigs maybe or you will a bicycle and I will ride a swan & next time when my heart is all mended again with snow repainted with bright new paint we'll ride you and I."

In the winter of 1947 Nancy, with her two children, Simon and Elizabeth, and her husband, Willard, moved to an apartment in a complex at 5901 Thirty-ninth Street in Long Island City, across the river from Manhattan. Nancy again was invited to visit Cummings and Marion, this time in their apartment at Patchin Place. She was fascinated by her mother's past, but Cummings wouldn't talk about it. When Nancy tried to ask him about her mother or the man she thought was her father, his friend Scofield Thayer, Cummings changed the subject.

At tea, Cummings asked Nancy if she would be willing to sit for a portrait. She happily agreed, but the two of them didn't start work on the picture until the spring of 1948. "Always the pictures came first," Nancy wrote years later in her book about her father, in which he becomes Charon, the aging boatman, on the river Styx. "In and out of dreams and memories; then the poems round and about them, afterwards prose to link with the broken key in the present: with absence, with Charon." Later, she explained that "the ferryman of the Styx represents not my father but my father's absence."

Nancy was a beautiful woman, with her mother's dramatic coloring and her father's grace and blazing blue eyes. Cummings first drew a small head of her and then started on another work, a larger, seated figure. When he and Marion returned from Joy Farm in the fall of 1948, the sittings began again. Nothing was revealed about the past. As Nancy sat for him, he entertained her with stories about his life and the lives of people he had known—omitting the one story that was of critical importance to his listener. He painted in his third-floor studio, and after the sittings the two of them went downstairs for tea. Marion seemed to hover at all times, so the conversation was cheerful and stayed on the surface. The afternoons when she crossed the East River to the row of tenements at Patchin Place and sat for Cummings became the bright spot of Nancy's week.

Cummings was one of the great talkers of the twentieth century, and his simply told stories and comic asides, which he used to lighten the silence as he painted, fascinated Nancy. He was, after all, a great poet, but he also seemed to be in every way a great man. He delighted in the sparrow and raged at the injustice of the universe. He was a successful writer, but he was as angry about bad editing as a beginner would be. "if I could make you realize how an artist feels when his work is mutilated by the very person he trusted to cherish it, you would be a wiser and sadder man," he wrote an editor who had corrected his syntax in October of 1948. "If I were a killer, you'd be in Hell now. Being only myself, am trying as hard as I can to forgive you. But don't commit the blunder of reviving your crime."

Taken up by the endless, mind-numbing dailiness of caring for two small children in an isolated apartment, Nancy found herself looking forward to the afternoons when she would sit absolutely still in his upstairs studio and listen to pigeons cooing, the distant traffic on Sixth Avenue, and the scratch of his pencil or the rough hiss of his paintbrush. Her marriage was difficult. Willard seemed lost without the structure of being a naval officer. He was trying to find work as a musician, teaching piano and playing occasional gigs. He was a brilliant composer, but that didn't seem to translate into a paying job. Without the war or any need for action, the Roosevelt family depression seemed to be bearing down on him. The four of them were living on the dwindling trust fund left to Nancy by the man she still thought of as her father—Scofield Thayer.

Nancy was almost thirty years old, and with some distress she realized that she was obsessed with, falling in love with, the charming fifty-four-year-old man who was painting her portrait. She thought about him all the time. With his cascades of brilliant language and his intimate smile, which seemed to say that the two of them were in a world of their own, he had taken up residence in her head and in her heart. Marion was usually with them, but Nancy felt that she and Cummings were so close that the presence of a third person didn't matter. Her connection with this older man had become one of the most important things in her life.

There were a hundred reasons why her feelings disturbed her. Marion was already acting jealous of her time with Cummings. At first this seemed unreasonable, but what if she was right? Nancy adored her children and believed in marriage. She decided to do the right thing and stop visiting Patchin Place, but she also decided to allow herself one last visit. It was a visit that changed everything—the culmination of a dozen coincidences.

On that afternoon, the afternoon she had decided was her last, Nancy sat as usual for her portrait. Marion hovered. Then Marion was called away by the telephone, or someone at the door. Alone with Cummings, Nancy immediately tried to take advantage of the few minutes she knew she had before Marion returned; she began to press Cummings harder about Scofield Thayer and the past. With Marion downstairs for once, Cummings was suddenly voluble. Something had shifted. He talked about her mother, Elaine, and her mother's sister Alexis. Flirtatiously he suggested that Alexis might have been in love with him. Laughter filled the studio. Again Nancy asked about Thayer, referring to him as her father, and Cummings looked at her strangely. After a short silence, Nancy blurted out her fears that she was falling in love with him.

Suddenly the third-floor room was as still as a church. The pigeons cooed, traffic rumbled by far away, to the west the afternoon light was fading, the room smelled of wood and paints. Cummings required absolute silence for his work. Now the quiet seemed to require a revelation. For the four years of their casual friendship, Cummings had known the truth about Nancy and she had been kept in the dark. Why hadn't he told her before this awful moment? Now, he asked Nancy: "Didn't anyone ever tell you that I was your father?"

To be told by a charming, famous, and talented man she thought herself in love with that he was in fact her father must have been nothing short of earth-shattering. "I hope never to forget the force of rejection, (at the moment of discovery) of what was too much dreamed about to be real—so that the force was the measure of the dream," she wrote to Cummings later. When Marion came back into the room, Cummings told her, "We know who we are."

The deep connection Nancy had felt to Cummings was not love at all, or at least not the kind of love that she imagined. Nancy was indeed shattered. She didn't believe it at first, but once it was out in the open all the pieces fell perfectly into place. She even looked like Cummings, with her ski-jump nose, slender body, and long, narrow face. The two of them embarked on a new relationship, one that would be difficult but based on the truth—unlike the secrets and lies that had been the foundation of all Nancy's previous beliefs. Nancy and her father had been apart for twenty years. In the remaining fourteen years before Cummings's death, they had a difficult, loving, and infuriating friendship. "The very thing which I'd have given my heart for 25 years ago, today knocks me down," Cummings wrote.

For Cummings, Nancy was confusing, but for Marion she was competition. "it seems to me that she is real, & that my life here (with M.) isn't," Cummings wrote later after one of Nancy's visits to Joy Farm, which ended awkwardly. Cummings had given Nancy a pile of old letters from

Thayer, Dos Passos, and Elaine. Nancy had confronted him with a card from Thayer written the day after her birth: "For Value Received." "What are all my salutings of Chocorua & worshippings of birds & smellings of flowers & fillings of hummingbirdcups etcetc?" Cummings wrote, sounding a little bit in love himself. "They're sorry substitutes for human intercourse generally & particularly for spiritual give-&-take with a child or a child-woman whom I adore."

Torn between being Nancy's father and Marion's lover—he apparently did not have the time or energy to be both—Cummings had to choose Marion, who had taken care of him for years. He might have been half in love with his own daughter, but he needed Marion. Physically she took care of him in a way that no one else was willing to do. He was too old to be alone. It was a painful situation all around, but Nancy Thayer was certainly the innocent—she had been lied to all her life, floated along on secrets; and now that she had stumbled onto the truth, it sometimes seemed more difficult than the lies. Cummings was torn between the past and the present. "While part of me is her tragic & immediate father," he wrote in his journal, "I am wholly and permanently someone else."

Marion was far less ambivalent. In the summer of 1951, Nancy visited Joy Farm again, without her family, and slept at night in her father's studio, which was also the guest room. One day she commented on the versions of a poem he had left scattered across his desk. Cummings bristled; no one commented on his unfinished work! The next day Marion asked Nancy to leave. "You know how hard it is for your father to have anyone around while he is trying to work," Marion dictated. "It is time to go."

Nancy, always forgiving, always trying to make it work between them, recouped her standing with Cummings later the same summer. When she had the energy and wit to send a red wooden wheelbarrow—like the one in his favorite poem by William Carlos Williams—to Joy Farm as an early birthday present, he practically crowed with delight: "thank you a millionmillion times for the marvellous gift!" Later, when her first book of poetry was published and got very little attention, he wrote her a fatherly letter about the stupidity of the public. Hailing her book as a miracle, he wrote "Anyhow:from my standpoint the only thing—if you're some sort of artist—is to work a little harder than you can at being who you are."

Are the sins of the fathers and mothers really visited on their children? Nancy's connection with her father, with the charming Cummings, did not break up her marriage in the way that Nancy had feared it might when she felt herself falling in love with him. Yet the marriage, which was already shaky, certainly received its death blows in that small, cluttered studio above Patchin Place off Tenth Street. Nancy's confused drive and furious intelligence came crashing up against her husband's troubles with disastrous results. "She was a critical person," Robert Cabot remembers. "She didn't give anybody any leeway. You could see it in the way she looked, she had a tight mouth. There was a lot of argumentativeness in her and a resistance to sloppy thinking."

Nancy was her father's daughter—he was also a critical man with a penchant for argument. As he got older, his critical brain seemed to grow while his ability to be loving and tolerant faded. As he wrote in a late poem that might have been addressed to Nancy:

old age sticks
up Keep
Off
signs)&

youth yanks them
down(old
age
cries No

Tres)&(pas)
youth laughs
(sing
old age

scolds Forbid
den Stop
Must
n't Don't

&)youth goes
right on
gr
owing old

Nancy and Cummings wrote to each other while both were living in New York, but even after Cummings's revelation their meetings were rare. Now, raising her two children with less and less help from Willard as their marriage disintegrated, she began to feel hurt all over again by Cummings's failure to give her the kind of welcome long-lost children dream of getting from their parents. Then, one night in New York City, Nancy went to a cocktail party for some friends of her husband's. For once, Willard stayed home with the kids. She wore a white dress.

Kevin Andrews, a summa cum laude Harvard classicist, was one of the Harvard class of 1947 who had dropped out of school to fight in World War II, been on the front lines in Italy, and returned to classes at the war's end. Handsome, dashing, and a little bit crazy, Andrews found life changed when he won a fellowship to study the ancient world in Greece after college. "Really . . . he went to Greece and never came back," remembers Robert Cabot, his classmate and friend. Andrews used his fellowship to work on a book about Greece, *Castles of the Morea*. Greece after World War II was impoverished and still at war, and the Marshall Plan, the American aid that was working so well in the rest of Europe, was being so badly administered in Greece that Andrews became convinced he should go to Washington and tell someone.

In Washington, he stayed with the Cabots and looked for work. Disguising his epilepsy, a disease that he had always had but that had become worse after college, he went the rounds of government agencies telling his story of the disasters in Greece. No one listened. No jobs were available. He headed north for New York, where he moved in with his mother and tried again to find a job, or at least a sympathetic ear.

Then, one night at a cocktail party in 1953, he looked across the room and saw a slender woman dressed in white. She was pretty, with long, dark hair and a look of utter detachment from the rest of the party. It was Nancy Thayer Cummings Roosevelt, and by the time he crossed the room to sit down next to her, he felt that he was being drawn to her by some mythic power. He was right. No one else had listened to him. She listened.

"Across that vacuous room, through the circulating trays of drinks and canapés, I glimpse a young woman. Alone, sitting in a window seat, obviously bored or uncomfortable with the scene," thinks Aidan, the character based on Kevin Andrews in Robert Cabot's wonderful novel about his friend, *The Isle of Khería*. "She is different definitely different. A poet, and something about her seems seeking to escape. That's for me. I drop whatever manners I still had, sit down beside her, announce that she and I would shortly be husband and wife."

Andrews talked incessantly about Greece, the country that he had used to build what became his entire identity. He was more than in love with the place and wanted desperately to share it with Nancy. He had sunk deeply into the life of the Greek villagers while writing *Castles of the Morea,* and he longed to return.

"I could lie in bed all day and know the village from its sounds," Andrews's biographer Roger Jinkinson wrote.

> In the morning there are cockerels, in the evening the sound of goats and sheep and all day dogs bark and children play. Then there are the voices of the women, their own private language low with chuckles and laughter round the oven as they bake bread, strong as they talk to a friend, or a sister, or a child further away. The tourist boat comes at its time and leaves with the flotsam and jetsam that is the European tourist trade; Danish, Dutch, German, Italian, a babble of barbarian voices and hysterical laughter. Now and then the ferry boat arrives, chains tumbling to the sea as the anchor seeks purchase against our strong winds. I hear the winds too. They play with my shutters; Trasmontana, Sirocco, Meltemi, Maestros. These names are ancient and Venetian; they remind us of what we were and tell us something of what we are. And then there is the sea, never silent, never still, the waves washing the stones in rhythms in the summer or pounding rocks when winter comes.

Nancy's love affair with Kevin Andrews was the final end of her marriage to Willard Roosevelt, but it improved her fragile relationship with her newfound father. By the time he and Nancy rediscovered each other, Cummings was becoming an old man who counted on his dragon of a companion to protect him from the world he had come to despise. He and Nancy both tried hard. In a letter to Nancy, Cummings remembered his own heartbreak when she had been taken away from him. "Perhaps some day you will remember the time (in Paris) I was allowed to take you for one whole hour to some sort of little foire—where we rode a variety of tremendous animals including chevaux de bois," he wrote to her. His heart was broken; he would "never forget how my staunch (then as now) friend Sibley Watson, by way of comforting our unhappy non-hero, gently reminded him that the great (to me) wise Freud says a child's self . . . is already formed at whatever age you were when we lost each other."

In August of 1953, Nancy, Kevin, and her two Roosevelt children had a happy visit to Joy Farm, where Cummings and a relaxed Marion were in residence after the ordeal of the winter in Cambridge and the anxiety of the Norton Lectures. *Castles of the Morea* had just been published in the United States, and Andrews had studied with John Finley, who had been one of Cummings's friends during his Norton semesters at Harvard. On his own turf and with Marion apparently placated by the presence of Nancy's new lover and her children, Cummings was an expansive and loving father and grandfather—a personality that was often less than evident during the fourteen years he and Nancy tried to forge a new relationship as father and daughter.

Although Nancy's affair with Kevin Andrews was good for her relationship with her father—at least at first—it was eventually dreadful for her relationship with her children. Soon after her fine summer visit to Joy Farm with Kevin, Nancy was divorced from Willard Roosevelt. The newly constituted family—Kevin, Nancy, Simon, and Elizabeth—embarked on a slow boat to Piraeus, the Athenian seaport, and the Greek islands. The trip was glorious—until the little family arrived in the hut on the remote island of Ikaria. Here, a clueless Andrews had imagined that Nancy and her children would learn to share his love of Greece. Ikaria, named after the mythical Icarus, who despite his father's warnings flew too close to the sun and plunged into the sea and drowned, is a tiny island off the coast of Turkey in the Aegean. Nancy and her children had never lived without heat, electricity, or running water, and they didn't like it.

Like much of Greece, Ikaria suffered horribly during World War II, occupied by the Italians and then the Germans and often besieged by famine. It was hardly one of the Greek islands in Homer's wine-dark sea, or even in Andrews's own *Castles of the Morea*. "You took us there in the dead of winter," Cornelia, the character based on Nancy, remembers in Cabot's novel. "Our home was a goatherd's hut thirty-five dangerous minutes up a precipitous rocky track. We had plastic sheets for windows, and the roof was just rusty tin on an occasional sagging beam . . . Our light was a single lamp, stinking and sputtering on watery paraffin."

By the second winter in Greece, in 1955, Nancy's children had rebelled against the physical hardships of life on a rocky island and the impossibility of fitting in to the local school, where no one spoke English and no one wanted to help the little American children learn Greek. Nancy had little choice, and she sadly sent her children home to live with their father in New York City. Her marriage to Andrews began to be troubled—how could it not? Living in Greece was not negotiable for Kevin Andrews; not living there was just as nonnegotiable for Nancy's children.

Eventually, Andrews consented to move to Athens, where the ragged family—Nancy and Kevin now had an infant daughter, Ioanna—lived in a farmhouse with an orchard above Athens on Mount Lycabettos, looking down on the Parthenon and the Acropolis. "It was a treasure of a place at the edge of a park," remembers Robert Cabot. "But their relationship was terrible. They were at each other's throats, they were violent and throwing things at one another." Cabot and Andrews went off on a climbing trip in the mountains and returned to Nancy's furious jealousy. "I think she thought there was some homosexual connection between Kevin and me—which there was, but it was one-sided. Kevin was a definite bisexual," Cabot recalls.

Reading over Nancy's correspondence with her father as well as Richard Kennedy's biography, which is based on extensive interviews with her, one comes away with the heartbreaking sense of how hard both of them were trying to repair their father-daughter connection, trying to heal. Their last visit together, however, was as ill-fated as Nancy's time with her children in Ikaria with Andrews. In the summer of 1960, Nancy suffered complications from the birth of her second daughter with Andrews—Alexis—and eventually her condition deteriorated so badly that she was flown to London, where she got the medical treatment she needed. This got her father's attention.

Frantically, Cummings tried to place a transatlantic call, and he finally reached her at the hospital in London. Belatedly he decided that, as her father, he should rush to her and be helpful. In those days, rushing was a slower matter than it is today, especially for Cummings and Marion, rushing to the aid of the daughter Marion had never quite accepted. At the end of September Cummings and Marion sailed for Europe on the *Vulcania*. More solvent than they had ever been, they treated themselves to a visit to Italy, which depressed them. By this time, Nancy had returned to Greece from London, and so Cummings and Marion headed south.

Finally, in Athens to visit Nancy—which had been the original goal of the trip, although typically Cummings had not mentioned this to Nancy—he and Marion checked in to the Hotel Grande Bretagne. Cummings immediately objected to the hotel's recent renovation, which, it seemed to him, had turned a grand hotel into a series of little boxes. Unmoved by the hotel's luxury status or by its astonishing view of the Parthenon, which seemed to float like an apparition from the ancient world just outside the windows, Cummings became his worst self—crotchety, impossible to please, sulky, and deferential to Marion.

To make things worse, his back immediately went into painful spasms, and the heating pad brought from New York didn't work with the Greek electrical system. The hotel staff was no help. Nancy and Kevin Andrews had no phone and no way of knowing that Nancy's father was fuming just a few miles away. By the time Marion had reached them by mail, Cummings's funk had achieved epic proportions—abetted by Marion, who was furious, too. When Kevin Andrews himself appeared with a Greek heating pad, Marion slammed the hotel room door in his face. She angrily plugged in the new heating pad without following Andrews's directions, and it blew a fuse. This was the limit! With the help of the hotel staff, the heating pad finally started to work, but Marion's mood was not amenable to a new plug—she had already blown her fuse. Finally Nancy, who had still not seen or spoken to her father, wrote him a heartbreaking note, delivered to the hotel. In it she called him by his given name, as he had requested, rather than calling him "Father." "We are as Kevin tried to say, at your disposal at all times but, not wishing to intrude & being perhaps rather too much aware of this possibility it seems best to leave the modus up to you—even at the risk of seeming, Estlin, less loving toward yourself than I feel; this has always seemed the lesser / or better / risk & very possibly I have always been wrong; I have very little to go on."

When Cummings and Marion finally appeared at the Andrewses' lovely farmhouse, anxiously shepherded by Nancy, Marion "behaved in a hoity-toity fashion about being invited to a mere family lunch with grandchildren present, implying that Cummings was too important a man to be asked to join the children at the family table," Kennedy writes.

On another day Cummings, Marion, Andrews, and Ioanna climbed Mount Hymettus to see a monastery. Whenever Marion was in the same room with Nancy, her displeasure was enough to make the experience unpleasant for everyone. A few days later, when Nancy and her father were finally alone in order to say the goodbye that turned out to be their final meeting, he seemed tremendously uncomfortable, Nancy told Kennedy. He commented on her love for her children. He said that he had come to see her and that he was glad she was well; this was the first time Nancy learned that he had traveled to Athens just to see her. The discomfort didn't lift until Cummings and Marion were leaving. Personal encounters were hard for both father and daughter. Letters were easier.

In a voluble letter to Nancy in London in 1961, the year before he died, Cummings complimented her on her poems, and asked her to help him with a translation of Rilke's poem "The Panther" if she had time. Writing about those years that, in retrospect, seemed like a golden dream for their father-daughter connection, he revisited the time before Elaine separated them and erased any memory Nancy might have had of her real father, before their twenty years apart, before their supremely uncomfortable reunion. In the story he included in the letter, he had gone to visit the MacDermots on the promise of getting to see her. What he was allowed during the visit was to watch her sing. "Your pluck was wonderful!" he wrote. "You hated being made to showoff, but your singing teacher's reputation was at stake & you didn't hate me. Long before, your mother had assured you your father was dead (or a little bird?) but you sang your best. The song was enchanting."

In another letter—he was much more loving in letters than in person, perhaps because Marion didn't vet his correspondence—he sent Nancy an old snapshot of himself in his twenties, a glamorous-looking kid with a lot of combed-back hair and a mustache. "Do you know at all, I wonder, what you sent me?" she asked in her reply. The photograph seemed to have produced a shock of memory; she wrote, "Strange that I should be able to forget so long."

Cummings trusted his analyst, Fritz Wittels, and he had come to respect the ideas of Sigmund Freud. Certainly the story of Nancy Thayer Cummings Roosevelt Andrews suggests that the damage done in childhood—especially the damage in relation to people of the opposite sex—plays itself out over and over in adulthood. "You can not turn the wheels of history backward," Cummings has Sophia say in *Eimi*.

Nancy Cummings had married two intensely intellectual, distinguished, and difficult men, and both marriages ended badly. Andrews, who was born in China, was a famously flamboyant guy, a "wild man" with epilepsy and a passion for all things Greek, who ended up swimming out into the sea and drowning—perhaps accidentally, perhaps as a suicide. He and Nancy had already separated. In 1968, complaining that she didn't want to raise her children in a country ruled by a corrupt junta, but really sick to death of her marriage to Andrews, Nancy took her children and moved back to London, where she spent the rest of her life. "I always had the feeling she was on the verge of depression," Robert Cabot remembers. "Later I saw her while she was living alone in her flat in London—a very solitary soul, quiet and judgmental still. She spent a lot of time doing yoga."

13

Readings: A New Career

At the same time that Nancy and Cummings were trying to find a way to be friends, if not father and daughter, the rest of the world was caught up in the prosperous, stuffy years between the end of World War II and the beginning of the 1960s. If the Cambridge ladies were uptight and divorced from the natural world, they found an echo in the so-called Greatest Generation. Cummings was a man ahead of his time, and his poems would enjoy another wave of popularity after his death in the 1960s. As the poet of chaos, playfulness, and topsy-turvy rule breaking, he once again found himself out of step. Politically, Cummings was conservative, even going so far as to agree with anticommunist alarmists—he had never forgotten his terrible time in Russia.

Yet Cummings was irrepressible. Although he was often financially desperate, he never lost his gallantry or his delight in the antics of a blue jay or in the water lapping at the shores of Silver Lake or in the cherries blooming in Washington Square Park. "The poet is no tender slip of fairy stock who requires peculiar institutions and edicts for his defense," he wrote to Mary de Rachewiltz, Ezra Pound's daughter, quoting his hero Henry David Thoreau in a passage from *A Week on the Concord and Merrimack Rivers* that might have been his own credo. "But the toughest son of earth and heaven, and by his greater strength and endurance his fainting companions will recognize the God in him. It is the worshippers of beauty, after all, who have done the real pioneer work of the world."

Asked to lecture in the poetry series at the Manhattan YM-YWHA by his friend John Malcolm Brinnin, Cummings perfected what would become his mature lecture style. His invitation to Bennington brought far more than a pleasant evening; it was the beginning of a satisfying and lucrative new career. Much like another of his heroes, Ralph Waldo Emerson, Cummings found that he was able to become a famous poet not by writing poetry but by reading poetry. Emerson's essays owe their popularity to the rigorous speaking schedule he used to support himself and his family at the end of his life.

By the time he took the stage at the Y in December of 1954, Cummings had developed a precise and powerful way of reading his poems to an audience. He never read behind a lectern. Before he read, the organizers and the venue got a list of very specific instructions. He would need a straight-backed chair, a table, and a gooseneck lamp. He would not answer questions, sign books, or agree to any of the social folderol that usually surrounds a reading—the dinner with the English department, the interview with the local reporter, the radio interview for the town station. There would be no photographs.

For the Y, for instance, Cummings had planned a two-part program, running from 8:40 to 9:10 and then, after a ten-minute intermission, from 9:20 to 9:50. The Y officials, however, not used to such precision, allowed the standees to swarm the unoccupied seats at 9 p.m., completely disrupting the reading. The mike was also, Cummings wrote Hildegarde Watson, "as stiff as a mule." The audience seemed half dead, Cummings told his old friend; whatever he did, they would not have noticed: "I could have roared as softly as a seashell or noiselessly dropped a demi-whisper into the very last row of the balcony."

A Cummings reading usually started with a few prose passages and proceeded to poetry. Often Cummings reserved a poem to use as an encore after the first round of applause had died down. "He was an enormously effective and careful reader," Brinnin told Richard Kennedy. Cummings began to draw large audiences, many of them young men and women whose experience of the poems was so intense that they seemed enrolled in a kind of Cummings cult. "must confess I attribute my physical ills to socalled nervous tension," he wrote, summing up the good and the bad for Hildegarde Watson. "If any quite unmitigatedly perverse human being insists on deliberately insulting the powersthatseem—instead of (come toutlemonde) dutifully soft-soaping same—what can he expect?

Certainly not something which happened yesterday; when a pretty young girl handed me a bunch of daffodills,saying 'you don't know who I am but I just wanted to give you these.' "

At the Y, Cummings met the series' assistant director, Betty Kray, who became a friend, dropping by Patchin Place for tea on Fridays and serving as Cummings's lecture agent as his audience grew. He began reading at places with a lot of prestige—the Museum of Modern Art, the Institute of Contemporary Arts in Washington, DC. At Betty Kray's urging, he began to travel to lecture and to charge higher fees—in 1955, a Cummings lecture cost $400, which quickly rose to $600 and beyond. In a typical season he read at the University of Chicago, the Chicago Art Center, Dartmouth College, the Metropolitan Museum, Queens College in North Carolina, Duke University, and Barnard.

A Cummings reading was a formal, dramatic event. It was more like a play than a reading. In the tradition of Dickens, who memorized his ninety-minute lectures and used his book only as a prop, Cummings brought a tremendous amount of theatrical skill to the art of reading. The writer Gerald Weales, who made a study of poetry readings, divided readers into three categories: performer, personality, and public speaker. Cummings was definitely a performer. On the shadowy stage, the goose-neck lamp was the only light. Cummings quietly entered and began to read, using his mimicking skills for different characters and voices to great effect. He could be side-splittingly funny and sadly sentimental within a few moments.

His voice—aristocratic, reassuring, and yet somehow filled with the wonder of childhood—was electrifying. He did all the voices, and he seemed to become the characters he had written as he read—his enjoyment of the work and the audience was easy to see. Whether he was reading something playful ("may I feel said he?") or angry or deeply serious and sad, his voice was brilliantly adapted to the material. Cummings played his voice, letting it go loud and soft, high and low, using vibrato and falsetto, as the poems demanded.

In a line like "my father moved through dooms of love," he would modulate his voice, drawing out the long syllables in a way that echoed with grief and longing. In the playful poems you could almost hear him smiling; in the sad ones he sounded close to tears. The words seemed to sob of their own accord. His pauses were electric; his vowels, endless and sad.

cy Thayer Cummings Roosevelt Andrews

Hildegarde Watson and Estlin Cummi‥

Cummings as he got older

chin Place

Cummings at work on the porch at Joy Farm

Cummings understood the power of sounds and the possibilities of language in a unique, pioneering way, and this came through when he read.

Until he began to read all over the country, Cummings had been a well-respected poet among poets. His was a name well known in the small community of ideas in literature, poetry, and art, especially at Harvard and in Greenwich Village. Now, partly because of his extraordinary readings, he began to become a national celebrity.

At the same time, his ailments began to catch up with him in a more dramatic and crippling way. His back remained fragile. His skin erupted in a variety of sores and rashes. Traveling was often difficult and sometimes impossible—he had to turn down $1,000 because traveling to the University of Texas would have required a four-and-a-half-hour plane trip. " 'arthritis'—without or avec a soupcon of 'fibrillation'—makes social planning something like a furbelow,& please do not think I'm complaining; if only because I am," he wrote Archibald MacLeish.

His vocal cords got wheezy. He took more Nembutal to sleep and he took all kinds of painkillers for the pain in his back, which persisted even when he was wearing the Iron Maiden. When Hildegarde Watson suggested a trip—probably paid for by the Watsons, who were almost as ready with their loans and gifts as Rebecca Cummings had been—Cummings painted an awful picture for her. "I always glimpse a miserably exhausted me—tortured in his 'iron maid'—waiting&waiting&waiting for some plane or train or boat or maybe hotel-room which doesn't dream of materializing." His misery, even to an old friend, as always was leavened by his own self-knowledge. "Tell me now, Hildegarde," he finished up his letter of complaint about travel, "what do you think: I am suffering from what 'the liberals' entitled 'failure of nerve,' or from something else most beautifully described by Quintus H as 'nec pietas moran': or may my unending timidities harbour a diminutive amount of truth?"

Reading also took an emotional toll. It was Cummings's absolute presence in the moment on the stage that made him so compelling. He paid the price in nerves and fear. "What I generally experience before a reading," he wrote to his sister, Elizabeth, "is a conglomeration of anxieties involving bellyache,heartrouble,arthritis, diarrhea, & (temporary) blindness." He also suffered from a frightening heart arrhythmia, a tachycardia that he controlled with doses of Quinidine.

His reputation as a lecturer increased, and he began to see that financial solvency might be possible if he could keep going. The University of North Carolina at Chapel Hill turned out for him. In Michigan, students lined up in a mob outside the auditorium where he was speaking, hoping for a glimpse of the famous poet. Typical of Cummings, when he was invited to be the featured reader at the Boston Arts Festival in 1957, he agreed to do it and then had second thoughts. "This invitation," writes Charles Norman in his authorized biography, "touched off a prolonged correspondence, in the course of which Cummings withdrew his consent twice, was twice prevailed upon to reconsider, reconsidered, and at length made perhaps his most triumphant appearance as a reader."

Lecturing was always torture for Cummings, torture mixed with the heady experience of being adored, especially by young people and students and even more especially by beautiful young women who memorized his work, sought to touch or speak with him for a moment, and in general brought an attitude of worship to everything he did. He had always spoken for the young, and now they seemed to hear him.

Still, his attitude toward money and fame remained quintessentially, gallantly, humorously Cummings. He wrote to Pound that he had "received an Honour which even I, egocentric though he may be,scarcely dare maintain we deserve." The honor in question was an event that another man might have construed as a disheartening failure: he was turned down for a grant simultaneously by the Bollingen Foundation and the Guggenheim Foundation.

After Pound was incarcerated in St. Elizabeths Hospital, he and Cummings wrote each other almost once a week. Their letters are a record of literary life after World War II in this country and they are also the record of Pound's slow recovery from madness. The letters are all about the difficulties of finding recognition from the establishment—the despicable establishment—and about new talents and intelligent people to whom they introduced each other and whom they tried to help. Sometimes the two great poets wrote about simpler things, like blue jays. Cummings loved blue jays, handsome and naughty, and in fact this led to one of their few arguments, which began with a Cummings poem (published in *95 Poems*):

crazy jay blue)
demon laughshriek
ing at me
your scorn of easily

hatred of timid
&loathing for(dull all
regular righteous
comfortable)unworlds

thief crook cynic
(swimfloatdrifting
fragment of heaven)
trickstervillain

raucous rogue &
vivid voltaire
you beautiful anarchist
(i salute thee

Pound disagreed with Cummings's critical assessment of the bird. He was a fan of blue jays. "whar yu git sech ideas re b.jays?" he asked in a letter with typical Poundian diction. Perhaps Cummings knew a lot about Russia, but Pound didn't think he knew much about birds. "I mean I accept yu as orthority on hrooshuns but queery analysis of b.j," he wrote.

Cummings defended himself with three long passages from books about birds. T. Gilbert Pearson's *Birds of America* calls the blue jay "an amusing rascal": "The Blue Jay is the clown & scoffer of birdland," Cummings quotes Pearson, who also calls the bird "cannibalistic." "Furthermore, he is one of the handsomest of American birds;also he is one of the wickedest." F. Schuyler Mathews's *Field Book of Wild Birds* asserts that "the Jay in spring is undoubtedly a reprobate"; and in Chester A. Reed's *Bird Guide,* "they have a very bad reputation."

Pound was still in many ways Cummings's mentor, and he scolded Cummings for using secondary sources in his writing about birds. Pound wrote that Cummings was wrong about birds and, worse, that he was quoting a sloppy writer, Gilbert Pearson, who used the word "cannibalistic" to describe a bird that was certainly not a cannibal. This, Pound noted, was "vurry poor langwidge." Furthermore, why wasn't Cummings reading the work of Louis Agassiz, the nineteenth-century Harvard professor and bird expert, who would never have made that kind of mistake? Always the teacher, Pound put his didactic advice in a small, characteristic poem:

> why even so the charmin' blue shd be
> VS yu
> I still don't make out
> does the humming's
> of boids
> move mr cummings
> no but
> other men's woidz
> erabout boids.

But Cummings's feelings about blue jays were unabated. "I find it interesting that—large & by—birds beautiful-to-hear dress quietly,& birds beautiful-to-see can't sing," he wrote to Pound.

With their experimental syntax, their running-together of words and punctuation on the page, their attention to the look of words against paper, their lapsing into other languages, especially ancient Greek, and their wild use of any symbol available on the typewriter, the Pound of "The Return" and the Cummings of "Buffalo Bill's" often got so wrapped up in the look or feel of the words that they even baffled each other. "O.K. wot *are* yu talking about?" Pound wrote to Cummings after a particularly dense letter combining Aristotle's writings on dolphins and whales—to be fair, Pound had brought the subject up first—with erudite mentions of Aquinas and *Hamlet*.

But Cummings's intense friendship with Pound had a less lighthearted aspect to it, which later came back to haunt him and which haunts his reputation even now. Like Pound, Cummings grew up at a time when anti-Semitism was accepted and even admired. Marion was mindlessly, socially anti-Semitic. Casting around for the reason he had not found a job during his miserable time in Hollywood, Cummings tended to blame the Jews. Before World War II and the dreadful knowledge of what had happened during the Holocaust, many Americans were anti-Semitic.

Then, in his book of poems *Xaipe,* published in March 1950 by Oxford University Press, Cummings did what he always did—pushed an extreme further than it had gone before, with disastrous results. One poem in the collection, a poem that had in fact been written and published previously before the war, was too offensive not to cause outrage.

> a kike is the most dangerous
> machine as yet invented
> by even yankee ingenu
> ity(out of a jew a few
> dead dollars and some twisted laws)
> it comes both pricked and cunted

The poem's original editor, Theodore Weiss, had objected to the last line, which Cummings subsequently changed to "it comes both prigged and canted" for inclusion in the book. Cummings's friend Allen Tate also objected to the poem. Cummings had tried to explain to Tate that the poem was being misunderstood. What Cummings meant was that the word "kike" had been created by Protestants to diminish Jews. Tate was unpersuaded.

Others, like his friend Paul Rosenfeld, tried to explain to Cummings why he should not include the poem. Even Hildegarde Watson, to whom the book was dedicated, asked him to reconsider its inclusion. As Christopher Sawyer-Lauçanno points out in his biography, the "firestorm" of anger about the poem wasn't really ignited until Cummings was chosen by the Academy of American Poets to receive its fellowship of five thousand dollars in the winter of 1950. *Xaipe* also won the Harriet Monroe Prize.

A public argument ensued. *Congress Weekly* devoted space to a symposium in which Cummings was attacked by an array of Jewish critics and defended by William Carlos Williams. He seemed somewhat clueless, as if he was mired in the years before World War II. "Cummings, the foe of tyranny and the defender of the underling, does not fit the definition of an anti-Semite," wrote Richard Kennedy. "But in the matter of this objectionable epigram, he showed puzzling insensitivity."

Others were more certain. "He was nothing but an anti-Semite," Harvey Shapiro said in my interview with him in 2010, and he was not alone in remembering Cummings's anti-Semitism as his principal characteristic.

Trying to re-create another time and place is difficult; trying not to let our own modern knowledge and understanding bleed into those descriptions of the past is almost impossible. On the one hand, a biographer's responsibility is to bring the past to life on the page in all its details—including the relative knowledge and ignorance of the community described. On the other hand, shouldn't the biographer give the reader and the subject the benefit of everything known at the time of writing? Should poems and books be understood in a vacuum—in the historical silence in which a writer connects viscerally and spiritually with a reader? Or should they be understood as pieces of the web of their own time and ours? When Cummings was writing poetry, I. A. Richards at Cambridge in England was arguing the former in his renowned New Criticism. Work should stand on its own, Richards wrote in his book *Practical Criticism* in 1929. What would happen if a reader knew nothing of the writer or the work—no biographical material or textual explanation?

Since Richards wrote, his ideas have been overwhelmed by the cult of personality; in our world it's unthinkable to read a poem without knowing who the author is, what he or she intended, and what the poem is about. Biography has spawned a cottage industry of literary medical men and women writing essays in which they diagnose the illnesses of a Coleridge (heroin addiction) or a Louisa May Alcott (bipolar disorder), or a Hemingway (clinical depression and alcoholism). In our attempts to understand the past, it is important to weigh the environment *then* against the knowledge we have *now*.

Cummings was raised in a community which was casually racist—casually until Jewish students began to go to Harvard, when it became systematically anti-Semitic under President A. Lawrence Lowell. The ideal man, represented by Cummings's barrel-chested, masculine father, was intolerant and often scary. Gender in this world was sharply defined. There was no homosexuality. Sodomy was literally illegal as well as culturally unacceptable. Men and women who found themselves attracted to people of the same sex lived in secrecy and fear. Women poured tea; men made judgments. Cambridge itself was a homogeneous microcosm of intellectual stuffiness and arrogance. It's worth noting that Cummings hated all this. He did not, could not, would not conform to the blustering masculine ideal of his childhood, and he left Cambridge as soon as he could to find a more tolerant, less anti-Semitic and racist environment in the freedom of Greenwich Village.

At the same time, Cummings had dedicated himself to questioning any rules that came his way—the rules of grammar, of matrimony, of the Harvard overseers—and by the 1950s it was no longer acceptable to be anti-Semitic in words or conversation. The unacceptable was like a red flag of invitation for a poet as provocative as Cummings. His anti-Semitism is indefensible. There is little point in comparing him with other public figures whose anti-Semitism was far worse. Language is powerful, as Cummings knew better than anyone, and the language he used is criminal and repulsive.

Perhaps the most sensible defense of Cummings's poem came from the American critic Leslie Fiedler, who wrote that "what is extraordinary is not that Cummings may be an anti-Semite (this he shares with innumerable jerks) but that he is able to make orderly and beautiful things out of his chaotic and imperfect heart. . . . Certainly when the attackers of Cummings (or Eliot or Ezra Pound or Céline) are revealed as men motivated not so much by a love for Jews as by a hatred for art, I know where to take my stand."

Two engagements that defined Cummings's new career as a popular and well-paid reader, a reader who had more lucrative requests for appearances than he could fulfill, were the prestigious Norton Lectures at Harvard in 1952 and the 1957 Boston Arts Festival lecture.

After finally accepting the offer of the Boston Arts Festival committee, headed by David McCord and including Archibald MacLeish and Paul Brooks, Cummings did a Cummings. Instead of a celebratory poem fit for a summer evening, Cummings wrote a bitter satirical attack on the United States in general and particularly on the way the country had failed to intervene in the Hungarian Revolution of 1956. Deeply moved by the Hungarians' refusal to buckle under to Communist Russia, and personally understanding what living in the USSR was like, Cummings was heartbroken and horrified when Russian troops rolled into Budapest and took over the revolution, imprisoning its leaders and brutally reasserting their power. This was the kind of thing that kept Cummings up at night. Cursed with a vivid imagination and a disintegrating body, he felt misery which was personal as well as political. Moved by the bravery of Hungary's rebellion, the old rebel wrote a poem in celebration and sadness. When the United Nations declined to intervene, he began doing the only thing he knew how to do—write a poem. Unfortunately, all this coincided with the Boston festival's request that he write a poem titled "Thanksgiving (1956)" especially for the festival. They were thinking of some pastoral poem, written by one of Boston's own. Instead they got rage:

> a monstering horror swallows
> this unworld me by you
> as the god of our fathers' fathers bows
> to a which that walks like a who
>
> but the voice-with-a-smile of democracy
> announces night & day
> "all poor little peoples that want to be free
> just trust in the u s a"
>
> suddenly uprose hungary
> and she gave a terrible cry
> "no slave's unlife shall murder me
> for i will freely die"
>
> she cried so high thermopylae
> heard her and marathon
> and all prehuman history
> and finally The UN
>
> "be quiet little hungary
> and do as you are bid
> a good kind bear is angary
> we fear for the quo pro quid"
>
> uncle sam shrugs his pretty
> pink shoulders you know how
> and he twitches a liberal titty
> and lisps "i'm busy right now"

so rah-rah-rah democracy
let's all be as thankful as hell
and bury the statue of liberty
(because it begins to smell)

Cummings, although professionally dedicated to questioning authority, was often a sweetheart in person. Sometimes he was crotchety, but
when appealed to rationally, he was an unusually understanding and
generous man. He was suffused by rage and delight at the same time.
American politics made him sick, but he was transported by the way a
hummingbird sucked pollen from the lilac bushes in the spring. He knew
that he was a finicky old man, and at his best he made fun of his own
eccentricities.

This was lucky for the Boston Arts Festival organizers. When they
explained to him that the poem was not suitable for the pastoral occasion
on June 23, and that they could not release it to the press to be published
as the festival poem, Cummings obligingly wrote another poem, another
kind of characteristic Cummings poem, a pretty, moving poem spoken in
the voice of a little church basking in the glory of God.

i am a little church(no great cathedral)
far from the splendor and squalor of hurrying cities
—i do not worry if briefer days grow briefest,
i am not sorry when sun and rain make april

The poem, in five stanzas of conventional iambic pentameter, ends with
a benediction:

. . . i lift my diminutive spire to
merciful Him Whose only now is forever:
standing erect in the deathless truth of His presence
(welcoming humbly His light and proudly His darkness)

At the festival itself, however, in front of seven thousand or so people crowded onto the Boston Common, Cummings read both poems.
He turned the occasion into a full-dress reading. When the first lines
of "Thanksgiving (1956)" were read, the audience seemed taken aback,

but by the end of the poem they roared their approval. As usual Cummings had found a way to say in poetry what everyone else was feeling: the American frustration with the Cold War and the blandness of the Eisenhower administration. "He had touched something deep in their feelings that needed expression," Kennedy writes. "He was reawakening that sense of helplessness and frustration that had descended upon the American public."

One of the benefits of leaving Cambridge for Greenwich Village was that Cummings came of age as a poet surrounded by the most interesting and talented writers of his generation. Hart Crane, William Carlos Williams, Marianne Moore were all his friends and neighbors. Djuna Barnes lived across the mews at Patchin Place, and Cummings actually climbed in through her window to rescue her once when she had locked herself in. Greenwich Village was also a stopping place for many poets who didn't live there—it was Cummings's good friend Allen Tate who brought his old rival T. S. Eliot to Patchin Place for tea.

14

Victory and Defeat

In the winter of 1961, Cummings's familiar world was threatened when Hugh Keenan, the owner of Patchin Place, decided he was sick of paltry rents from dozens of tenants and planned a complete renovation of the ancient mews, with its narrow curbs and lush ailanthus trees and rent-controlled apartments. Thanks to the generosity of friends and Cummings's furious sensitivity to sounds and smells—he refused to let Marion clean with bleach—Cummings controlled all the rooms at 4 Patchin Place except the second floor in the front.

This wasn't the first attack on the tiny mews, which had become Cummings's refuge from the dirtier, noisier city. Robert Moses had designated Patchin Place as well as the brick spire of Jefferson Market for demolition, but that edict had been overturned. Now, Marion went to court to fight Hugh Keenan. Finally, someone apparently alerted Mayor Robert Wagner to the fact that the famous poet E. E. Cummings was being evicted, and Keenan's permits were revoked. "To a human being, nothing is so important as privacy—since without privacy, individuals cannot exist: and only individuals are human," Cummings gratefully wrote the mayor in March of 1962. "I am unspeakably thankful that the privacy of 4 Patchin Place will be respected; and shall do my best to be worthy of this courtesy."

As sweet as he was to Wagner, Cummings was still furiously antigovernment. In May, when President and Mrs. Kennedy requested Cummings's presence at a black-tie White House dinner, Cummings angrily turned them down and made fun of Mrs. Kennedy's invitation ("not transferable!!!") to a young protegée in a letter.

Cummings slept late, and on a typical day he woke up in the late morning and wandered downstairs for breakfast. Because of his delicate intestinal tract, he took Donnatal for digestion. After breakfast, like clockwork, he jammed an old hat on and walked along Tenth Street to Washington Square Park, where he sat on a bench, did some sketches in his notebook, and then wandered back to Patchin Place. There he retired to his third-floor studio and worked most of the day.

At teatime Cummings would come downstairs for a cup of Lapsang Souchong, perhaps spiked with brandy. "Marion would be in and out from the tiny curtained-off kitchen with the tea things," wrote Richard Kennedy in a lyrical description of Cummings's days in New York. "Estlin would be perhaps eating a pear in the French manner—with a fork piercing its top as he sliced chunks off the side. Or he might be tilting back and forth on his straight-backed rush-bottomed chair, offering his latest complaint about a decision of the Supreme Court or describing his latest putdown of an authority figure. . . . If the weather were pleasant there might be an evening stroll." Cummings drank and smoked throughout the day, sometimes taking a painkiller if his back was sore. At night he took Nembutal to sleep.

Life at Joy Farm had also changed for the better, or at least for the more comfortable. Between his lecturing and reading fees and a few more grants and prizes, money was less a problem than it had been for a lot of his life. Cummings always returned to his better self when he swung the car's wheel up the dirt road to Joy Farm. Now he had electric wiring installed so that Marion could print photographs and have a refrigerator. Lincoln Kirstein's sister Mina arranged to have a heating system installed. Cummings's sister Elizabeth with her husband Carlton Qualey and their children came back to the farm every summer, so it remained a family place.

In the summer of 1962, Marion and Cummings were just finishing a collaboration on a book of fifty of her photographs, with gnomic captions by Cummings, titled *Adventures in Value*. Cummings was thrilled by the book, and he also kept writing poems for a volume to follow *95 Poems*, which had been published in 1958 and had won the prestigious Bollingen Prize.

Many of the poems he wrote that year are about his twin obsessions: aging and the natural world. Even the creatures of Patchin Place—mice, squirrels, and pigeons—seemed to grow closer to Cummings's consciousness as he aged. One of his last poems immortalizes a dying creature in a way that sings Cummings's own sense of being a dying creature.

Me up at does

out of the floor
quietly Stare

a poisoned mouse

still who alive

is asking What
have i done that

You wouldn't have

It was in New Hampshire that Cummings seemed to bond intensely with the copious creatures of the field and the singing birds of the air. More and more, the sixty-seven-year-old Cummings had lost interest in his own species and become fascinated with the New Hampshire flora and fauna. The fearless raccoons and the porcupine mother who seemed to be teaching her child to eat apples, a red fox in the bank above the lake, woodchucks, mischievous chipmunks with their striped backs, all got his attention in a new, vivid way. Cummings still had the Remington .38 pistol Sibley Watson had gotten him when he was on fire with murderous hatred for Frank MacDermot and wild with a despair that made him think of killing himself. Once he had been half-crazy, a feral man with nowhere to turn. Now the thoroughly domesticated Cummings used that haunted gun to protect the farm's chipmunks from a neighborhood cat.

The New England summer birds became his pride and joy. He too was a singer; he too was given a short season in which to spread his melodic song.

christ but they're few

all(beyond win
or lose)good true
beautiful things

god how he sings

the robin(who
'll be silent in
a moon or two)

Poring over his bird books, he studied a recording of bird songs to help him identify the *to-wit-to-wee* of the thrushes, the high and low notes of the nuthatches, the oriole's complicated symphony, the scornful creak of the roguish blue jay, the high shrill of the occasional tanager, the steady trill of the purple finch, and the low buzz of the hummingbirds that came up to the porch in the morning to drink from the tiny tubes of sugar water Cummings put out for them. Sometimes the birds seemed to be singing to him.

"o purple finch
                please tell me why
this summer world(and you and i
who love so much to live)
                must die"

"if i
        should tell you anything"
(that eagerly sweet carolling
self answers me)
                "i could not sing"

Joy Farm, with its built-in exercise—building, chopping wood, clearing brush—was where Cummings always felt at his best.

By September, New Hampshire mornings are cold, but during the day the warming sun still hits the green of the meadows. As summer ends there is a kind of sunset effect—like sunsets, many things are more intense just before they end completely. The growing season is so short and the winter to come will be very long. It's a time to prepare, to harvest the last potatoes and split wood.

On the morning of September 2, after he fed the hummingbirds, Cummings was delighted by an out-of-place, late-blossoming, bright blue delphinium in Marion's flowerbed. In the afternoon, he went out to the barn like many other New Hampshire men in that season, to split some wood for the winter. It was a hot day, filled with the smells of new-mown hay and the cool darkness of the barn. The motion of wood splitting— the wedge, the axe, the downward strokes—was another rhythm clouded in the musty smells of the wood and the barn hay. As he was finishing for the day, Marion came to the kitchen door in the fading light and called out that it was time for dinner.

He told her he would be there as soon as he sharpened the axe. He stacked the wood he had split, whetted the axe blade against the grind-stone so that it would be sharp for the next day, and put it up against the wall just as he had been taught to do by his father when he was a boy. He went inside the house and walked upstairs to wash for dinner. Marion heard him crash to the floor in the hallway. He was unconscious, felled by a cerebral hemorrhage. Marion called an ambulance, but he never regained consciousness and died in the hospital the next morning.

Three days later, Cummings was buried in the family plot in Forest Hills Cemetery in Boston. In spite of his fame, it was a small, private funeral. Nancy was in Europe but sent her two teenage children, Simon and Elizabeth. Marion was too devastated to let many people know. His tombstone is a slab of New Hampshire granite engraved with his name and dates.

Marion lived for less than seven years after Cummings, dying of throat cancer in 1969 when she was just sixty-three. She still took photographs in those years, but her real profession was Cummings's legacy. She oversaw the publication of his final, posthumous book, *73 Poems,* and sold his hundreds of boxes of papers, drafts, and letters to the Houghton Library at Harvard. His paintings went to a summer camp in Rhode Island that Nancy's children had attended.

Cummings's Reputation in the Twenty-first Century

Cummings's reputation waxed and waned during his lifetime, from that of a Harvard prodigy to that of a man who couldn't get published without a loan from his mother. Soon after his death, the 1960s and '70s embraced him all over again as a poet of freedom and playfulness as he had been embraced in the 1930s. He was the Henry David Thoreau of poets, rediscovered by the 1960s students who revered individualism and worshipped the idea of freedom.

In the past twenty years, however, Cummings's reputation has waned. "He was cool in the 1960s and cool when you were young," says the poet David Daniel, echoing what Harvey Shapiro said about Cummings. "Somehow he has the feeling of being a kid's poet, so we never have to think about him." Of course Cummings, for all his youthful playfulness, is a consummate adult when it comes to poetry. His high jinks with poetic forms are based on a knowledge of those forms—in English, Latin, and Greek. Cummings is rarely taught in schools anymore. His understanding of the history of poesy, of scansion, meters, rhyme schemes, forms, and techniques like internal enjambment, in which a word in the middle of a line rhymes with a word at the end of the next line, is what allowed him the experiments that sometimes seemed so spontaneous and young. In fact they were studied, written, and rewritten, and based in what had gone before.

Cummings's sales are a barometer of the national mood. In confident times his poems are beloved. Their questioning, their humor, and their rule-breaking formalism seem to jibe with a democracy ready to ask hard questions and make fun of itself. In precarious times, readers seem to want an older, more assured poet, someone who speaks with authority rather than scoffs at it.

These days he is too popular for the academy and often too sassy to be taught in high school. Many people remember him for his use of the lower case, but few understand that this lowercasing was a fraction of the experiment with form and syntax that was at the heart of Cummings's modernism. Educated about poetics and the various forms of language, he chose to twist the forms he knew well to yield more powerful poems. As a result, he is one of the great and most important American poets.

Furthermore, although modernism is out of style, we live in a time when its mandate—to make it new, as Pound said, and to notice the world—is more important than ever. Cummings and his colleagues felt that they were being inundated with unprocessed information. They hoped that their poetry would make sense of the world.

Patchin Place

When I turn in to Patchin Place these days it's like going back in time. Cummings is still very much alive. Narrow sidewalks line an alley, trees shade houses with white lintels, and the iron tracery of fire escapes hangs above neat wrought-iron fences and gates. The house where Cummings lived has been opened up into a big, light living room and kitchen with hardwood floors and white sofas. The place where Dylan Thomas and Cummings sat and talked about language in front of a smoky fire while drinking gin out of cheap glasses is now the living room of a family with two children and a dachshund, but the tenement feeling is still there in the way the old wooden stairs twist, and in the feeling of many small rooms.

You walk up the warped risers to Cummings's old studio, which is now a boy's bedroom and has become a shrine to basketball. Where Cummings paced and agonized over how to be a formalist with the maximum amount of informality, where his long-lost daughter told him that she loved him, a young boy does his homework. Pigeons coo. Doors open and close as patients visit the psychiatrist next door. The late-afternoon light still streams in from the west through the old panes. Through the window it is still Cummings's view—the backs of older buildings, the open garden with slate everywhere, the low roofs of the Village where it looks as if families of Italians are still making wine in barrels. Further west toward the Hudson River the sun is beginning to set.

Acknowledgments

Biography is a collaboration with the past, with the biographers and historians who have gone before, and this book is no exception. Estlin's first biographer, Howard Norman, who wrote *The Magic-Maker* in the late 1950s with his subject perched roguishly on his shoulder, did a lovely job. I am in debt to him for much of his analysis of Cummings's work—coached by Cummings—and for revealing Cummings's edits of his own story. Cummings's next biographer, Richard Kennedy, in the 1970s did extensive interviews with everyone he could find at a time when many of the characters in Cummings's story were still alive. He was a masterful archivist, researcher, and interviewer whose book, *Dreams in the Mirror*, will be the baseline for any subsequent Cummings biography—and is certainly the foundation of my own. Cummings's most recent biographer, Christopher Sawyer-Lauçanno, wrote an eloquent and thorough book, *E. E. Cummings: A Biography*, published in 2004 and based on the Cummings papers at the Houghton Library at Harvard, and the papers and letters that Marion Morehouse sold to the Houghton Library after Cummings's death. Sawyer-Lauçanno, a poet himself, did a beautiful job of integrating Cummings's life story with the story of his work. Sawyer-Lauçanno was also helpful to me in person, sharing research and insights into Cummings's life. In telling E. E. Cummings's story I stand on all their shoulders. I have been enlightened by their research and insights, their descriptions, and their storytelling.

My personal thanks begin with my father, who introduced me to his friend Estlin in stories and then in real life. My son Warren who, fortunately for me, is between college and graduate school, was an immeasurable help. He read and reread the manuscript and the poems, editing and re-editing until they were correct. Ingrid Sterner also did a masterful job of editing and fact-checking. Kevin Bourke and Patrick Dillon at Pantheon did astonishing work above and beyond the normal call of duty. Bob Morris and Ira Silverberg somehow came up with the idea that I should write about Cummings, and my extraordinary, adorable, and loving agent, Gail Hochman, supported the idea.

I am also indebted to the Houghton Library at Harvard, and to many others who have written brilliantly about Cummings: Richard Kostelanetz, Hildegarde Watson, Catherine Reef, and Wyatt Mason among others. Aileen Gural, who lives with her lovely family in Cummings's former house in Greenwich Village, was astonishingly generous in opening her home and in finding people who remembered him.

My friends, my spiritual Board of Trustees, and my family all make it possible for me to write. The world I live in—New York in the twenty-first century—is a rich and thrilling place for a writer. My lovely editor Victoria Wilson was a brilliant and supportive part of the book. Thank you all!

Notes

I. ODYSSEUS RETURNS TO CAMBRIDGE

3 "There was a hush": Author's interview with Joanne Potee, West Hartfield, Mass., December 2011.

4 series of six lectures: Norman, *The Magic-Maker*, p. 370. Norman's account of Harvard's wooing Cummings to give the Charles Eliot Norton lectures is the most complete and includes the correspondence between Cummings, Finley, Buck, and other Harvard officials. Since Norman's biography was approved by Cummings, albeit reluctantly, I have taken its numbers as accurate.

5 "Please keep many fingers crossed": *Pound/Cummings,* p. 331. Letter dated October 24, 1952.

5 One drunken tryst: Sawyer-Lauçanno, *E. E. Cummings,* p. 457.

5 "He strolled in": Watson, *The Edge of the Woods,* p. 144.

5 "He didn't look nervous": Author's interview with Hugh Van Dusen, New York City, February 2012.

6 "Cummings was not at all the man": Author's interviews and correspondence with Ben La Farge, September and October 2010.

6 "I found it somehow aesthetically": Ibid.

6 the greatest model: Edward Steichen, *A Life in Photography* (New York: Doubleday, 1968), p. 86.

6 This girl's too tall: Sawyer-Lauçanno, *E. E. Cummings,* p. 364; Kennedy, *Dreams in the Mirror,* p. 338.

7 "We were all very polite": Author's interview with Hugh Van Dusen.

7 "The fifties view of him": Author's interview with Harvey Shapiro, 2010.

8 Marion wrote a friend: Kennedy, *Dreams in the Mirror,* p. 441. Marion Morehouse letter to her friend Evelyn Segal, October 1, 1952. Kennedy has the date of the first lecture wrong; it was October 28.

8 "Let me cordially warn you": Cummings, *i: six nonlectures,* p. 3. All the following quotes are from this edition.

9 "many times worshipped": Ibid., p. 3.

9 "Lucky the students": Houghton Library, Harvard College Library. Janet Flanner IMG 2436.

10 "As a child he was puny": Cummings, Journal entry, Houghton Library, Harvard College Library. Restricted material.

11 "It was both scary and exciting": Qualey, *When I Was a Little Girl,* p. 105.

13 "Have yet to encounter": Kennedy, *Dreams in the Mirror,* p. 443.

2. 104 IRVING STREET

15 "to have you in": Kennedy, *Dreams in the Mirror,* p. 9. Kennedy quotes this tidbit without attribution.

16 the Cummings house was also filled with pets: Qualey, *When I Was a Little Girl,* p. 33.

16 "Eeenie, meemie": Ibid., p. 29.

16 *The Rhymester:* By Tom Hood, originally published in London, republished in Boston in 1882.

17 "if there are any heavens": Cummings published this tribute in *ViVa* in 1931, when his mother was seventy-two years old. His tribute to his father, "my father moved through dooms of love," wasn't written until fifteen years after his father's death and was published in 1940 in *50 Poems.*

18 "Only a butterfly's glide": Cummings, *i: six nonlectures,* p. 32.

18 "the ignoramus listening": Ibid., p. 30.

20 "I stand hushed": Sawyer-Lauçanno, *E. E. Cummings,* p. 24.

20 Harvard's first instructor in sociology: Kennedy, *Dreams in the Mirror,* p. 493, note II. 15.

21 "No father on this earth": Cummings, *i: six nonlectures,* p. 9.

21 Joy Farm: Norman, *The Magic-Maker,* p. 29.

23 "He would let my brother": Qualey, *When I Was a Little Girl,* p. 75.

25 "He must have felt": Ibid., p. 91.

25 "I felt his weight": Ibid., p. 92.

25 "Rex, you and I have loved each other": This poem, quoted in Sawyer-Lauçanno, *E. E. Cummings,* p. 41, is in Charles Norman's papers at the Harry Ransome Humanities Research Center at the University of Texas.

26 "I keep them to remind me": Kennedy, *Dreams in the Mirror,* p. 49.

27 Cambridge Social Dramatic Club: Ibid., p. 86.

27 "a lively, spree-drinking": Ibid., p. 74.

27 "I will wade out": Ibid., pp. 108–10.

3. HARVARD

31 Lowell "represented the conservative": Jerome Karabel, *The Chosen: The Hidden History of Admission and Exclusion at Harvard, Yale and Princeton* (New York: Houghton Mifflin, 2005), p. 459.

31 Under President Lowell, the university would: Bethell, *Harvard Observed,* pp. 43–54, is a source for this discussion of President Lowell's attitudes.

31 "The anti-Semitic feeling": Karabel, *The Chosen,* p. 28.

33 "I am certain of nothing": Norman, *The Magic-Maker,* p. 44.

33 "sitting next to some little": This repulsive statement from Theodore (Dory) Miller is quoted in Kennedy, *Dreams in the Mirror,* p. 53, but Miller's identity is hidden. He is referred to only as "Cummings' first Greek instructor." His name is in Kennedy's endnotes.

34 someone from another era: Watson, *The Edge of the Woods,* p. 81.

34 "Homosexual feelings toward Watson": Sawyer-Lauçanno, *E. E. Cummings,* p. 82. On this subject, when Sawyer-Lauçanno asked the poet John Ashbery if he would talk about Cummings, Ashbery asked, "Are you going to out him?"

35 "Practically everything I know": Norman, *The Magic-Maker,* p. 43.

35 With his gang of friends: Reef, *E. E. Cummings,* p. 20.

38 "I led a double life": Sawyer-Lauçanno, *E. E. Cummings*, p. 56.

39 "Is that our president's": Foster Damon on Amy Lowell, quoted in Reef, *E. E. Cummings*, p. 22.

39 Lowell kept his face immobile: Kennedy, *Dreams in the Mirror*, p. 84.

39 "He defends (his friends)": "Ezra Pound," *Wikipedia*.

40 "gave me [the rudiments] of my writing style": Sawyer-Lauçanno, *E. E. Cummings*, p. 72.

43 "Mr. Ezra Pound": *Pound/Cummings*, p. 1.

4. THE WESTERN FRONT

46 "It was something absolutely new": Houghton Library, Harvard Library Collection, quote from Malcolm Cowley from John Urlich research.

47 "In New York I also breathed": Cummings, *i: six nonlectures*, p. 52.

48 "We were young": Reef, *E. E. Cummings*, p. 26.

49 "We are alright": Cummings, *Selected Letters*, p. 14. Letter dated April 17, 1917.

49 "colossally floating spiderwebs": Cummings, *i: six nonlectures*, p. 53.

50 "I don't know why": Cummings, *Selected Letters*, p. 14. Letter dated April 7, 1917.

51 "Hope the war isn't over": Ibid., p. 16. Letter dated April 18, 1917.

51 "We were eager": Norman, *The Magic-Maker*, p. 29.

51 "for those who wish": *Harvard Crimson*, March 1917.

51 "waste a torpedo": Cummings, *Selected Letters*, p. 18. Letter dated May 4, 1917.

51 "The amazing vulgarity": Ibid, p. 19. Letter dated May 4, 1917.

52 "Last night I sat": Cummings, *Selected Letters*, p. 26. Letter dated May 1917.

53 "the finest girls": Ibid., p. 17. This is the last letter from the Hôtel du Palais, dated June 4, 1917.

54 aristocratic cutups: Kennedy, *Dreams in the Mirror*, p. 90.

54 "show those dirty Frogs": Ibid., p. 146.

55 "Perhaps the real heroes": Dyer, *The Missing of the Somme*, p. 53.

55 "Since 1916, the fear of gas": "Robert Graves," *Wikipedia*.

56 "I hope M. le Censor": Cummings, *Selected Letters*, p. 29. Letter dated July 7, 1917.

57 "This made me angry": Ibid., p. 30. Letter dated July 7, 1917.

5. THE ENORMOUS ROOM

58 "Death is not an adventure": Remarque, *All Quiet on the Western Front*, p. 54.

59 *"J'aime beaucoup les français"*: Cummings, *The Enormous Room*, p. 19.

60 "An uncontrollable joy": Ibid., p. 23.

60 "I fell on my *paillasse*": Ibid., p. 60.

60 "You can't imagine, Mother mine": Cummings, *Selected Letters*, p. 38. Letter dated October 1, 1917.

62 "Pardon me, Mr. President": Cummings, *The Enormous Room*, pp. xi–xiv.

62 he had lost his smile: Kennedy, *Dreams in the Mirror*, p. 159.

64 "The artist keeps his eyes": Cummings, *Selected Letters*, p. 54. Letter dated September 11, 1918.

67 "His neck was exactly": Cummings, *The Enormous Room*, p. 56.

67 "Your father turned": Norman, *The Magic-Maker*, p. 111.

67 "He uses some new alloys": Ibid., p. 122.

68 "my mattress resembled an island": Ibid., p. 62.
68 "splendid comrades": Cummings, *Selected Letters*, p. 40. Letter dated Nov. 1917.
69 "Indeed for the first time": Cummings, *The Enormous Room*, p. 71.
69 "You know Cornelius Vanderbilt": Ibid., p. 73.
69 "he knew probably less": Ibid., p. 84.
70 "He makes us see and smell": Kennedy, *Dreams in the Mirror*, p. 223.

6. GREENWICH VILLAGE: ELAINE AND NANCY

71 "independent republic of Greenwich Village": Wetzsteon, *Republic of Dreams*, p. 1.
72 after an accident: Milford, *Savage Beauty*, p. 18.
72 And they wrote about it: Schulman, *Romany Marie*, p. 11.
72 When she decided to sleep with them: Milford, *Savage Beauty*, p. 198.
72 was also having an affair: Wetzsteon, *Republic of Dreams*, pp. 124–5. This triangle between Reed, O'Neill, and Louise Bryant was the subject of the 1981 Warren Beatty movie, *Reds*.
73 "ST—the world, money, Freud": Houghton Library, Harvard College Library, restricted folders of E. E. Cummings, 1 of 1 204.
74 "the first time I saw Elaine": Houghton Library restricted papers of EEC.
74 "What an unsettled luncheon": Watson, *The Edge of the Woods*, p. 83.
74 "Those of us who weren't": Kennedy, *Dreams in the Mirror*, p. 193.
75 "I see E. not as she is": Houghton Library. Cummings archive Bms Am 1892.7 (198).
75 "there's no way out": Ibid.
75 "If I hadn't changed": Ibid., folder 3.
75 "go in, oh please": Ibid. (189.7 198).
75 "I didn't want to possess her": Ibid.
77 "Out of a very ancient wheelmine": Cummings de Forêt, *Charon's Daughter*, p. xi.
78 "One solitary recollection": Ibid., p. xi.
79 "I am essentially an artist": Sawyer-Lauçanno, *E. E. Cummings*, p. 223.
82 "I love her more than anything": Houghton Library, Harvard College Library. Cummings archive Bms Am 827—from folders.

7. ANNE BARTON AND JOSEPH STALIN

85 "Homo duplex": William James, *Varieties of Religious Experience*, p. 234.
85 "before breakfast self": Houghton Library, Harvard College Library (restricted), Bms Am 1892.7 (217).
86 "fortune does us neither good nor evil": Ibid.
86 "You can only see": Kennedy, *Dreams in the Mirror*, pp. 285–6.
87 "Myself seems to be": Cummings, *Selected Letters*, p. 111. Letter to Rebecca Cummings, dated September 13, 1926.
89 "When two brakemen jumped": Cummings, *i: six nonlectures*, p. 12. Cummings interviewed the brakemen the next day.
89 "My sister and I entered": Sawyer-Lauçanno, *E. E. Cummings*, pp. 304–5.
90 the classy writer Hazel Hawthorne: Morrie and Hazel were benevolent fixtures of my childhood. Hazel in particular became a babysitter for me and my brother some nights and a few weekends after we had moved to the suburbs. One Valentine's Day when my

parents had gone off somewhere leaving us with Hazel, a huge card with an intricate set of springs and feathers was delivered to me. She was a friend.

91 "As she quickly rose": Watson, *The Edge of the Woods*, p. 99.

92 "Think that I am not a bit the sort": Norman, *The Magic-Maker*, p. 225.

92 "We knew from Freud": Wittels, *Freud and the Child Woman*, p. 38.

93 "They had been stewed": Sawyer-Lauçanno, *E. E. Cummings*, p. 323.

93 "lucid madness": Ibid., p. 226.

93 "every now and then": Norman, *The Magic-Maker*, p. 254.

95 "Inexorably has a magic wand": Cummings, *Eimi*, p. 8.

95 "The whole trouble with you": Ibid., p. 51.

97 She got drunk and embarrassed Cummings: Houghton Library, Harvard College Library. Cummings archive, Bms Am 176.

97 Hart Crane had died: Crane had been traveling with Cowley's ex-wife Peggy. The way my father told it, Crane had burst into the beauty parlor where Peggy was having her hair done, saying he had to talk. Peggy had dismissed him. He had left the room and thrown himself overboard.

8. *EIMI* AND MARION MOREHOUSE

98 "I have been": Lincoln Steffens, *Autobiography* (New York: Harcourt Brace, 1931), p. 875.

98 "Are the Russian people happy?": Norman, *The Magic-Maker*, pp. 284–5. Interview with Don Brown in Paris, in 1931.

98 "Cummings went to the Soviet Union": Sawyer-Lauçanno, *E. E. Cummings*, p. 355.

99 "subhuman communist superstate": Madison Smartt Bell, introduction to *Eimi*, by E. E. Cummings, p. xii.

99 "next:in the very diningroom": Cummings, *Eimi*, p. 63.

99 "He avoids the cliché": William Carlos Williams, "Lower Case Cummings," *The Harvard Wake* 5 (Spring 1946), p. 22.

100 "i is small": Bell, introduction to *Eimi*, p. xiii.

101 "a four hundred page garland": Karl Shapiro, "The Bohemian," *The Harvard Wake* 5 (Spring 1946), p. 45.

101 "If only Cummings would condescend": Norman, *The Magic-Maker*, p. 298.

103 "As soon as you": Cummings, Journals from the Houghton Library, Harvard College Library, Restricted 3 of 7, p. 190.

103 "During one of your early": Cummings, Journals from the Houghton Library, Harvard College Library.

103 "the curse becomes a blessing": Ibid.

104 "When you refused to let her": Ibid.

107 "Marion's my new pride": Cummings, *Selected Letters*, p. 123.

110 "I only wish I": Kennedy, *Dreams in the Mirror*, p. 347.

110 "There in Africa": Cummings, *Selected Letters*, p. 27.

9. NO THANKS

113 "In the previous dozen years": Kennedy, *Dreams in the Mirror*, p. 350.

114 Stewart was the literary representative: Bennington class roster, 1935, Bennington College Library Archive.

115 "We have been able to avoid": Letter, Robert Devore Leigh to Joseph Willits, March 12, 1935. Bennington College archives c. Oceana Wilson and Joe Tucker.

115 overthrowing the rules and the rulers: Bennington, Vermont, is dominated by a plinth—the Bennington Needle or the Bennington Monument—erected on the highest point in town in memory of the soldiers of the American Revolution.

115 "I too was at Bennington": *Pound/Cummings*, p. 138.

116 "Three or four times a week": Brockway, *Bennington College*, p. 78.

116 In the official Bennington version: Bennington College Archives, Crossett Library.

117 "Mr. Cummings' poetry": *The Bennington Banner*, April 27, 1935; courtesy of the Bennington College Archives.

117 "E. E. Cummings is far more incomprehensible": Norman, *The Magic-Maker*, p. 309.

118 "Once with *The Enormous Room*": Ibid.

123 "so slightly acknowledged": Sawyer-Lauçanno, *E. E. Cummings*, p. 406.

124 "My poems are essentially pictures": Reef, *E. E. Cummings*, p. 99.

124 "The poems to come": Cummings, *Collected Poems 1922–1938*, n.p.

126 "This is the poetry of a man": Ibid., p. 100.

127 "When Cummings writes": *Harvard Wake* 5 (Spring 1946), p. 61.

10. EZRA POUND AND *SANTA CLAUS*

129 A letter from the Yale admissions committee: The applicant was my uncle Thomas Winternitz whose father, my grandfather, had been the dean of Yale School of Medicine and was ousted as a result of anti-Semitism.

131 "relinquishing self-expression": Houghton Library restricted material.

132 "It resembles armour": Kennedy, *Dreams in the Mirror*, p. 390.

132 "Dew yew figger": *Pound/Cummings*, p. 143.

132 "Insteroot (ov Awts n Lers)": Ibid., p. 146.

132 "I saw him in New York": Ibid., p. 145.

133 "attractively curly-headed": *Pound/Cummings*, p. 138.

133 "a thick and sanguinary steak": Ibid.

133 "We don't know if he's a spy": Ibid., p. 139.

133 "I find poor Pound": Ibid.

134 The letter is an almost incomprehensible jumble: Ibid., p. 152.

134 "Spring is coming": Ibid., p. 156.

134 "Ars longa": The complete aphorism by Hippocrates, which might well have been a Cummings credo, reads:

> Art is long,
>
> life is short,
>
> opportunity fleeting,
>
> experiment dangerous,
>
> judgment difficult.

136 "Marion's been in the hospital": *Pound/Cummings*, p. 167.

137 "I like getting letters": Ibid., p. 168.

137 "changed her clothes": Cummings, *Selected Letters*, p. 166.

II. REBECCA AND NANCY

140 "the genuine 101%": Cummings, *Selected Letters*, p. 158. Letter dated March 29, 1941.

140 *When I Was a Little Girl:* The book's dedication reads: "Written for John and Mary and their children and children's children."

141 "an extraordinary human being": Letter to Hildegarde Watson. Letter dated January 22, 1947.

142 "Nancy was early treated": Kennedy, *Dreams in the Mirror*, p. 413. This is from one of many interviews Kennedy had with Nancy—she was as open as possible with him and any account of her life must be heavily indebted to Kennedy's extraordinary and timely work. I stand on his shoulders. Any presumption that this book could have been written without his magnificent research and his biography is entirely my own obfuscation.

142 "deb delights, London 1938": Cummings de Forêt, *Charon's Daughter*, p. 7.

144 "New York 1943": Ibid., p. 9.

146 "Marion, for whatever reasons": Kennedy, *Dreams in the Mirror*, p. 416.

147 *Santa Claus: The Harvard Wake* 5 (Spring 1946), pp. 10–19.

148 "he pushed all the tears": Sawyer-Lauçanno, *E. E. Cummings*, p. 174.

148 "Nancy and I had a wonderful time": Ibid., p. 309.

152 "I knew a couple of lemmings": Norman, *The Magic-Maker*, p. 267.

12. "I THINK I AM FALLING IN LOVE WITH YOU"

154 "There are three roofers": Letter dated April 5, 1952. Houghton Library Archive. Collection of William James correspondence.

155 "seemed extraordinary, like a bell": Kennedy, *Dreams in the Mirror*, p. 417.

155 "goodbye dear & next time": Cummings de Forêt, *Charon's Daughter*, n.p.

156 "Always the pictures came first": Ibid.

156 "the ferryman of the Styx": Bernard Stehle lecture at AIAC in 2006.

158 Nancy blurted out her fears: This is the story Nancy told her close friend Robert Cabot—a story Cabot told me in 2011. The story Nancy had previously told Richard Kennedy and which he used in his biography leaves out her confession of love.

158 "I hope never to forget the force": Sawyer-Lauçanno, *E. E. Cummings*, p. 498.

158 "it seems to me that she is real": Sawyer-Lauçanno, *E. E. Cummings*, p. 474.

159 "While part of me is her tragic": Ibid., p. 472.

159 "You know how hard it is": Kennedy, *Dreams in the Mirror*, p. 429.

159 "thank you a millionmillion times": Cummings, *Selected Letters*, p. 214.

159 "Anyhow:from my standpoint": Ibid., p. 263.

161 "Across that vacuous room": Robert Cabot, *The Isle of Kheria* (Kingston, NY: McPherson & Company), p. 196.

162 "Perhaps some day": Cummings, *Selected Letters*, p. 269.

164 "It was a treasure of a place": Author's interview with Robert Cabot, November 22, 2011.

165 "We are as Kevin tried to say": Kennedy, *Dreams in the Mirror*, p. 533.

165 "behaved in a hoity-toity fashion": Kennedy, *Dreams in the Mirror*, p. 474.

166 "Your pluck was wonderful": Cummings, *Selected Letters*, p. 268. Letter dated January 15, 1961.

166 "You hated being made to showoff": Ibid., p. 269. Letter dated Jan. 15, 1961.
166 "Do you know at all": Kennedy, *Dreams in the Mirror*, p. 476.

13. READINGS: A NEW CAREER

168 "The poet is no tender slip": Cummings, *Selected Letters*, p. 273. Letter dated Feb. 19, 1962.
169 "as stiff as a mule": Ibid., pp. 238–9. Letter dated December 8, 1954.
169 "He was an enormously effective": Kennedy, *Dreams in the Mirror*, p. 447.
169 "must confess": Cummings, *Selected Letters*, p. 245. Letter dated April 8, 1955.
170 three categories: Norman, *The Magic-Maker*, p. 128.
171 " 'arthritis'—without or avec a soupcon": Cummings, *Selected Letters*, p. 189. Letter not dated.
171 "I always glimpse": Ibid., p. 212. Letter dated 1949. This is a reference to the *Odes* of Horace who, in an ode refers to fleeting time, advancing age, and the disaster that devotion will not delay wrinkles.
171 "What I generally experience": Sawyer-Lauçanno, *E. E. Cummings*, p. 512.
172 "This invitation": Norman, *The Magic-Maker*, p. 359.
172 "received an Honour": *Pound/Cummings*, p. 273. Letter dated April 22, 1950.
173 "whar yu git sech ideas": Ibid., pp. 283–4.
175 the "firestorm" of anger: Sawyer-Lauçanno, *E. E. Cummings*, p. 482.
175 "Cummings, the foe of tyranny": Kennedy, *Dreams in the Mirror*, p. 434.
177 "what is extraordinary": Ibid.
180 "He had touched something deep": Kennedy, *Dreams in the Mirror*, p. 458.

14. VICTORY AND DEFEAT

181 "To a human being": Cummings, *Selected Letters*, p. 274.
182 "Marion would be in and out": Kennedy, *Dreams in the Mirror*, p. 478.

Bibliography

Andrews, Kevin. *Castles of the Morea*. Boston: Houghton Mifflin, 1953.

———. *The Flight of Ikaros: Travels in Greece During the Civil War*. Boston: Houghton Mifflin, 1959.

Bethell, John T. *Harvard Observed: An Illustrated History of the University in the Twentieth Century*. Cambridge, MA: Harvard University Press, 1998.

Brockway, Thomas P. *Bennington College: In the Beginning*. Woodstock, VT: Countryman Press, 1981.

Broyard, Anatole. *Kafka Was the Rage: A Greenwich Village Memoir*. New York: Crown, 1996.

Cummings, E. E. *Eight Harvard Poets*. 1917; repr. Binghamton, NY: Vail-Ballou,

———. *The Enormous Room*. New York: Modern Library, 1998.

———. *Eimi: A Journey Through Soviet Russia*. New York: Liveright, 2007.

———. *Selected Letters of E. E. Cummings*. F. W. Dupee and George Stade, eds. New York: Harcourt, Brace and World, 1969.

———. *Complete Poems, 1913–1922*. New York: Harcourt, Brace, Jovanovich, 1923.

———. *Fairy Tales*. Illustrated by Meilo So. New York: Liveright, 1950.

———. *Little Tree*. Illustrated by Deborah Kogan Ray. New York: Dragonfly Books, 1923.

———. *Collected Poems, 1922–1938*. New York: Liveright, 1963.

———. *i: six nonlectures: the Charles Eliot Norton Lectures, 1952–1953*. Cambridge, MA: Harvard University Press, 1953.

———. *Complete Poems, 1904–1962*. George James Firmage, ed. New York: Liveright, 1991.

Cummings de Forêt, Nancy. *Charon's Daughter*. New York: Liveright, 1977.

Dyer, Geoff. *The Missing of the Somme*. New York: Vintage Books, 1994.

Firmage, George. *E. E. Cummings: A Bibliography*. Middletown, CT: Wesleyan University, 1960.

The Harvard Wake 5 (Spring 1946). Issue devoted to Cummings.

Jinkinson, Roger. *American Ikaros: The Search for Kevin Andrews*. London: Racing House Press, 2010.

Kayton, Bruce. *Radical Walking Tours of New York City*. New York: Seven Stories Press, 1999.

Kennedy, Richard S. *Dreams in the Mirror: A Biography of E. E. Cummings*. New York: Liveright/W. W. Norton, 1980.

Kostelanetz, Richard, ed. *Another E. E. Cummings: A Mind-bending Selection of the Avant-Garde Cummings Poetry and Prose*. New York: Liveright, 1998.

Mason, Wyatt. "Make It Newish: E. E. Cummings, Plagiarism, and the Perils of Originality." *Harper's Magazine,* May 2005.

Milford, Nancy. *Savage Beauty: A Life of Edna St. Vincent Millay*. New York: Random House, 2002.

Millard, Candice. *The River of Doubt: Theodore Roosevelt's Darkest Journey.* New York: Anchor Books, 2005.

Mitchell, Joseph. *Up in the Old Hotel.* New York: Vintage Books, 2008.

Norman, Charles. *The Magic-Maker: E. E. Cummings.* New York: Macmillan, 1958.

Pound, Ezra, and E. E. Cummings. *Pound/Cummings: The Correspondence of Ezra Pound and E. E. Cummings.* Edited by Barry Ahearn. Ann Arbor, MI: University of Michigan Press, 1996.

Qualey, Elizabeth Cummings. *When I Was a Little Girl.* Privately printed by Carlton Qualey, 1981.

Reef, Catherine. *E. E. Cummings: A Poet's Life.* New York: Clarion Books, 2006.

Remarque, Erich Maria. *All Quiet on the Western Front.* New York: Ballantine, 1982.

Sawyer-Lauçanno, Christopher. *E. E. Cummings: A Biography.* Naperville, IL: Sourcebooks, 2004.

Schulman, Robert. *Romany Marie: The Queen of Greenwich Village.* Louisville, KY: Butler Books, 2006.

Watson, Hildegarde Lasell. *The Edge of the Woods: A Memoir.* Privately printed by James S. Watson, 1979.

Wetzsteon, Ross. *Republic of Dreams: Greenwich Village—The American Bohemia, 1910–1960.* New York: Simon & Schuster, 2002.

Wittels, Fritz. *Freud and the Child Woman: The Memoirs of Fritz Wittels.* Edward Timms, ed. New Haven, CT: Yale University Press, 1995.

Index

PHOTOGRAPHIC CREDITS

Rebecca Cummings in 1892 by Charles Sydney Hopkinson (Courtesy of the Massachusetts Historical Society)

The Cummings house at 104 Irving Street, Cambridge (bMS Am 1892:11 (92) Courtesy of the Houghton Library, Harvard University)

A portrait of Cummings at age eight, c. 1902, by Charles Sydney Hopkinson (bMS Am 1892:10 (21) Courtesy of the Houghton Library, Harvard University)

Cummings, age ten, with his father Edward and his younger sister Elizabeth, in 1904 (bMS Am 1892.10 Courtesy of the Houghton Library, Harvard University)

The family at Joy Farm with, from right to left, a maid holding Rex the dog, Elizabeth on a donkey, Estlin on horseback, Rebecca in white, and handyman Sandy Hardy leading the cows, c. 1904 (bMS Am 1823.8 (46), Courtesy of the Houghton Library, Harvard University)

Estlin with his beloved dog, Rex, and Elizabeth in the hammock (Houghton Library MS Am 1823.8 (46))

Dean LeBaron Briggs, the Harvard professor who taught Cummings form (© Harvard University Archives, Call #HUP Briggs, L.R. (12))

James Sibley Watson, Cummings's closest friend and patron (© The Estate of Hildegarde Lasell Watson)

Young women at a burlesque theater in 1916 (Courtesy of the Library of Congress, LC-USZ62–113672)

Scofield Thayer, Cummings's friend and patron and Elaine's first husband (© The Estate of Hildegarde Lasell Watson)

Memorial Hall and Sanders Theatre at Harvard College

Elizabeth Cummings, Estlin's sister, in her teens, c. 1917 (bMS Am 1892.11 (92), Courtesy of the Houghton Library, Harvard University)

Cummings's Harvard graduation photograph, 1915 (Houghton Library MS Am 1892.11 (92))

A Cummings self-portrait, from the 1920s (© Houghton Library, Harvard University)

Cummings's notes on the stationery of Collier & Son where he was working: "Buffalo Bill is Dead" (Houghton Library MS Am 1823.7 (21))

INSERT 2

William Slater Brown, 1917 (Courtesy Slater Brown)

Cummings's drawing of the view from one of his Paris windows in the 1920s (© Houghton Library, Harvard University)

Cummings's drawing of Marie Louise Lallemand, his Paris friend from 1917 (bMS Am 1823.7 (16), Courtesy of the Houghton Library, Harvard University)

Paris artists in the 1920s. Ezra Pound stands in the middle row to the right. (Courtesy of the Library of Congress, LC-USZ62–113902)

American ambulance drivers in France near the Western Front in 1927 (© American Red Cross)

Dépôt de Triage at La Ferté-Macé, where Cummings and Slater Brown were incarcerated (Courtesy Slater Brown)

Scofield and Elaine Thayer in the summer of 1916 (bMS Am 1892 (681), Courtesy of the Houghton Library, Harvard University)

Edward and Rebecca Cummings in the mid-1920s. Edward was killed in 1926. (bMS Am 1823 (642), Courtesy of the Houghton Library, Harvard University)

Elaine near her Washington Square apartment just after Nancy was born, 1920 (Courtesy Nancy T. Andrews)

Private Cummings after his return from France at Fort Devens, Massachusetts, 1918 (Houghton Library MS Am 1892.11 (92))

Cummings in Paris, age twenty-seven, early 1920s (Courtesy Nancy T. Andrews)

Nancy Thayer Cummings, age five, in 1925 (Courtesy Nancy T. Andrews)

INSERT 3

Morrie Werner . . . (© Houghton Library, Harvard University)

. . . and Anne Barton: two portraits by E. E. Cummings (bMS Am 1892.9 (1), Courtesy of the Houghton Library, Harvard University)

Rebecca Cummings at Joy Farm in old age (bMS Am 1892.11 (92), Courtesy of the Houghton Library, Harvard University)

Marion Morehouse, early 1930s (bMS Am 1892.11, Courtesy of the Houghton Library, Harvard University)

Cummings photographed in his studio at Patchin Place by James Sibley Watson (bMS Am 1892.11 (92), Courtesy of the Houghton Library, Harvard University)

The glamorous Marion Morehouse shot by George Hoyningen-Huene, 1933 (Hoyningen-Heune Collection)

Cummings's drawing of Marion Morehouse (bMS Am 1892.1, Courtesy of the Houghton Library, Harvard University)

Nancy at Joy Farm, 1950 (Courtesy Nancy T. Andrews)

A Cummings self-portrait from 1947 (Houghton Library MS Am 1892.17 (107))

Marianne Moore drawn by Hildegarde Watson (Houghton Library MS Am 1892.11 (92))

Ezra Pound after his stay at St. Elizabeths in 1957 (bMS Am 1892.11 (92), Courtesy of the Houghton Library, Harvard University)

Marion Morehouse in the 1930s (bMS Am 1892.11 (92), Courtesy of the Houghton Library, Harvard University)

E. E. Cummings before World War II (© Manuel Komroff Papers, Rare Book and Manuscript Society)

Cummings with his own painting of Mount Chocorua in 1950 (© Houghton Library, Harvard University)

Nancy Thayer Cummings Roosevelt Andrews (Courtesy Nancy T. Andrews. Taken by Alexis Orr)

Hildegarde Watson and Estlin Cummings (Letters of Cummings, also Houghton Library MS Am 1892.14 (4))

Cummings as he got older (bMS Am 1892.11 (92), Courtesy of the Houghton Library, Harvard University)

Patchin Place (no credit)

Cummings at work on the porch at Joy Farm (© Houghton Library, Harvard University)

ALSO AVAILABLE FROM

Vintage Books & Anchor Books

WALT WHITMAN'S AMERICA
by David S. Reynolds

Combing through the full range of Whitman's writing, David Reynolds shows how Whitman gathered inspiration from every stratum of nineteenth-century American life: the convulsions of slavery and depression; the raffish dandyism of the Bowery "b'hoys"; the exuberant rhetoric of actors, orators, and divines. We see how Whitman reconciled his own sexuality with contemporary social mores and how his energetic courtship of the public presaged the vogues of advertising and celebrity. Brilliantly researched, captivatingly told, *Walt Whitman's America* is a triumphant work of scholarship that breathes new life into the biographical genre.

Biography/History

THE UNABRIDGED JOURNALS OF SYLVIA PLATH
by Sylvia Plath

A major literary event—the complete, uncensored journals of Sylvia Plath, published in their entirety for the first time. Sylvia Plath's journals were originally published in 1982 in a heavily abridged version authorized by Plath's husband, Ted Hughes. This new edition is an exact and complete transcription of the diaries Plath kept during the last twelve years of her life. Sixty percent of the book is material that has never before been made public, more fully revealing the intensity of the poet's personal and literary struggles, and providing fresh insight into both her frequent desperation and the bravery with which she faced down her demons.

Autobiography

ANNE SEXTON
by Diane Middlebrook

Anne Sexton began writing poetry at the age of twenty-nine
to keep from killing herself. She held on to language for dear
life and somehow—in spite of alcoholism and the mental
illness that ultimately led her to suicide—managed to create
a body of work that won a Pulitzer Prize and that still sings
to thousands of readers. This exemplary biography, which
was nominated for the National Book Award, provoked
controversy for its revelations of infidelity and incest and
its use of tapes from Sexton's psychiatric sessions. It rec-
onciles the many Anne Sextons: the 1950s housewife; the
abused child who became an abusive mother; the seduc-
tress; the suicidal woman who carried "kill-me pills" in her
handbag the way other women carry lipstick; and the poet
who transmuted confession into lasting art.

Biography